Of course I love you...
NOW GO TO YOUR ROOM!

Of course I love you...
NOW GO TO YOUR ROOM!

Diane Levy

RANDOM HOUSE
NEW ZEALAND

National Library of New Zealand Cataloguing-in-Publication Data

Levy, Diane.
Of course I love you... NOW GO TO YOUR ROOM! / Diane Levy.
ISBN 1-86941-514-0
1. Parent and child. 2. Behavior modification. 3. Child rearing.
I. Title.
649.64—dc 21

A RANDOM HOUSE BOOK
published by
Random House New Zealand
18 Poland Road, Glenfield, Auckland, New Zealand
www.randomhouse.co.nz

First published 2002. Reprinted 2003 (three times), 2004 (twice)

ISBN 1 86941 514 0

Design, layout, and cover design: Vasanti Unka
Printed by Griffin Press Ltd, Australia

Contents

To the parents in my life

Sally, Emanuel, Hilel, Marta and Geoffrey (z"l)

from whom I have learned so much

To our children

Robert, Tanya and Deborah

who have taught me so much

and

To my beloved

Vernon

who is truly the wind beneath all our wings.

Introduction

I remember my rat with great affection. My rat and I graduated with a major in Psychology in 1967. I painstakingly taught my rat to tell the difference between horizontal and vertical lines.

It was not a pleasant process for either of us. We would both enter a dimly lit enclosure with a small 'leaping-from' platform, a 'landing-on' platform — complete with food pellet — under the 'correct' set of lines, and nothing under the 'wrong' set of lines except a net to safely catch a mistaken rat. The hapless subject was placed on the first platform and eventually overbalanced, was pushed or just got bored, thus heading toward a set of lines. Correct choice equalled a safe landing and a food reward. Incorrect choice equalled an unpleasant but safe fall into the net below.

Slowly, slowly, the rat learned to tell the difference between horizontal and vertical lines. Quickly, quickly, I became convinced that behavioural psychology was the answer to every aspect of animal — including human — behaviour. Hadn't I always been told that psychology was the study of behaviour? Hadn't I now confirmed for the whole scientific world that any behaviour could be modified by positively reinforcing the desired behaviour and negatively reinforcing the undesired behaviour?

And so I spent nearly 20 years with this as my basic tenet. I was well reinforced in this position. Praise (positive reinforcement), punishment (negative reinforcement), star charts were the way this was applied to the human sphere, and parents and teachers were encouraged to modify children's behaviour.

My interest, comfort and curiosity in where God fitted in with science was heavily reinforced in childhood memories of our Rabbi reciting the

Ten Commandments each Saturday. It was one of the few portions of the Sabbath service that was in English, and therefore comprehensible to me. 'I the Lord thy God am a jealous God, visiting the iniquities of the fathers upon the children unto the third and the fourth generation of them that hate me and showing loving kindness unto the thousandth generation unto them that love me and keep my commandments.'

Even God was keen on reward and punishment. I tried as a parent, I tried as a teacher, I tried as a wife, I tried as a committee member, I tried as a chairman, I tried as a counsellor and I tried as a Family Therapist.

The problem with this theory was that it almost worked often enough to encourage us to think we had the answer. When it didn't work, we thought we hadn't done it well enough, often enough, sincerely enough or — a greatly punishing word for any parent — consistently enough. Clearly, the answer was to try harder.

Today I cannot understand why it took me another 30 years to think of my rat again. The rat that took so long and worked so hard to learn to tell the difference between horizontal and vertical lines was also capable of choosing and collecting the right foods in the right quantities, avoiding — on the whole — dangerous things like precipices and cats and fires and humans, finding its way back to where it had left from, nest-building, finding a mate, setting up for offspring and caring for those offspring. All without my help and all without carefully and deliberately administered reward or punishment.

Simultaneously, I began to examine the arrogant assumption that I should manipulate the behaviour of any other person — of whatever height — through the means of reward and punishment.

I started to look at the world around me and began with fresh eyes to notice that the reward and punishment theory just did not stack up for complex animal and/or human behaviour. Leaving aside the biggie — Why do bad things happen to good people? — there were still plenty of examples.

Traditionally, in our culture, financial reward was supposed to act as an incentive and a measure of a person's worth.

Then how come people who could amplify sounds so that our ears and our hearing were forever damaged were being paid megabucks, while the people who could heal our ears were being paid much less, and the people who earlier had tenderly wiped our ears, taught us to wipe our own and tried to persuade us not to subject our ears to the amplified sound were paid nothing at all?

The problem for me was: If I abandon praise and punishment as the basic tools of parenting, what is left?

Then there were three big breakthroughs. The first involved thinking about how to listen to children and how to support them without solving their problems. This happened when I found a way of taking Jean Liedloff's observations of the 'primitive' Yequana Indians and reshaping the parental behaviour to be suitable for use in New Zealand in the 21st century.

The second and biggest breakthrough came when I began to understand the difference between those parents who were using Time Out successfully and those for whom it was not effective. Where it was used as a punishment (to replace smacking), parents were finding themselves totally disempowered when a child enjoyed the peace and refused to emerge. Where, however, parents were using the Time Out as a space for children to spend whatever time was needed for them to change their minds and decide to behave in a way that fitted the family's way, children not only became more self-disciplined, but also appeared happier.

This was reinforced when I turned again, with new understanding, to Hal Urban's book 20 Things I Want My Kids to Know. His final chapter is built around his premise that 'being good is the most essential ingredient of emotional and spiritual health'. At last I had an explanation for why, when I sent parents away with strategies that appeared to make them meaner and stricter parents and their children more compliant, they would return a fortnight later and say, somewhat puzzled and bemused, 'They seem to be so much happier.'

The third breakthrough happened when I attended a Virtues Project seminar run by Dan and Linda Popov and acquired a language that made recognition of our children's virtues more significant and powerful than praise of their actions.

The outcome of these breakthroughs is that I see our parenting goals underpinned by two main tasks:

- To support our children as and so that they experience a wide range of emotions (happy, angry, sad, frustrated, furious, delighted) in socially appropriate ways.
- To limit our children's inappropriate behaviour so that they behave in socially appropriate ways and develop self-discipline.

While these two parenting goals are being accomplished, our children will develop the skills and the virtues they need to lead wholesome and independent adult lives. Best of all, these approaches include lots of low-energy strategies for exhausted parents so that we can raise pleasant children, in whose progress we can delight and whose company we can all enjoy.

NOTE: The English language has not given us a single simple pronoun that means 'he or she' and I find it tedious and disruptive to always write 'he or she'. To get around this, my first choice will be to use 'they'. If this is not appropriate, I will use 'he' in the odd-numbered chapters and 'she' in the even chapters. I leave it to you, dear reader, to juggle with concepts regarding your sons being referred to by feminine gender and those regarding your daughters being referred to in the masculine gender.

Parenting itself is such a difficult juggling act that this should be comparatively easy!

Part One:
You've Got 20 Years

1. The 20 Year Plan

It takes about 20 years to raise a child. This is no guarantee that your child will have left home after 20 years, nor even an implication that he should have done so. These days, many children are leaving home before the age of 20, and conversely many stay in the family home to complete tertiary education, to save money, or simply because they like being there. Notwithstanding current mores, it is by about 20 that our children should be capable of living independently and, if living at home, should be living as an independent and useful adult family member.

Within that 20 years you will have taught — or led your child toward the learning of — all the skills that an adult child needs to function in the world away from home. You hope it also means you have raised a young adult who knows when to ask for help, when to consult and when to act independently.

Notice that I have not said: 'You will have taught your child what to do and what to think.' The world is simply too complicated for us to have provided our children with the answers to all the questions and decisions that come their way. It is our role, our privilege and our responsibility to teach them how to assess situations, how to think for themselves, how to make wise decisions, and how to avoid dangerous situations.

The good old days

We parents of today's children are often heard to say, 'I would never have dreamed of talking to my parents or teachers like that.' Grandparents will mutter, 'The children are much brighter these days, but so cheeky and with so little respect.' A question that I, as a parent and a family therapist, frequently ponder is: 'Are our children getting more difficult to manage?'

We keep saying it is a different world from the one we grew up in, and certainly very different from the world of our grandparents. But just how different is that? Let me recount to you a story I heard on talkback radio a few years ago.

The chief-of-police was retiring, and told this account of his first few weeks as a young 'bobby' about 40 years ago.

One evening his chief called the young bobby into his office and told him that bowling clubs in the area were being burgled for their alcohol. 'Here's how we are going to catch them,' the chief said. 'Every evening after your beat is finished, you are going to stake out a bowling club. You will stay overnight in the pavilion each night until these guys are caught.'

So that evening, after he had come off duty, he took his bike and a bag with a thermos, a hottie and a blanket, and spent the entire night in a bowling club pavilion. The first night nothing happened. The second night nothing happened. On the third night he heard the sound of breaking timber and went to investigate. Two men were indeed breaking into the club.

He told them they were under arrest and they were to accompany him to the police station. And so the three of them set off amiably to the police station. One burglar pushed the policeman's bike, the other carried his bag with the thermos, hottie and blanket, and the policeman carried their kit of burgling tools. When they got to the police station, he locked them up.

It's a different world

Try to imagine that scenario today. Contemplate the respect held, only 40 years ago, by the policeman for his chief, by the burglars for the law.

Now contemplate the comparatively lawless, anarchic and 'godless' society in which we raise our children today. As parents and grandparents we no longer feel as if we have the backing of the state, the government, the church or the police as we go about the task of raising our children and creating an extended family.

This is one of the reasons I believe parenting is so difficult today. We tend to parent in isolation and without the backing of the society around us.

In this difficult world, I believe we must become more skilled, more thoughtful and more deliberate in raising our children. It no longer works to just get through each day — although there will be many days where just getting through is a major achievement. We need to develop a long-term view so that we become more skilled at handling our children on a day-to-day basis.

I hope this book will remind you of skills you already have and give you some additional skills.

Don't be too tough on yourself

In every other field, particularly when you consider the trades and professions, years of training are given before we are 'let loose'. There may be several years of academic study at a tertiary institution, years of apprenticeships, step-by-step introduction into the practical aspects, careful supervision of your early attempts, repeated reviews of your performance, mentors, supervisors and bosses to turn to. There are also opportunities to keep up to date on new ideas and thinking.

Consider parenting. The only prerequisite is a child: after that you are on your own. So we, as parents, have to see to our own study, training, supervision, mentoring and updating. We must arrange the taking of leave, and cover for our absence. Although society pays lip service to parenting as 'the most important job in the world', the facilities and support on offer give the lie to this.

We are on our own.

Let's get cleverer. Let's keep learning.

Four major parenting tasks

In raising a child there are four major tasks. As parents we are responsible for making sure our children achieve or acquire:
  i) emotional independence
  ii) self-discipline
  iii) skills
  iv) morality

Emotional independence

When a baby is born, he depends on us entirely to meet his emotional needs. Carrying him around helps him feel comfortable and right. When he cries, much of his distress can be alleviated by the warmth and reassurance of a (walking) adult. Patting his back helps. Muttering soothing, loving sounds helps. He calms down. His world is safe. He needs us to meet the emotional needs he feels.

Jean Liedloff offers a lovely description of the 'rightness' of being carried around by a loving parent in the wonderful book *The Continuum Concept*. (I will refer to this book again and again — it is one I re-read about every six months. It keeps me in touch with the need to allow children to do their own emotional growing while being supported by caring adults.) Jean Liedloff talks about cuddling as a way for our baby's little body to discharge or transfer energy to our own larger body. We can absorb his distress without it having a major effect on us. Once his energy is discharged, our baby can feel peaceful again — right with the world.

Emotionally Dependent ⟶ Emotionally Independent

In adulthood, our best method of discharging rage and anger is quite similar. A cuddle, a shoulder to cry on, a listening ear all enable us to discharge some feelings and begin to deal with the rest.

When we are young we experience emotions with our whole body. When you go in to a six-month-old baby after he has had a good sleep, he greets you with delight. It is not just the big smile and the gurgles of delight. He waves his arms, squirms with delight and fans his toes. He expresses his emotion with his whole body in a head-to-toe response.

Similarly, the enraged two-year-old has a whole-body response. He hurls himself on the ground. He pounds the floor with his fists and knees and sometimes even his head. He screams his outrage at the world. All of him is angry and upset.

Think of the adult response. When we are delighted to see someone, we show it by raising our mouth in a smile and the skin around our eyes may crinkle with delight as well. It is a very localised response. Similarly with rage. We shout or go grimly quiet, we may clench our fists or wave our arms or stamp our feet. It is a localised response.

Our babies begin by being entirely emotionally dependent upon us. By the time they are adults we want them to be emotionally independent — not emotionally dead, but independent. We want them to be able to experience and handle, in socially appropriate ways, the full range of emotions: from joy to sorrow, from happy excitement to rage.

When these emotions are too tough to handle alone, we also want them to be able to seek out the family member or friend who will listen and who will care.

Self-discipline

Richard Gordon, who wrote the *Doctor in the House* series, described a baby as 'a very short person with no discipline at either end'. It is our task, as parents, to take these very short undisciplined people and help them grow up to be somewhat taller self-disciplined young adults.

Notice that I say 'self-disciplined' rather than simply 'disciplined'. Discipline is not sufficient to prepare them for the adult world. It simply does not serve our children well enough to learn to do as they are told, provided there is a responsible person who is watching.

We need to raise children who can choose goals, keep themselves on task and experience satisfaction at tasks completed and dreams realised.

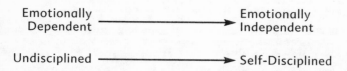

Emotionally Dependent ⟶ Emotionally Independent

Undisciplined ⟶ Self-Disciplined

With emotional independence and self-discipline our children can acquire the next two requirements for adult life: skills and morality.

Skills

You may think it is unfair to describe a newborn baby as unskilled. I agree. Our newborn babies are miraculous in the things they can already do. But the number and complexity of the skills that they will need to have developed to live independently in adulthood are huge and it is our responsibility to make sure they achieve them before we launch them into the world.

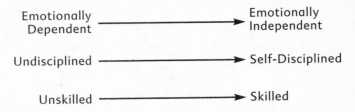

Morality

Babies begin as essentially amoral beings. They do not know right from wrong. By the time our children are living independently, we need to know that they have been inculcated with the family's morals, values and ethics. They also need to be developing their spiritual side.

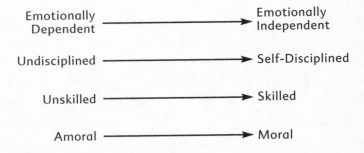

Emotional independence and self-discipline: the keys

This book concerns itself with these first two parenting tasks. I am assuming that, if they develop the emotional independence and self-discipline, our children will follow a natural imperative to acquire the skills they need and will pay attention to our wisdom if we believe that they are missing out on skills necessary to their well-being. Emerging from this and parallel to this will be their development of moral and ethical behaviour and spirituality.

When I began coaching parents some would come to me to talk about their child stealing and/or running away, I used to deal directly with the problem. Now I am less inclined to see these as problems to be dealt with in isolation through a 'stealing programme' or a 'staying safe programme'. I am more likely to ask: 'What are the chances if you ask him to do something, that he will?' Often, when we tackle the issues of anger or non-compliance, the other behaviours disappear.

Learning to make safe mistakes

I raised our first two children in the era of bright, shiny, interesting kettles. Telling them not to touch because it was dangerous meant nothing to them. Telling them not to touch because it was hot was often incorrect information, so that would lose me credibility. Telling them they were never to touch seemed unreasonable. There were already so many things they were forbidden to touch that I was finding it hard to enforce this.

What was a mum to do? How could I give them a safe mistake to learn from?

I filled the kettle with very hot — but not dangerously so — water and showed them I could just lightly touch something to check out the temperature. I said 'Hot' every time I touched the kettle. Of course, the first time they held their little hand on a little longer than was wise they got a fright. But no damage was done and they had learned a valuable lesson.

This model — of allowing our children to learn through safe mistakes — is way ahead in the success stakes compared with telling them, making rules and punishing infractions. It does, however, require forethought and planning. Most of us find it a lot easier to yell after the event.

I think this contrast encapsulates the choices of parenting. There is the swift and easy response — yell. And there is the carefully planned response that requires thought, restraint, patience and often hard work. It is this that will give our children a learning experience to stand them in good stead.

The choice is ours, but it is not an easy choice.

Parents must reflect the real world

Our children are so precious that it is hard to let them make mistakes. When they fall, we want to pick them up. When they plead for 'just one more story', what harm can that do? When they get a wonderful social offer in the middle of homework, we want them to go and enjoy themselves. ('You're only young once.') When they are tired and want to skip music practice, we hate to watch them struggle.

But our job is to reflect the real world that we are raising our children to operate in. Once they are out there, they will need to know: i) how to pick themselves up and carry on; ii) that pushing people does not necessarily endear you to them; iii) that sometimes they need to finish their work before they can play; iv) completion is often the biggest struggle.

Very few people are prepared to continue to tolerate a bad-tempered, unreliable friend, pupil, colleague or partner. There has to be a good story behind the first time someone said, 'Only his mother could love him.'

However, often, at a particular moment, our children need support more than they need a life lesson. It takes a great deal of parenting wisdom to distinguish a support moment from a learning moment.

So, I would like to moderate this heading. It is a parent's job to reflect the real world — in amounts that our children can handle.

I love the title of Bruno Bettelheim's book, *The Good-enough Parent*, in which he says that as long as we get it more or less right more often than not, our children will turn out okay. This always gives me enormous comfort after I have given way to yelling and screaming.

One of the great arts of parenting is reflecting the real world in amounts that our children can handle.

Learning to make wise choices

When our children are newborn we make almost all their decisions for them. If we want them to move from one place to another we simply pick them up and take them there.

By the time our children are 20, we are largely confined to making decisions about what we will or will not do: 'I am or am not prepared to share my front-door key, my car key, my bankcard.'

Before adulthood there is that lovely phase called adolescence, where half the decisions are ours and half the decisions are theirs — and there is often little agreement about which half is which.

One way of viewing parenting is that it is the task of teaching our children to make wise choices. The world our children will encounter when they are adults will be so complex that it will be, as it has always been, impossible for us to give them all the answers about how to react in a particular situation. The best we can hope for is to give them plenty of opportunities to make decisions when they are younger so they know their own minds and can think through cause and effect.

They need to have made enough safe mistakes in their short lives so that they can call on their learning from these to prevent them from making unnecessary further mistakes.

When things go wrong for my daughter Deborah — I don't remember being this clever with our first two children — the observation I least like to hear coming out of my mouth is 'I told you so' and the question I most like to hear is 'What did you learn from that?' It will be a great parenting day for me, when I can restrict myself to the latter.

The working mum or What will my child tell his shrink?

The biggest lack we seem to experience is the lack of time. Although many of us say we don't want our epitaph to read: 'I wish I'd spent less time at the office', we don't live our lives that way. Today there are many, many couples both of whom work outside the home, and many, many single parents doing the herculean task of being both the prime parent and the family breadwinner.

'It takes a village to raise a child' is no longer a new insight. We all know it and wonder how on earth we can possibly find that village when we are so busy trying to run home, work, school, after-school activities, fitness and everything else that there is simply no time to form the sort of friendships and acquaintances that will keep our children safe and supported.

I often see men today in their thirties and forties who weep when they tell me that their dad looked as if he had the time but was always too busy 'at the office' to be around at significant moments. The critical factor seems to be that he 'looked as if he had the time'. I don't see the same response from adult children who describe parents as working long hours so they could keep a roof over their children's heads and food on the table.

We simply don't know how our children will later interpret their mother's pursuit of a career, her desire to maintain her place on the corporate or professional ladder, her wish to earn enough to give her children possessions and experiences way beyond a child's needs.

I don't want to lay blame at the doorstep of the working mother. I had the privilege of being a full-time mother for the first five years of my children's lives and then spent much of the time working from home. I am living proof that it is possible to be physically there and still not spend enough time with my children — and to still look back with regret at all the busyness I allowed into my life.

The last 10 years in my practice have seen an increasing number of three-adult appointments where the third party is the nanny. This arrangement has a lot of merit in that there can be consistency among all the adults who are looking after the children.

However, while there are many nannies doing thoughtful and dedicated work for the children and adults they work for, it cannot be repeated too often that a nanny can care for and educate your child, but she cannot raise your child. That is a parent's privilege and responsibility.

Bearing in mind my favourite bumper sticker, which reads: 'A mother's place is in the wrong', if you want to review what you are doing and where you would like to make changes, one way is to imagine what your child may be saying about your parenting 30 years from now. Are you being the sort of parent you want to be? If you reckon you're about 50 percent of the way there, you're doing well.

The 60 minute parent

So if I have only 60 minutes with my children, what am I supposed to do? My best suggestion for the parents with very restricted time available to be with their children is: 'Use that time to be a parent.' Other people can be your child's nanny, friend and playmate. Only you can be their parent.

Use your time available to meet your child's needs — not necessarily their wants.

I am taking it as a given that your children live in paradise. They live in a war-free zone and they live in a democracy. They have a roof over their heads, enough food to eat, access to excellent education and adequate toys and clothing. They are in the privileged portion of this planet.

Your first responsibility is to give your children the emotional support they need so they will have the courage to have the experiences and do the learning they need to become emotionally independent adults.

Your second responsibility is to set suitable boundaries and expectations so they can safely tread the path from 'undisciplined to self-disciplined'.

If you have one hour or 24 hours a day, use the time for these basics. Now let's look at how.

2. The Family Structure

Each person in a family is of equal worth. A family should be, if at all possible, a place where everyone's needs are met. However, some people are more capable, more experienced and initially taller than the others. We call these people parents. It is their responsibility to look after those less capable, less experienced and shorter people whom we call children.

A family is not a democracy. Not every person's opinion is equally worthy and not everyone gets an equal vote. Those who are taller and have more experience and wisdom get to vote. They take into account the needs and wishes of the children but, ultimately, the decision-making and the responsibility are theirs.

A good family structure involves one or two (other numbers are also acceptable, but two is the most common number in Western countries) adults of roughly equal power, and a strong boundary that shows that these people are the ones with the power, control, wisdom and experience to care for and raise the others. Within a good family structure the children will also be of roughly equal power and their needs will be met equally over time.

It is usually easier to be a two-parent family because, when crunch time arrives, there is twice the power. Even if one parent is not at home, the at-home one represents the power of two.

Single parents usually have to work much harder to maintain the boundary between parent and children. Matters of discipline can be very wearying to parents who are in charge 24 hours a day with no relief in sight. I am in awe of how well the majority of single parents manage such a difficult, exhausting and unrelenting task.

When there is a strong family structure, everyone within the family seems happier. Duh!

A weak family structure

Noelle..

In some families, on some days, it feels as if one of the children is running the show. Whether through temper tantrums, non-compliance, hitting siblings, being over-sensitive or simply going slow on every request, there is often one family member whose ways dominate the family.

Everything becomes much more difficult when they are in 'one of their moods'. Everyone treads on eggshells to try to keep that family member happy. Sometimes when that person is absent the whole family feels more cohesive and life feels much simpler.

The other children seem to have less power than their rambunctious sibling. Their parents will often ask them to give way to the tricky one for the sake of peace, or so that everyone can get on with whatever it is that needs to be done.

The boundary between the adult sphere and the child sphere becomes blurred, and it is often worse when one parent is absent so there is only the 'power of one' to keep the family running.

Within this type of family structure everyone is somewhat unhappy.

I'm too short to run a family

This structure does not feel good for the family as a whole, but what about the target child? I have always thought that, when one child dominates a family, the least he could do is feel happy, but it is often this child who is the unhappiest.

What we often overlook is that this arrangement is not good for the child involved. The fact that children who rule households not only seem obnoxious but are also unhappy is testimony to this.

Children need suitable limits set for their behaviour. If it isn't obvious to them what the limits are, they will push and push at the boundaries to try to find them.

Often when parents come to see me about children's behaviour that is out of control we begin with the basics. No hitting or swearing. Children need to do as they are told. We set up strategies to ensure that the parents are in charge and that the child complies when asked to do something. In other words, we get mean.

Although it is designed to work that way, and although I know it is going to happen, I am always a little surprised when parents come back a fortnight later and tell me that, yes, their child is better behaved and, yes, he is much more co-operative. And then they always add, somewhat bemused, 'He seems so much happier.'

Our children need our love and our support. They also need us to provide boundaries for their behaviour, for their well-being and for their happiness.

The insecure child

A child who is dominating the family inappropriately will often appear insecure. The parents are puzzled because they cannot pinpoint events in their child's life that would lead her to be insecure. This is a child who has always been in familiar places, never been left with strangers, has had a minimal number of educational shifts, has always had the same three or four baby-sitters. Why is she so insecure?

The first set of questions I am likely to ask may seem surprising. 'What is her compliance like? How hard is it to get her to do simple household tasks? What is she like at getting ready in the morning? How hard is it to get her to do her homework?'

By this stage we are often getting a picture of a small tyrant who is often non-compliant even when coaxed or cajoled. The whole family often has to wait until she deigns to be ready. If asked to greet her beloved grandparents, she mumbles at her shoes or refuses to greet them. Homework is a nightmare. But the biggest problem is her insecurity. Sometimes even her teachers will wonder why this child appears so insecure.

When your child is dominating the household, when she looms this large in the family, it is no wonder she looks around and says, 'If I am the most powerful person in this family, who will look after me when I am in trouble?' Of course she feels insecure.

It always surprises parents when I say, 'First let's work on the compliance and then I am sure she will become more secure.' Putting in boundaries gives children security.

Setting boundaries

Non-compliance can manifest itself in many ways. How many of us have children who will blindly run off in carparks, ignoring the traffic? How many of us have children who run off from us in playgrounds with complete disregard to the dangers involved? How many of us have children who, when asked to get out of the car, will refuse and lock themselves in?

We may think the problem is the running way. However, when we think it through a little further, we can see these children are failing to respect the boundaries their parents set and, out in the public arena where control issues are more difficult, they know they can exploit this to the full. These children need to have boundaries set, not only to keep them safe, but also to ensure their well-being and happiness.

It is quite hard to see that running way is another form of non-compliance.

But imagine that I could interview your child and ask, 'If Mummy says to hold her hand in the carpark, are you supposed to run away?' I imagine your child would look quite horrified and say 'No'. So you see your child doesn't have a 'running-away problem' but rather a lack of respect for the boundaries you set to keep her safe.

Don't be surprised if my next step would be to work with you on her compliance at home. Once your child is doing as she is told more often at home, you have increased the chances that she will be more compliant out. She will be less likely to do things that she knows she is not supposed to do.

By making the boundaries clearer and stronger, by establishing yourself as the most powerful person in her daily life, you will have taken care of the runaway behaviour and have a happier child as well.

When parents fight

So how can a family that is working well, with parents in charge and children nurtured, guided and protected, turn into a family where one or more children dominate and the boundaries are weakened or shattered? Even more important, when the boundaries are shattered and one or more children is out of control and ruling the roost, what would it take to restore the boundaries and put everyone in a much happier position? The key to this is a phenomenon known as Karpman's Triangle.

Karpman's Triangle

In my early counselling days I was taught about the positions of Persecutor, Victim and Rescuer. The rapid switching from one to another was known as Karpman's Triangle. Stephen Karpman published the original article in the *Journal of Transactional Analysis*.

Karpman's Triangle describes the situation whereby one person in an interaction takes one position (Persecutor, Victim or Rescuer) and then the next person takes up one of the available remaining positions. The positions can now spin around between these two people or more can join the triangle. Once a family has begun this way of interacting its powerful structure is lost, the parent-child boundary has dissolved and a lot of unhappiness results. If a family can haul itself out of the triangle a powerful structure can be restored.

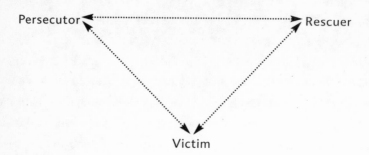

Picture the scene

It has been a long day. Mum is preparing dinner, the children have done their homework and are stationed in front of the TV. Dad comes in and greets everyone and shortly afterwards Mum calls the family to dinner. The TV programme has about five minutes to run.

Dad, meaning to be helpful, pushes the TV off button.

'You kids get to the table now. Your mum has called you.'

(Feel free to interpret Dad's move as being helpful to Mum. I would, but the children behave as if he is a b-i-i-g Persecutor. This conveniently gives them the opportunity to be pathetic Victims.)

Children (expert Victims) whine:

a) 'That's not fair.'

b) 'There's only five minutes to go.'

c) 'We'll miss the ending.'

d) 'I'm not hungry.'

e) All of the above.

Mum, feeling like Rescuing the Victims, Persecutes Dad.

'Now look what you've done. They are all upset and they won't eat their dinner. Surely another few minutes wouldn't have hurt. The programme would have been over and then they would have come happily to the table.'

Dad, firmly the Victim now, wonders why he bothered coming home early. The office is starting to look extremely attractive. He mutters, 'I was only trying to help.' Quickly switching to Persecutor he continues:

'Anyway, you let the kids watch far too much television.'

Mum, now the defensive Victim: 'Well, it was all going very smoothly till you walked in.'

Child (Rescuer to the rescue) sidles over: 'I love you, Daddy.'

Both parents (yelling in unison): 'Get up to the table.'

Child (Victim) sits and grizzles.

The atmosphere at the table is awful and the children stir their food around their plates, sullenly whining. They all resist the opportunity to tell about some good things that have happened in their day.

This is such a typical family scene. One minute we are sailing along just fine; the next minute we find ourselves in a situation where everyone is mad at everyone else and the atmosphere is thoroughly unpleasant.

If we review what happened, there were a few points at which this situation could have been avoided or retrieved.

Changing shifts or 'I was only trying to help'

A few years ago our oldest child, Rob, was in hospital. He was there for a week so we went to visit him many times. A peculiar thing happened if we went in around 3–3.30 pm: the ward appeared to be deserted. There was not a doctor, nurse or other health professional in sight. They all appeared to have vanished.

If we looked hard enough we could see them all huddled in one room. You see, during a change of shifts, the nurses don't just race in and start distributing medication. They spend time with the previous shift finding out about what has happened, who needs more of the same, who needs something different. Only then do they proceed to action.

Similarly in families, we have different shifts with different systems. Assuming a mum at home and a dad at work, this family has three distinct shifts. There is the two-parent morning shift, the daytime Mum-only shift and the after-work two-parent shift.

In the scene above, Dad came in with the true intention of being helpful. When Mum asked the children to the table, he was being genuinely helpful when he switched off the TV, but it all went horribly wrong after that.

You see, Mum had the daytime shift and she and the children knew whether she allowed the children to finish off watching programmes and whether 'Dinner's ready' meant immediately or come at the end of the programme. She also knew who had had a tough day and was fragile, who had set the table in order to be free to watch TV, whose turn it was to choose the late afternoon programme.

So one way of avoiding tripping into a Karpman's Triangle is to make sure you have full information. When you come on duty, check with 'Matron' what has happened in your absence. When you arrive home and it is shift changeover, a really good question, rather than just barrelling in and 'helping', is: 'Is there anything I can do to help?' Whoever has been on the last shift, will know what needs doing.

Avoiding the triangle

You may be wondering who started the triangle. The children did. They were asked to do something by a parent and promptly threw themselves into Victim position and began whingeing. Dad leapt into the Persecutor position and Mum followed soon after with a Persecutor position of her own and it all went downhill from there.

One alternative would have been for Dad to avoid joining his children in the triangle. He could have said, 'Hang on, let's see what Mum says.' Mum could have said, 'I have given them permission to watch that programme. I know it sounded like a call but it was actually a countdown. Could you make sure (because Mum knows children's complete inability to turn off such a seductive medium) the TV goes off as soon as the programme is over?' Dad could have gone back and said, 'Your kind mum has given us a five-minute reprieve,' watched to the end of the programme with his children and then hustled them off to wash their hands and come to the table. Mum could have said, 'Thanks for your help.'

Notice that, this time, Dad declined the invitation to join the triangle, put in a firm boundary and presented as a unit with Mum. The power of two adults pulling together would have been a great model for the children and would have restored the strong family balance.

Alternatively, Mum could have said, 'Yes. Dinner is hot and ready and they need to come now. Thanks for your help.' Dad could have gone back and said, 'Your Mum's been working at getting a nice meal on the table. We need to go now.' There would have been a bit of grizzling but, again, seeing that they had two parents pulling together and no one willing to Rescue the grizzlers, they would have rapidly become civilised and a pleasant meal could have been had by all. If one child was determined to stay Victim — 'It's not fair' is a great Victim whine — and then carry on until they were Persecuting the family, the parents could put a stop to her attempts to pull the family into the triangle by sending her to her room until she was ready to join the family in a reasonable frame of mind.

Leaving the triangle

Back to Scene One. Mum could have noticed Dad being sucked into the triangle when the children whined about the TV going off. She could have held off being the Rescuer, thereby reinforcing Dad's position as the Persecutor and making sure the family fully entered the triangle.

Together they could step out of the triangle and restore the position of two-parent power by Mum standing shoulder to shoulder with Dad and saying, 'You heard what your Dad said. Now turn off the TV and come to dinner.'

If in doubt, restore the strong structure

But shouldn't the children have done what their mum said? Shouldn't the children have done what their dad said? Wasn't it reasonable that the children just had five more minutes of TV since they had watched most of the programme? What about the fact that dinner was ready?

All these are valid points, but there is one overriding factor. The most important thing is that the children have the protection of strong boundaries created by their parents pulling together. Often we hear the other parent asking our children to do something that may not be our first priority. Should we point this out or should we back the other parent?

If in doubt, go and stand shoulder to shoulder with the other parent and say, 'Do what your father (mother) says now.' (I also need to point out that staying in your chair and yelling from two rooms away, 'Will you kids just do as your mother says. Now,' will not work. You need to get out of your chair and stand alongside the other parent.)

If we have to choose between getting what we, individually, want and sticking together, sticking together will give your child far more protection and security than two parents fighting over whether or not their child should have a second chocolate biscuit or put on their shoes before going out the door.

Of course if your spouse is about to beat up your child or do some other sort of damage you will move to protect your child. But most of the things we get into adult disagreements about are not life-or-death or even bodily-harm situations.

I cannot emphasise enough how important it is for your child to have parents who pull together and for your family not to fall into the triangle more often than is necessary.

This is also a good message for grandparents and other relatives. Think carefully before you contradict a parent in front of a child. You may be right or wrong in what you are suggesting but, unless the child is in danger, it is better for children to have adults in agreement.

If parents seriously disagree

Wait till the child is asleep. This is bound to happen within 12 hours and mature adults are supposed to be able to delay gratification! Then you can have as big a row as you like. You can be Victim, Persecutor, Rescuer or all three simultaneously. Just don't do it in front of your children or within their hearing.

Vernon and I have certainly had times when we disagree over child-rearing. We have opposite temperaments: I am always ready to look at ways in which the children can be social and have fun and Vernon is more likely to look toward their responsibilities and what tasks need to be done.

It has taken a lot of practice and a lot of courage, when our children need an instant answer, to be able to say to them, 'Dad and I are seeing this differently. Give us time to sort it out.' We don't return until we can give them a yes or no from the two of us. It might engender the odd sneered

'You always do what Mum/Dad says,' but our children know that when we have sorted out the difference in our opinions, an answer from the two of us holds firm.

It is inevitable that when you marry a person of the opposite temperament you are bound to see things differently. It is a fine role-model for children to know that parents of varying views can come to a united policy about their children. They just don't need to witness the process.

3. Wisdom vs Power

Picture the scene

You are standing at the kerb, holding your four-year-old's hand.

Child (positively wriggling with enthusiasm): 'Mummy, Mummy, I can cross the road all by myself.'

Mum (hanging on tight): 'No, sweetheart. You are much too little.'

Child: 'But Mummy, Mummy! I am such a fast runner! No cars will get me.'

Mum: 'Yes and you have such lovely strong legs but, think about it, you can run five, maybe six kilometres an hour and the cars are going at 50. You cannot possibly outrun them.'

Child: 'But Mummy, the policeman came to kindy and I will look to the right and I will look to the left and I will look to the right again.'

If you consider this scene, you will see that the mother is exercising overview, experience and wisdom. She knows the likelihood that a four-year-old would stop to look before crossing, and she also knows a young child cannot judge traffic speeds.

The child is showing enormous intelligence with his reasoning powers and considerable power with the force of his arguments. There is only one problem. What he is suggesting is brainless. It is a brainless thing to think that, at four, he can cross the road safely every time and this is not an area of life where he can afford to learn through making mistakes.

Now let's take the scene one step further. Your child lets go of your hand and runs out across the road. Let's ignore Option One because that is too awful to contemplate. Let's go to Option Two. He gets across safely.

Now you have a seriously dangerous child on your hands. He has used his power and his intelligence to prove to himself that he was right. But just because he got across safely, it doesn't mean Mum was any less wise in her explanation. Just because he got across safely doesn't make it any less of a brainless thing to do.

Experience
Overview
and
Wisdom

Intelligence
Power
but
Brainless

Just because our child was lucky this one time doesn't mean our advice wasn't good. It simply means we have to be far more vigilant with this child around kerbs because he uses his power and his intelligence to override his parent's wishes and this has led him to do something extremely dangerous.

We now know that the next time we approach a road we will have to hang on to him very tightly. We have to raise our level of awareness and supervision. We have to embark on a careful programme of teaching road safety.

First, we have to be prepared to carry him across the road if we cannot trust him to walk holding our hand. Once he accepts our hand-holding, we can offer him our hand to take. Once he can reliably cross the road holding our (passive) hand, we can move on to a gentle back-of-the-T-shirt grip. Once he accepts that, we can allow him to cross holding on to our skirt or jeans. Once he can do that safely, we can progress to his walking alongside us as we cross. Once he can do that safely and reliably, he is ready to learn some of the rules for crossing the road by himself, under close supervision. It will probably not be until he is closer to 10 that he will have the experience and judgement to cross a busy suburban road safely.

Good arguing or fine reasoning?

From a very early age our children are encouraged, both at home and at school, to be able to formulate a good morning talk, a good speech, a good debate. No wonder they are so good at marshalling their reasons. They are also encouraged to think laterally.

We are talking about fine skills here and I think that they are to be encouraged. We want children who will think before they act, be able to reason their way through issues, be able to see both sides of an argument and be able to express their ideas clearly and cogently.

However, we do not need these fine skills to be used against us in matters of reasonable compliance and safety.

Often, when our children advance excellent reasons as to why they should do certain things, they sound very plausible. When we advance our own counter-argument, we may not sound very convincing — even to ourselves. This doesn't mean we are wrong. It may mean our children's debating skills are better. It may mean our children are more naturally powerful by temperament than we are. More often, it means there are more far-reaching consequences than we think our children can comprehend or than can be easily and rapidly explained.

We would probably be better off giving them the reasons. We do them a disservice if we do not. Even if they do not fully comprehend our reply, we have respected their intelligence. If we overreach their comprehension, that is often sufficient reason for them to back down.

When I was teaching Year 12 biology I was occasionally challenged with a whined 'But why do we have to do this?' I would begin with a carefully explained monologue on where this topic fitted in the syllabus, why the particular skill was necessary and what underpinned the particular theory. By the time the pupil's eyes had glazed over I would follow up with 'And the second reason is because I said so.' It never failed to amaze me how often the pupil would say 'Okay' and wander off.

'My writing is better than yours — see!'

It probably happens in every Year One class, every year. The teacher shows her class how to write a lower case 'a'.

'Now, class, we start here and then go over the top, make a backwards circle and then make a stick.'

There always has to be one child in the class who will put up their hand and say, 'Please, Miss! I like to make the stick first and then do the circle … and see, my one looks just as good.'

Of course he's right — for the moment. His 'a' does look as good as the teacher's. So his response displays initiative, power and intelligence. However, the teacher, with her overview, experience and wisdom, knows that within 18 months she — or another teacher — will be teaching cursive writing and will need the child to be in the habit of starting his letters in the most appropriate place.

Most issues like this also have a compliance component. Often the child is also challenging the teacher's authority.

What do I mean by brainless?

Here are some examples of 'brainless' statements:

- You're not my friend.
- You're not the boss of me.
- You can't come to my party.
- I can go out in the rain without a jacket and I won't get sick.
- I don't have to do any homework — the teacher said so.
- If I start my project too early, I'll find it hard to stay interested.
- All my friends are allowed to go to R16 movies.
- I can stay up late Friday, Saturday and Sunday and I will be fine on Monday morning.
- I can go to that party and all my friends will look out for me if I drink too much.
- If you won't let me get my ears pierced, how about a belly-button ring because no one would know about it?

This last one has a familiar sound for me.

Once we have grasped the idea that our highly intelligent children will use their intelligence and power to try to convince us that their less than wise ideas have merit, we can respond appropriately. Instead of reasoning, a vague mumble and a private resolution to deal with this later will save you from an unwinnable argument.

My all-time favourite 'brainless' comment from a highly intelligent, powerful child whose parent had just annoyed him is, 'You're not coming to my party.' Don't fall into the trap. Don't respond, hands on hips, with the impeccable parental logic and sarcasm of, 'So who do you think is going to do all the cooking?' Vaguely mumble, 'That's a shame,' amble off and forget it.

Another great hook for parents who forget about their wisdom and experience is, 'You're not my friend' or its stronger version, 'I hate you.' This is not the time to head into 'Mummy's so sad she's going to cry,' or 'That is a terrible thing to say — and so hurtful.' Above all, don't hook into a low-level debate: 'No you don't, Yes I do, No you don't, Yes I do' ... Try: 'Oh, that's a shame,' and wander away. Save your energy for getting his teeth cleaned.

A lovely example of not hooking in was told to me by the wise grandmother of a four-year-old.

Grandchild: 'You're not my friend.'

Grandmother: 'What's a friend?'

Grandchild: 'I don't know.'

And he giggled and ran off to do something much more fun and important.

A modern brainless challenge

It is only in the last 10 years that children have started responding to simple compliance requests with 'You are not the boss of me.' It is an unwise parent who begins to take this seriously and wonder if in fact she has the right to ask the child to carry someone else's plate from the table, or whether homework is a good idea or merely a device by teachers who cannot fit all their teaching into a busy day. 'You're not the boss of me' may simply be a very powerful way of saying 'I don't want to do that' or a very intelligent way of diverting you from the task at hand to a discussion of issues of power and control.

It might be fun to try to impart all the information about why a parent needs to guide a child for 20 years from an undisciplined baby to a self-disciplined adult ...

And that the most successful people in our society are those who can tolerate frustrations, delay gratification and get on with the task at hand ...

On the other hand, recognising that your child has just said no to a simple parental request and responding accordingly is a great shortcut. Read on!

On the edge

Hardly a week goes by when I don't get a worried call from a parent asking whether a six- or seven-year-old (usually a boy) can be suicidal. When I enquire a little further I hear that the child has said, 'I wish I were dead,' or 'I'm going to kill myself.'

This is a ghastly thing for a parent to hear. There is a lot of publicity about the high suicide rate among young males (particularly) in New Zealand and about how we need to begin prevention early in the raising of our children.

However, when I talk to parents about what preceded this outrageous statement I find it has often started when a parent has asked a child to do something relatively simple — like feed the dog or make his bed or tidy up his books. The child has not wanted to do it, a lot of arguing has ensued, the task is still not done, the child is angry and/or upset and, as a final rejoinder, he has flung at his parents, 'I wish I were dead.'

This is a very obstreperous way of displaying power and intelligence, and a particularly brainless alternative to making his bed. Use your wisdom, overview and experience. Swallow the dramatic response ('What a ghastly thing to say. Do you realise how precious life is? Do you realise how precious you are to all the family? How can you say such a dreadful thing?'). Swallow the sarcastic response ('I would hate you to do that — and could you make your bed first?').

Use your wisdom, power and experience and deal with it as a particularly colourful, modern-day way of your child saying, 'No! I don't want to make my bed,' and then getting upset about the arguing that ensues.

4. Increasing a Child's
Self-esteem?

Which came first?

Many, many clients arrive with an assumed explanation of their child's behaviour: 'My child has low self-esteem.' Who has given them this diagnosis? Sometimes doctors, sometimes health nurses, sometimes teachers, sometimes family members, sometimes it is their own. If I ask them about their own self-esteem some will say, 'I have low self-esteem too and I don't want my child to suffer in the same way.'

Parents and teachers often give 'low self-esteem' as the explanation why a lovely child, from a perfectly good home with a roof that doesn't leak, more than enough clothes to wear, good food available, access to excellent education and with one or more devoted parents, seems unhappy, unfulfilled and fails to achieve her potential.

When we talk a little further, it becomes clear that this child is not motivated to work, may be quite disruptive and unco-operative, may have difficulty meeting and greeting teachers and grandparents, is often grumpy and bad-tempered, is tearful or angry when asked to do simple tasks for the family, cannot remember where she left her jumper. The solution to all or any of these problems — say parents and teachers — is to increase her self-esteem, then her behaviour will improve.

I see it the other way around. When a child is contributing to family and school in an age-appropriate way, when the child can warmly and politely greet people, when a child is mainly cheerful and only gets upset about things that are (again, age-appropriately) worth getting upset about, when our child can tolerate a reasonable level of the ordinary frustrations of life, only then are we likely to be dealing with a child of quietly confident, high self-esteem.

The low self-esteem spiral

No one wants to see their child enter or slide down a spiral of low self-esteem. It all begins with the child who says 'I can't'.

Once our children have said 'I can't' often enough and convincingly enough that they and their parents believe it, they begin to carve out an area of unnecessary incompetence. If they have added several areas of unnecessary incompetence to their repertoire, we begin to have a child with the attitude and belief of: 'I can't do much.'

The more our children convince themselves that there are things they can't do, the more their opinion of themselves drops and they begin to view themselves as not particularly capable. They lose that 'bright-eyed, bushy-tailed' look and begin glowering at the world or being bored a lot of the time. We begin to wonder what we could possibly do to make them happier. We worry about their self-esteem and what we could do to boost it. All our attempts seem to meet with failure. Our child is beginning to believe that they are 'no good'.

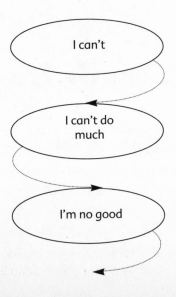

Children with low self-esteem are likely to start not to care for their bodies or their brains. Beyond the ordinary experimentation that is part of teenage-hood and greying parental hair, they ease the pain of incompetence and boredom through drinking excessively, taking drugs, indulging in risky and brainless behaviour and immersing themselves in music with depressingly negative lyrics and inner ear-damaging volume. They hang about with peers of a similar ilk and their sexual activities are more about rebellion and trying to be part of the crowd than they are about developing greater intimacy in relationships. I date myself by referring to this as the Sex, Drugs and Rock'n'Roll phase.

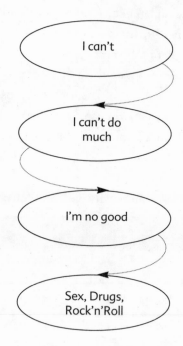

As our children become more and more preoccupied with an antisocial peer group and antisocial and unhealthy activities, they begin to pull away from 'pro-social' friends and family activities. Often they appear depressed and we worry that their attitude has slid from 'Don't worry, Mum, I'll be fine' to 'What's the Use?'

If they keep going down this ghastly spiral they may appear to be drop-ping out of even trying to be on a pathway to being skilled, self-disciplined, emotionally independent and ethical. We feel as if we are losing them and seem powerless to stop the slide. And of course our biggest fear, when our child is not leading a productive and useful life and is becoming increasingly miserable and indifferent, is teen suicide.

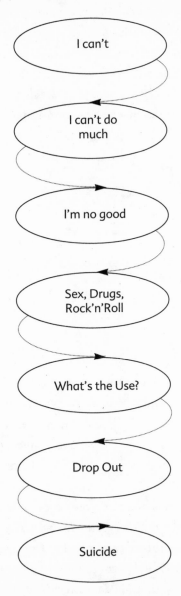

Not surprisingly, we are all keen to prevent this downhill low self-esteem spiral. The further up the spiral we can catch the behaviour, the easier it is to hook our child off it and onto an upward spiral of optimism and confidence.

The high self-esteem spiral

Whenever our children discover there is something they can do, they are potentially on the upward spiral of developing great self-esteem.

Enough examples of 'I can' in their lives and they begin to realise there are many things they can do.

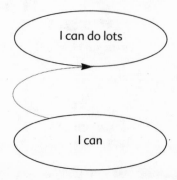

Once they are competent (through their self-feedback) and appreciated (through our feedback) for many pro-social activities, they begin to see possibilities: 'I can do anything.' This is not from any arrogant 'the world owes me' position, but rather from a position of 'I can do anything I put my mind to and work at hard enough'. Presumably they will have also learned that there are some things it is unrealistic for them to reach for, and to tolerate the frustration of that where necessary.

With the ability, the will and the experience of setting goals, working hard and reaching them, our child is entitled to believe: 'I'm great.' There is nothing boastful about this; I certainly don't mean it in an 'I'm better than ... ' way. In fact, when we look around us at the adults we would put in that 'I'm great' category, they are characterised by their quiet confidence that they can plan, work hard and achieve their goals and dreams.

Children who are developing emotional independence and self-discipline, whose skill base continues to improve and who are developing desirable

44

values and ethics, are likely to have a whole world of opportunity available to them. The world is theirs for the taking.

Moving from down to up

So, how do we get our children off the downward spiral and onto the upward spiral?

We have all tried so many times to deal with children who say 'I can't' by trying to convince or persuade or encourage or entice them into believing 'I can'. We cajole, explain, offer incentives and rewards, threaten dire consequences and offer punishment. It doesn't work, but we keep doing it anyway. Finally, at the end of our tether, we shout, scream, chase and smack.

The outcome is an exhausted parent and a resentful child. Even if the task eventually gets done, it is rare for the child to have a feeling of 'I can' no matter how many times we say, 'See, I told you you could do it. Now why did you have to perform all day and get everyone all het up, when you managed to finally do that in 10 minutes?' The child does not feel she has chosen the successful path; she feels that her resistance was worn down — for the moment!

While parental logic says that the child has learned from this and next time will do it right away, child logic appears to guide them towards a repeat performance. So the child learns to cry, yell, run, avoid and delay. And the parent learns that it easier to do it herself and only pick the fights when it is essential.

Most of these battles take place in the privacy of our own home where we can walk away and not insist. Apart from our long-suffering neighbours, most of the world is not aware that battles rage over the competence or otherwise of children to help around the house, wash behind their ears, find the floor of their bedroom or remember to take their gym clothes to school. And if all else fails, we can do a lot of these things for our children.

The big exposure comes over homework. That is when the world gets to see that we cannot persuade, cajole, threaten or entice a child to learn five spelling words faster or more quietly than our child can go through the tears and temper rituals of 'I can't, it's too hard, I am too tired, I am too upset, I'll do it later, I need to watch *The Simpsons*, I hate my teacher, I hate YOU.'

'I won't, I can't'

The first trick lies at the top of the low self-esteem spiral. It lies in what precedes 'I can't'. Before a child is convinced that they can't, and before a child has succeeded in convincing us that they can't, there has been a large amount of 'I won't' going on. It may be disguised as …

- It's too hard.
- I'm too tired.
- It's not my turn.
- I don't know how.
- She made me do it.
- I hate you forever.
- I am crying uncontrollably.
- I am leaving the room.

... but believe me, it means 'I won't'.
'I can't' is almost always preceded by 'I won't'.

So by allowing our children, often enough, to get away with 'I won't' we inadvertently pitch them toward the downward spiral of low self-esteem.

'But,' I hear you say, 'you have no idea how often I have encouraged them that they are capable and competent, that they can do whatever it is that they are finding difficult or distasteful. You just don't understand how hard I have worked at raising their self-esteem.'

And so have I. I have tried and tried and tried.

But we were both wrong.

There is only one way for a person — of whatever height — to feel proud of themselves. That is to struggle and overcome challenges and to discover that 'I can!' People with high self-esteem have a lot of 'I cans' in their lives — a lot of achieving the things they found hard, of struggling with difficult situations, of overcoming obstacles.

'I have to, I can'

Up till now we have talked as if the high self-esteem spiral began with 'I can'. But there is a shadowy figure that precedes 'I can' in the lives of our children. Often, in order to get our children to do ordinary everyday tasks we have to override their resistance and insist that they do the task. Often, they discover 'I can' as a result of 'I have to'.

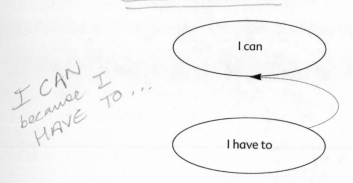

I CAN because I HAVE TO ...

It would be a wonderful world if we could leave our children to make their own discoveries, to learn solely by experience, to learn that struggling gets you to places you never imagined you were capable of, that it is in that struggle that we learn to be competent and self-reliant.

But we live in a real world where we simply cannot risk our children learning about traffic by playing on the motorway, where they cannot learn about sabotaging their educational opportunities by getting to 15 and then

48

discovering they cannot read, or by beating up their peers and then discovering that life is lonely without friends.

There are two good reasons we cannot let our children learn by the law of the jungle.

The first is that we produce very few offspring. This means that each and every one is very, very precious and that, if we are to perpetuate our species, we need to take good care of them. Frankly, a female frog who produces — with a little bit of help from a male, or more precisely several males — hundreds of offspring in a breeding season does not need to take particularly good care to ensure that at least one male and one female survive to perpetuate the froggie dynasty.

In fact, if you look at the animal kingdom you will see that the fewer offspring an adult breeding pair produces in a lifetime, the greater care they take of their young. Watch nature programmes on TV with a parenting eye and you'll see how carefully the larger mammals guard, lead and teach their offspring.

So the first reason we cannot allow our children to learn simply from experience is that it is too dangerous out there. We need to save them from dangerous mistakes.

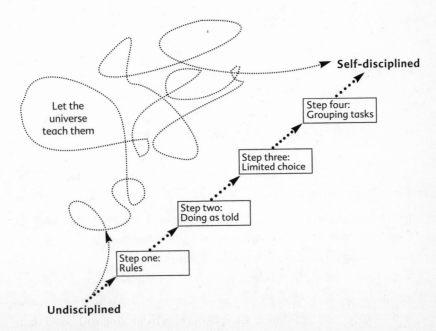

The second reason we need to teach our children, rather than let them learn simply through experience, is that there is just not enough time for them to learn that way. There are so many things they need to know in order to live safely and independently by the time they have reached adulthood that there simply is not enough time for them to 'reinvent the wheel' over every activity in their lives.

The only way they can pack in enough learning and gain enough life skills to live independently is to take some things as a given, simply because a teacher or parent says so. I am not talking about the joys of discovery; I am talking about the simple things that can make a day heaven or hell:

- Come here so I can tie your shoelace, please.
- Get your lunchbox, please.
- Don't put your sister in the dishwasher, please.
- Put on your seatbelt, please.
- Do your homework now, please.
- Be home by 11 pm, please.

To summarise: Our children need to do some things their parent tells them to assist them in their growing up:

(i) because it is dangerous out there; and

(ii) because there is a lot to learn.

So the shadowy figure that precedes 'I can' is, very often, 'I have to'. Often, our task as a parent is to manage a child who is saying, 'I can't', recognise that they mean, 'I won't', and insist upon 'I have to', so that we and they can delight in the fact that 'I can'. This pattern, repeated many times, means that we can nudge them off the low self-esteem spiral and onto the high self-esteem spiral, see page 52.

We had a memorable example of this when Deborah was about 10 years old. I asked her to empty the dishwasher which she had done many times before. This particular day she whined and grizzled and bargained: 'It's too hard. I'm too tired. I'll do the top shelf if you do the bottom shelf. I can't bear to do cutlery. If you do the cutlery, I'll do the rest.'

I stuck to my guns. She stuck to hers.

Eventually Mummy Power won and the wretched dishwasher was emptied — in about four times as long as it would have taken me to do it myself. Both of us felt aggrieved: Deborah because she had been made to do something she didn't want to do; me because I didn't think I should have to struggle so hard to get a simple piece of co-operation.

The following day I overheard Deborah saying, with considerable pride, to one of her friends, 'It's my job in the family to empty the dishwasher and my mum trusts me with all the glasses and the fine china.' I bit my tongue. It wasn't her job to appreciate what that bit of raised self-esteem had cost me in frustration and determination!

From 'I won't' to 'I have to'

The only way I know to safely raise children who grow to be young adults who are emotionally independent, able to tolerate frustration, self-disciplined, skilled both practically and socially, pleasant to be with and ethical is to begin with the premise that it is our responsibility, as parents, to make them do some things they may not necessarily want to do.

In wishing to take our children from the low self-esteem spiral of 'I can't' to the high self-esteem spiral of 'I can', we first have to take them from 'I won't' to 'I have to'. The acceptance of imposed discipline is the beginning of their swiftest and safest pathway to self-discipline and will enable them to live the sort of life that is likely to give them pleasure and satisfaction.

Learning to tolerate the frustrations of doing things we don't want to do is one of the most important skills of the self-disciplined. That is why the recurring theme of this book is 'getting children to do as they are told'.

Sometimes when you hear their pleas, their shouts of outrage, their wails of protest, it is hard to remember that we are not asking them to pull out their toenails and put them on a plate for us. The pathway to self-discipline will be fought over simple, ought-to-be-painless requests such as:

- Let's change your nappy now.
- Please get your jumper now.
- Leave the cat alone.
- The table needs to be cleared now, please.
- We need to check your homework notebook.
- What are the safety arrangements for Saturday night's party?

Of course, we don't expect any thanks or recognition for this until they are older than 25 or have children of their own. Getting our children to do as they are told is a tough but essential part of parenting and compliance to reasonable requests leads to increased self-esteem.

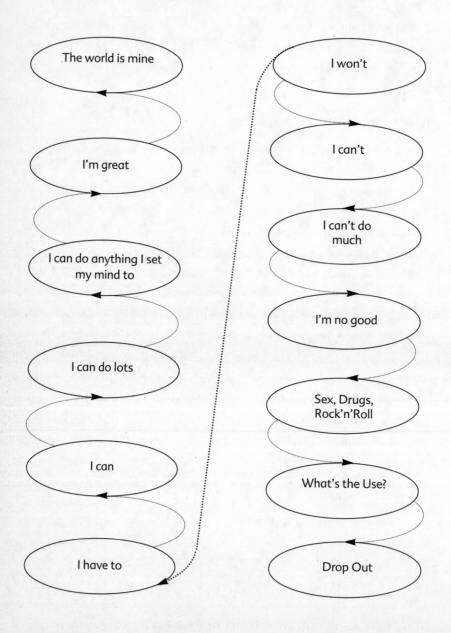

5. Why It All Turns to Custard So Quickly

Most of us try so hard as parents. We take care of our children's physical needs, we take care of their emotional needs, we take care of their intellectual needs, we set up times for them to have fun and we set up times for them to rest.

Some of us feel lucky that we have children who enjoy life, are focused and purposeful, have a reasonable amount of gratitude for things done for them and enjoy being part of their family.

Others of us are struggling on a daily basis with children who appear to fight us every step of the way, groan and moan when we ask them to do something, appear as if nothing will make them happy and behave as if they didn't deserve to be born into this awful family.

Sometimes, we have both sorts of children in the same family. How does this happen?

Often it can be because we are trying too hard. We are taking full responsibility for our children's actions and feelings — and they are taking little or no responsibility.

A vicious circle

It all begins with our child being upset or angry or not wanting to act on a simple request such as 'Get dressed' or 'Please set the table'. Our child, instead of taking care of it, immediately hands the problem over to us.

How do we know we have just been 'handed over to'? We know when we try to make the situation better or find a compromise and our child still refuses. Somehow, a simple issue has become large and complex and insoluble and we are hooked in.

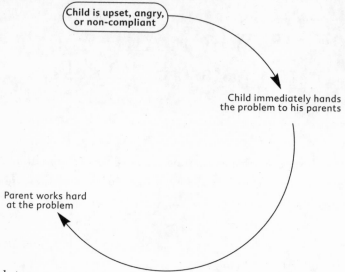

We explain

Our first step is usually to try to explain to the child why it is necessary, or how much more smoothly things will run, or why it might be good for him to allow another child to use a pencil for a minute.

If he doesn't like that explanation we are likely to try another, and possibly a third. We make the assumption: 'If only I can explain it the right way, he will be reasonable and see it my way.' What we fail to realise is that our child has already decided that no explanation, no matter how reasonable, is going to make him take the problem — not to mention the solution — back. He is determined that the problem is not going to be his.

I would like to be clear that we are not dealing with a nasty, calculating manipulating child. All this happens at a subconscious level. Our child has learned through previous experience that while he keeps us involved in explanations, he doesn't actually have to do anything.

We distract

If explaining has not proved successful, we try another tack. We suggest ways it could be done more easily, or we suggest that, if he just does it quickly, it will all be over with very soon. We suggest that he stop thinking about how upset he is and think about how good he will feel when it is all over.

If he is upset about something we may suggest he think about something else, or that it is not really important, or we may give the other person's point of view.

If he is angry we may suggest he uses his anger in another way — rather like a therapist in the movies — maybe by punching his mattress or his pillow.

If we really like to live dangerously we may say, 'You probably need more sleep.'

We may try to suggest that there are more important things in the world to be angry about, or we may try to tell him about things that have happened to us that were really worth getting angry about.

We cajole and encourage

If none of this works we may move on to trying to sweet-talk him into seeing it our way. We try to make whatever it is much more palatable. We appeal to his better nature, his strong arms, his caring about the family, his need to contribute. We return to 'I' messages to let him know how we feel and how pleased we will be when it is sorted out. We suggest that it is character-building and that there are many sound reasons why our point of view will work well for him in his life.

Notice how hard we are working. Notice how little work our child is doing.

Of course he may be putting a great deal of effort into resistance and arguing, but he is not putting any effort at all into doing whatever is required of him. He has handed the problem to us. We took it over willingly. And now we are working very, very hard at solving it.

We threaten

It is still not working, so we up the ante.

We tell our child what will happen if he doesn't begin to behave appropriately. We think up a punishment and hope it will not be too hard for us to see it through, or that our child will not become so upset that he will render himself incapable. We wonder why we had children in the first place. We tell him people may not like him if he carries on so. We tell him that his grandparents will be disappointed in him.

We punish

If none of this is working, there is always the last resort. We shout, we smack, we send him to his room, we cancel outings, we cancel parties, and we ground him. We ban his favourite TV programme for a week, for a month, and then wonder if we are going to be able to see it through — and what about the other children. Is it fair that they should also be penalised when they weren't involved? Is it really fair that the miscreant should be excluded, knowing that the others can watch?

Our child gets angrier and becomes resentful. He complains that we are unfair and we have favourites and we don't understand. He collapses into such hysteria that he becomes incapable of any action. He shouts, 'I hate you! You are the meanest mum in the whole world.' He hits and swears, and then we have that behaviour to deal with too.

Where are we now?

The whole atmosphere has turned to custard. Everyone is upset and aggrieved, the atmosphere is awful and we feel a mixture of anger and despair.

The outcome of a recurrence of this scenario is threefold:
- Our child becomes less competent.
- As parents we feel incompetent.
- The penalty is distance.

Our child becomes less competent

The more our child resists doing the tasks expected or requested of him, the more he becomes angry at the least little thing. The more he becomes upset at minor irritations, the less competent our child becomes. We want our children to increase their spheres and levels of competence so they can have the joy, satisfaction and increased self-esteem that come from tackling and overcoming challenges.

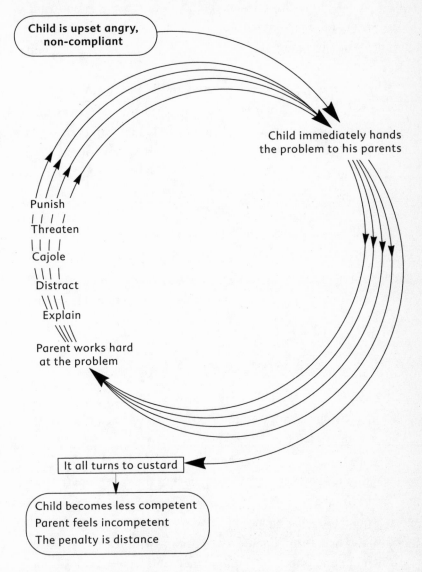

As parents we feel incompetent

When our children are behaving badly — when they whine and grizzle over any request, when they are aggressive to each other and rude to us —we begin to wonder if we know what we are doing. We feel incompetent as parents and it feels much worse when our children's behaviour embarrasses us in public.

The penalty is distance

When my children are misbehaving and I am angry, it is certainly unpleasant and I do try hard to change things, but it is not painful. The situation I find most painful is when they have annoyed me to such an extent — or I have annoyed them to such an extent — that I don't want to be in the same room.

When I have tipped over from anger to indifference, when I wish them every good fortune in their lives but wonder if they could live on another planet while they are doing it, when I am so fed up with them that I would rather not breathe the same air, then it feels the most painful.

Feeling angry is unpleasant; feeling indifferent is painful. And if we keep going around in the circle of explaining, distracting, cajoling, threatening and punishing, the penalty is distance.

This sort of scenario is awful for everyone involved and yet we all get into it from time to time. When it is happening too often for us to be able to shrug it off with a 'Let's just cancel today', it is time to look at alternatives.

Keeping the problem with our child

We may well start with the same scenario: a child who is upset, angry or non-compliant.

Our task is to keep the problem with the child. I need to be clear that this is not saying, 'That's your problem.' That approach is bound to have a child feeling resentful or deserted.

First, we need to be sure we don't take over the problem. We can support our child in dealing with it, we can give him the space to deal with it, but we must not take over our children's problems if we want them to become good problem-solvers. We need to find a way of keeping the problem with the child so he has the experience of dealing with it.

When children solve age-appropriate problems, whether they are problems of feeling angry and using that energy in pro-social ways, problems of feeling upset and being able to handle the frustration and come up with a better plan, problems of not wanting to do things that need to be done and overcoming that feeling in order to be productive and skilled family members, our children grow in competence. The more they grow in competence, the more they value themselves. The more they value themselves, the greater their self-esteem. The greater their self-esteem, the more they try new things and aim at excellence.

The outcome of a recurrence of this scenario is threefold:

- Our child becomes more competent.
- As parents we feel competent.
- The reward is closeness.

We want our children to be on an upward spiral of increasing competence that leads to increased self-esteem. Instead of being in a vicious downhill spiral, they are on a virtuous upward spiral.

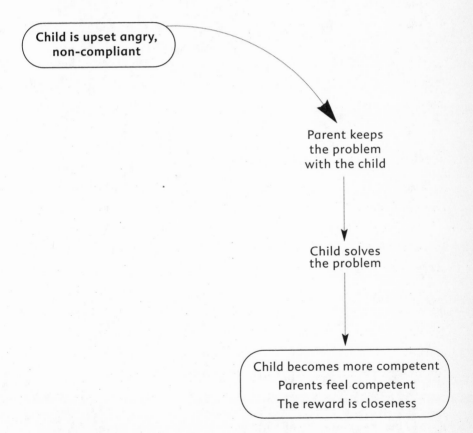

A competent child, at whatever their level of competence, is a child we can rejoice in. I would define competence not as a goal but as an upward path. As long as our children are increasing their skills — whether they be social, domestic or academic — we have reason to take pride in their achievements. A child whose manners, ability to tolerate ordinary frustration and interactional skills are progressing in an appropriate direction is usually a pleasure to be with.

If your child is a pleasure to be with, this is one of the best ways of knowing that your parenting is taking them in the right direction.

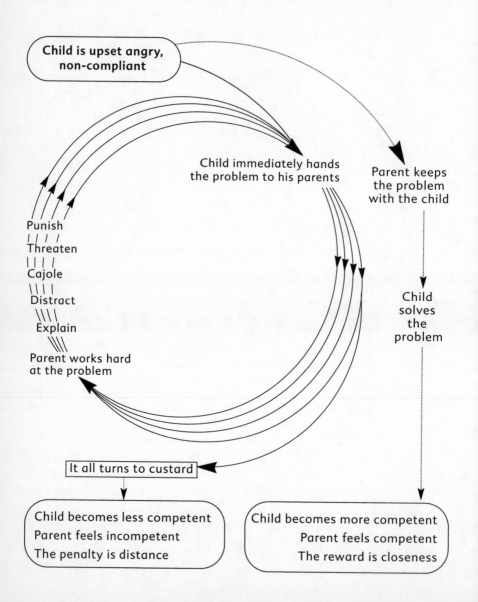

Part Two:
Understanding Personality

6. Personality Theory

About 10 years ago, a friend of mine said to me, 'You must listen to this tape.' I listened with enormous enjoyment. Florence Littauer was very funny and very entertaining. I listened several times and began to note examples all around me. I became intrigued but could find none of the books she spoke about.

Six months later Florence Littauer came to New Zealand, and since then there have been very few clients with whom I have not shared some of her ideas.

Her understanding of personalities is easy to convey, and so helpful. What I like most is that it is not the province of the psychologist or the personnel consultant, but available to us all to help us better understand others and ourselves.

This chapter is about my understanding of Florence Littauer's ideas, but I recommend that you buy her books. My favourite 'starters' are *Personality Plus* and *Your Personality Tree*. *Raising the Curtain on Raising Children* gives wonderful descriptions of the interactions between parents and children according to their personalities and temperaments. If you have problems finding them in ordinary bookshops, you will easily find them in Christian bookshops.

(A word of explanation. People have sometimes asked if I am trying to convert them to Christianity in recommending these books. They are deeply Christian books, but the information is greatly useful regardless of your religious persuasion.)

Aristotle and Hippocrates

About 2000 years ago Aristotle was a great Greek thinker and philosopher. He postulated that all matter in the world could be described as either:

- Hot or Cold; and
- Wet or Dry.

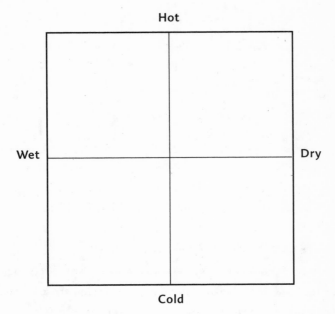

Around the same time there lived a Greek physician called Hippocrates — the same physician from whom today's graduating doctors take the Hippocratic oath. Hippocrates realised from his dissections that all people were largely physically alike, so he pondered how they could have such different temperaments. He postulated that the difference in temperament came from the influence of various body 'humours' (fluids) and named the temperaments accordingly:

Sanguine

Hippocrates thought there was a group of people whose temperaments were largely influenced and characterised by their blood. They were frothy, bubbly and fast-talking.

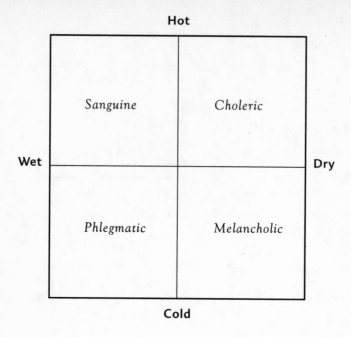

Choleric

People influenced by 'the exudations of their liver' were a bit testy, quick to anger and impatience and knew exactly what they wanted. Today we still use the word 'liverish' to describe such people.

Melancholic

Melancholia meant 'black bile' and Hippocrates thought these people were influenced by the contents of their gall bladder. They were likely to be fussy, precise and often find the world somewhat disappointing.

Phlegmatic

This term is possibly the most distasteful for the squeamish among us. Hippocrates described the phlegmatic individual as being somewhat slow, ponderous and stuck (sticky) in their ways.

The modern version

Florence Littauer has taken Hippocrates' definitions and 'revved them up' for the 21st century.

Sanguines want the world to be FUN

People of a sanguine temperament want to have fun. Their idea of fun is to do whatever they do with a lot of other people.

Both our daughters are strongly sanguine. They can go out with friends all day, be home for half an hour, then set about making social arrangements for the evening — and they can do this for several days in a row. People are the life-blood of sanguines.

Sanguines have a lot of natural charm. In fact, I use this as a 'definer' when I am trying to get some idea of what sort of child a parent may be speaking about. 'Is she charming?' I ask. If the parent beams or gives a wry grin ('Oh, yes!'), the odds are high that we are dealing with a sanguine child who is driven by the need to have fun.

Cholerics want to have CONTROL

The choleric child wants to have control of all situations. Your sanguine child will wake up saying, 'What are we doing today?' meaning 'Are we going to have fun? Are we going to do something that involves lots of people?' Your choleric child will ask, 'What are we doing today?' meaning, 'Are we going to be following the plan I had in mind?'

At this point you may have no idea what particular plan she had in mind, but you already feel a little anxious about the consequences of giving the wrong answer. If you do, you are likely to be met with, 'I'm not going to do that!' It will take the form of half-statement, half-challenge.

It is a wise parent who walks away muttering something non-challenging like, 'We'll work it out', and doesn't begin the day with a confrontation with a choleric.

Melancholics want the world to be PERFECT

They not only want the day to go just right, they want to know the exact sequence of events and be assured that all will go according to plan.

I used to be in a carpool with a lovely little melancholic child who would get into my car each morning saying, 'Good morning, Mrs Levy.' This in itself was a melancholic approach to the world. All the other children would hop in with a 'Hi, Diane', but she wanted to get it just right. Then, each morning, she would ask, 'Are we going to be late?' My track record wasn't that bad and I used to have to stifle the sanguine urge not to be offended because she didn't just love everything about me. 'No, Elizabeth,' I would say patiently, albeit through gritted teeth. 'There is plenty of time.' 'Oh, good!' she would say contentedly. Then: 'Who is picking me up?'

If I didn't understand about temperaments I may have throttled her after the twentieth or hundredth pick-up. Luckily, I tumbled quite early on to her need for order and sequence. As soon as she knew, in her own mind, where she was going, what time she would get there and who would pick her up, she was free to settle down and enjoy the company of the other children.

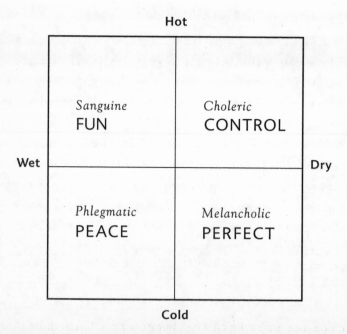

66

When your melancholic child begins the day by asking, 'What are we doing today?' don't be surprised if, no matter how enthusiastic you are, she looks slightly downcast and says with a clear message of disappointment, 'Oh. Okay then.' It is in the nature of the perfect child to see the cup as half empty rather than half full.

There used to be an annual fair in Auckland that we took our children to. I would often begin by setting parameters, like: 'You can each have four rides and three things to eat.' As we were driving home, I would say something typically sanguine, like, 'Well, kids, did you have a good day?' Now I don't expect 10-year-olds to meet the needs of their sanguine mother and her need for approval but my sanguine daughter Tanya's reply of bouncing up and down in her seat saying 'It was great!' was much easier to take than the melancholic Robert's 'I didn't get to go on the ghost-train'.

About 10 years later, when I heard Florence Littauer speak, I finally understood that his reply meant he probably had had a perfectly good day but that his melancholic nature would lead him to notice what hadn't happened. It is hard work for an exhausted parent to translate this shorthand!

Melancholic children are quietly enthusiastic but they do have a natural tendency to focus on what went wrong rather than what went right. So if you ask them about their day, you can expect their reply to focus on the less-than-perfect elements. If your pick-up-the-children-from-school ritual, or your bedtime ritual, includes: 'Now, everybody tell me three good things that happened today,' you invite a 'Nothing' reply from your perfect child and you risk making her feel left out, with her needs unmet.

It is better to ask an open-ended question such as: 'How was your day?' and to accept her negative comments without a sermon on gratitude or a suggestion that she should look on the bright side. Then she can feel accepted by you for who she is.

Phlegmatics just want PEACE

Parents whose first child is of a phlegmatic temperament look in bewilderment at the struggles of other parents. The phlegmatic baby whimpers gently when she is hungry, can wait while you unbutton your shirt, suckles contentedly and does not protest much when put in her cot. Often those of us whose controlling baby has let us know on the way down the hall that walking towards the cot is a lousy idea think that the other mother, and definitely the baby, must be from a different planet when she 'just loves her little bed'.

The phlegmatic toddler goes along with most things as long as she is not over-stimulated, and is generally a peaceful delight to have around. She may be more inclined to sit on her mother's knee than join in with all the rowdies in the sandpit, and she is more likely to hand over the toy that Master or Miss Choleric want. Every now and again, just to prove that you have a real baby, she may refuse to relinquish something she regards as hers and seriously dig her toes in, but most of the time she is pleasant, easy-going, co-operative and a general delight.

She is the baby that most people describe as 'our easy one'. She is motivated by the desire for a peaceful life. As she gets older her desire for the peaceful life may make it hard to get her to do some things but she does not appear to be non-compliant. Rather, we forgive her for what she hasn't done because she is so nice about it. When we remind her she says, 'Sure, Mum. Sorry, Mum.' This doesn't necessarily mean she goes and does as asked, but she does go off and we tend to believe that she meant to do it but just forgot.

If we get upset with the peaceful child she looks bewildered and hurt and tries to correct the mistake. Often, she knows that if she quietly and pleasantly waits and looks helpless enough, or starts but earnestly does it badly enough, someone — and the odds are that the someone will be an impatient choleric adult or child — will rescue her by grumpily doing it for her because they cannot bear to watch such incompetence.

What a great personality. I rarely have parents who come to me saying, 'I have this delightful, pleasant, easy-going child. Can you fix her?' If there are going to be problems they are more likely to show up in adolescence when she is taking doing nothing in a pleasant and charming way to an unacceptable extreme.

Influence over others

Most people, of course, are a combination of temperaments, often with one predominating. Each temperament has a different style of influencing others to do it their way.

Sanguine children, driven by the primary need to have fun, seek to influence by charm. Their whole bearing towards us says, 'Let me charm you into seeing it my way.'

The choleric child, driven by the primary need to control, seeks to influence through anger. Their demeanour suggests: 'Do it my way — or else!'

Anger can take the form of shouting and tantrums — we know that. It can also be passive. The choleric can go very, very quiet. If you have the urge to say, 'dangerously quiet', you are talking about 'passive anger'. This feels even more scary and you are wise to recognise this shut-down as a powerful bid to control the situation — and the parent.

Think about how your baby summoned you in her first year. If the general flavour of her crying was: 'Get here right now — or else,' you can be fairly sure you are dealing with a choleric child.

(Many babies seem to be bedevilled by colic in their first few months, which can make it difficult to determine their temperament. Often it is easier to tell in retrospect.)

The melancholic child, driven by a primary need to have things just right, i.e. perfect, influences others by mood. If she cannot make the world a perfect place, she tends to retreat into a black mood. Since her parents only want her to be happy, they may pursue her into her hidey-hole and try to make her feel better.

Sanguine **FUN** Influences by: CHARM	*Choleric* **CONTROL** Influences by: ANGER
Phlegmatic **PEACE** Influences by: PROCASTINATION	*Melancholic* **PERFECT** Influences by: MOOD

Big mistake. Let her have her mood if she cannot influence you to do it her way, let her return for a cuddle (without lecture or inquisition) when she needs it, then let her drift off and get on with it.

The phlegmatic child, driven by a primary need for peace, influences in such a subtle way that, until it is pointed out, we often miss it. Once we see it, it is obvious that it has been there all along. If there is something the peaceful child doesn't want to do, she doesn't argue or fuss. She just doesn't get around to it, or she goes about it very, v-e-r-y slowly. She is the master of procrastination.

Usually she does this so subtly and so gracefully that we don't even know it is happening. We find ourselves getting increasingly irritated and angry without a particular focus, not even aware that the reason we are becoming so grouchy is that we have asked several times for something to happen and nothing is. Furthermore there is no one in sight, so we become more and more frustrated. As we reach a pitch of frustration, the first person near us 'gets it'. It is unlikely to be the causative peaceful child because she is very sensibly cruising out of the way.

What are their needs?

If thinking about your children's way of influencing, or their primary need, still does not clarify what their temperament is, you may find it useful to think about their needs. You will also find the list of basic needs useful when you have an upset, angry or unco-operative child. It is often useful to think in terms of 'Which of their needs is not being met?'

Sanguine needs

Your sanguine child, who is driven to find ways of making life fun, needs someone to be an *audience* for her fun, her achievements and even her mistakes. If her mistakes make a good story then she is happy to entertain you with these mistakes. However, she also needs a lot of your *approval*, so will only tell you about the mistakes that will draw you closer to her. Watch out for the crowd of sanguines each outdoing the others to tell of the biggest mistake (and watch the melancholics look bewildered at why anyone would want to display their imperfections in public).

I frequently do the typical sanguine thing of freely confessing all my parenting mistakes so that others can feel they are not the only ones. My two sanguine daughters, Tanya and Deborah, understand this perfectly and, since they are audience-driven and therefore not unhappy to have stories told about them, do not feel that stories about 'Where it all went wrong' denigrate them, or their parents, in any way. When Deborah was about eight, I was writing a fortnightly column. If she spotted me at the computer her first question, asked with enormous hope, would be, 'Are you writing about me?'

Sanguine

FUN

Influences by:
CHARM

Needs: Attention
Approval
Acceptance
Affection

On the other hand, my husband Vernon and son Robert, both of whom have melancholic (perfect) characteristics, cannot understand why anybody would want to publicise their mistakes.

Sanguine people are driven by the need for *acceptance*. They feel hurt if the group leaves them out. If you tell your sanguine child about a plan that does not involve her, don't be surprised if you get the 'what about me?' face. Sanguine children are loving and generous and want everyone else to be happy too, but their primary concern is for their own entertainment and need to belong.

When you take children to a playground it is easy to pick out the sanguine child. She is the one who is directing a continuous stream of 'Look at me, did you see what I did, do you know what I am about to do, do you know what I am going to be doing after that' to the caregiver who is desperately thinking, 'I came to the playground so she would have something to do that *didn't* involve me.'

I can still remember my parents describing my endless chatter as '*wie ein Wasserfall*' — like a waterfall — and I remember them begging me on long car journeys: 'Just five minutes' quiet.' Being sanguine, I would have liked to co-operate. I just didn't know how! (Still don't!)

I remember my Year Two teacher, Mrs Walsh, at the end of the school year saying to me, 'I'm going to miss my little chatterbox.' All my school reports mentioned that 'Diane could do better if she talked less and paid a little more attention'. I am still enchanted that I was invited back to my school to speak at an Old Girls' dinner and was able to quote my old reports and to explain that I now earned much of my living from speaking!

Choleric needs

While your choleric child's primary need is for control and you certainly cannot always cede the control of the family to the youngest member, it is a wise parent who watches out for the *other* needs of the choleric child and does her best to meet them.

The easiest need to try to meet is the need for *admiration for real work*. Whereas your sanguine child is happy to be admired just for standing there in her socks, your choleric child will not respond well to praise she doesn't feel she has rightfully earned.

Top of the list of real work is anything that grown-ups consider to be work. When Deborah (who has a choleric streak) was four she was a willing collator of many-paged documents. If Mummy said, 'I need your help for a grown-up job,' she would work away solidly until it was completed. The sanguine side of her liked adult company while the choleric side of her was trying to be so fast and so efficient that she was 'beating' me.

Rob also loved to do adult tasks but, being of a melancholic tendency, preferred to have his own space to do it in. His preference was to work on his own until the task was completed to his satisfaction and then receive the recognition. As a very focused (choleric) adult he is still inclined to say, 'Just tell me what you want done — and by when,' and you can rely on him to remember, and to do it well — but in his own way and his own time.

Choleric children are characterised by their need for their version of *loyalty* and can turn most situations into a loyalty crisis. In this regard, there are generally only two positions in their lives: you are either *on their side* or *not on their side*. If you make any decision that doesn't fall in with their idea of what should happen they may interpret that as a lack of loyalty towards them. The positive side of this need for loyalty, is that there is no more loyal friend and family member than a choleric who is on your side.

With choleric children, you have to be scrupulously fair about whose turn it is to sit in the front seat and all other situations that involve making choices between children. Be careful about making up rules on the spot, such as 'She can go first because she is the guest', because the next time your child is the guest she will expect that same right to be applied to her.

Your choleric child has a strong drive to be the best and the fastest. She wants everything to be scrupulously fair — particularly if it can be fair in her favour!

Florence Littauer does not include the need *to blame* as one of the choleric needs. But in my experience, because the choleric child knows exactly what she needs and how it is supposed to happen, then if it doesn't work out that way she feels someone must be to blame and she gives them a hard time.

Choleric

CONTROL

Influences by:
ANGER

Needs: Admiration
for real work
Loyalty
To blame

Parents of choleric children often tell me that it feels as if the child is trying to punish them because she (the child) got up on the wrong side of the bed. It's true. If they got up on the wrong side of the bed, or if something is worrying them, or if someone has made them angry, the choleric needs to find someone to pick on — to *blame* — for these occurrences.

When Rob was little he was often so angry or unhappy that I frequently thought, 'What this child needs is a dog.' Unfortunately ours was not a pet household so it never eventuated, but I am sure a dog would have been of enormous comfort to him. He could have poured out his woes about the unfairness of the world and saved his parents and sister from being 'blame targets'.

Since cholerics' primary form of influence is anger it is not surprising that, when they are worrying about something in their world that they cannot control, the nearest person often feels as if they have had their head bitten off.

Melancholic needs

Your melancholic child is driven by the need to make the world perfect — meaning ordered and predictable. She needs things to be in their place and she needs to know that there is a timetable that will be more or less adhered to. Melancholics do not do well with a 'let's see what happens' approach.

When she is unable to rely on the plan or when the plan goes wrong, your melancholic child is likely to retreat and be in a bad mood for a while. The best thing you can do is to respect the melancholic's need for *space* and *silence*.

Particular flashpoints are after kindergarten or school. By that time your melancholic child has used up all her words and all her tolerance and is ready for some wide-open spaces, or some privacy and quiet. She wants some sort of 'space bubble'. If you can provide her with the space and silence she needs she will emerge ready to play and have fun.

If you have social activities after school or kindergarten, think creatively about how you can meet your melancholic child's need for space and silence while the gregarious children cannot see enough of one another.

> *Melancholic*
> **PERFECT**
>
> Influences by:
> MOOD
>
> *Needs:* Space
> Silence
> Sensitivity
> Support

One of the best pieces of advice I can give to keep your melancholic children sweet is to meet their third need, which is to show *sensitivity* towards their needs and feelings and *guard their space*. Feel free to say to other children, 'Sophie just needs some quiet time on her own. I am sure she will be happy to join in as soon as she has had a break.'

For sanguine parents this is difficult because we are always worried that our children may miss out on some fun. For choleric parents it may be hard because we have made plans that everyone must stick to — and they are going to have a good time, or else. Phlegmatic parents just want to keep everyone happy and peaceful so we may find it hard to put one child's needs ahead of another's wants and may wind up entreating our melancholic child to 'just fit in' as we would undoubtedly do.

It would be nice to think that the melancholic parent would understand the needs of the melancholic child, but if you have sorted out the perfectly planned afternoon and all the details involved in making the afternoon run perfectly, you may find it hard to deal with the one who is messing up your plan by not wishing to take part.

Meeting the needs of several personalities at once is hard work. One of the toughest jobs of parenting is trying to sort out the needs from the wants, and then trying to meet lots of people's diverse needs. Once we get the idea that our melancholic children have a *need* for space, silence and sensitivity towards them — it is not just that they are being difficult — we can go about supporting their needs more effectively and without rancour.

Although all our children need our support, our melancholic children *need* our support more often because of their temperament. There is only one answer: give it.

Phlegmatic needs

Your phlegmatic children are driven by the need for peace and their most powerful way of ensuring they have attained it is by not getting around to doing anything they don't want to do. They are the masters of vanishing, fading into the background at times of turmoil and looking concerned when we finally get outraged, then scurrying off saying, 'I'll do it right now, Mum.' This doesn't necessarily mean they will do it, just that they have serious intentions of doing it — if only it weren't so difficult or inconvenient. Surely, if they keep out of the way for long enough the whole issue will have vanished.

More than anything else these children need to live with *lack of confrontation*. They are great mediators but, if it is not possible to sort the issue out, they need a degree of protection from everyone's rages and squabbles — particularly when the sanguines and cholerics are enjoying the fun of arguing. Phlegmatics are happy to let everyone else go at the debate hammer and tongs, and even really enjoy that energy level if it is good-natured and *not directed at them*. But if it turns nasty, or if it confronts them personally, they are very unhappy.

Phlegmatics often have a lively, dry wit and are not above stirring up arguments. Then they quietly retreat to a safe spot and watch the battle rage.

Because phlegmatic children are generally co-operative, good-natured and easy-going, it is easy to overlook their need for a *sense of worth and value*. While they don't need a continuous stream of attention, it behoves us to remember to go over every now and then, give them a hug and say, 'How would I manage without you?'

Phlegmatic adults are easy-to-get-on-with, go-with-the-flow sorts of people. They are anxious to make life good for everyone so when they make arrangements for a crowd it can be agonising as the phlegmatic change the arrangements several times so that everyone can be accommodated and be happy.

Should you want to hurt a phlegmatic — and I cannot imagine why anyone would — ask her advice, listen to her carefully considered reply and then rubbish it or ignore it. This will seriously hurt the phlegmatic as it cuts across her need for a sense of worth and value.

Watch out for quiet sadness in your phlegmatic children. Their first choice will always be to stay still and be very good so the world will treat them kindly. When this strategy doesn't work and they are picked on or left out, they need you to notice and value them so they can get on with the job of solving the problem themselves or seeking your help. Make sure you notice.

Phlegmatics have a great need for things to be ordered and happen in a predictable way. This is not the perfectionist tendency of the melancholic, but rather a way to avoid tension. Having good systems in place is important to the phlegmatic because it lowers the chances of things going wrong and tension developing as a result.

Phlegmatic
PEACE

Influences by:
PROCRASTINATION

Needs: Lack of confrontation
Sense of worth
Sense of value

A final word

When I first heard Florence Littauer speak about personalities I had a great flash of understanding about the differences between the ways in which Vernon and I operate. My first thought was: 'So he's not doing all that just to annoy me.'

Since then, I have explained this way of looking at people to many,

many clients and friends. For all of us, the blinding insight has been the same: 'So he or she is not doing this just to annoy me.'

More often than not, people behave the way they do because they are meeting some need of their personality. We may be able to respond to that need, we may not — but it's not helpful to see others, whether they be the children or the adults in our lives, as going out of their way to annoy us. It is more helful to think about which needs of their personality they are trying to fulfil.

Energised by People

Sanguine **FUN** Influences by: CHARM *Needs:* Attention Approval Acceptance Affection	Choleric **CONTROL** Influences by: ANGER *Needs:* Admiration for real work Loyalty To blame
Phlegmatic **PEACE** Influences by: PROCASTINATION *Needs:* Lack of confrontation Sense of worth Sense of value	Melancholic **PERFECT** Influences by: MOOD *Needs:* Space Silence Sensitivity Support

Drained by People

7. Attractions and Combinations

In order to look at the interactions within our family, it is useful to look at the personalities of our family tree and to see how they are inter-related. For the purposes of this chapter I am going to use my own family, mainly because they are the most familiar to me, but also because there are a sufficient number that most of the combination personalities are represented.

The attractions of opposites

Whether we acquire children through birth, IVF or adoption, we are not able to choose their personalities. However, most people choose as a partner someone who is their diametric opposite. My husband Vernon is primarily melancholic. He likes things done a particular way, in a partic-ular order. Things not done that precise way are deemed to be 'wrong' and in need of correction. He can be relied upon to know where his keys are at all times and where mine are most times. He always begins international calls to beloved family members and dear friends by asking what is the time and about the weather. He is reserved and needs a lot of time and space on his own. When he comes home after a day's work, he vanishes. When the children were little, vanishing was impossible, but now that we have two adult children living overseas and one teenager at home he can vanish safely. No one has ever discovered where he vanishes to but a melancholic who seriously needs space can always find it.

Vernon was and still appears to be greatly attracted to my sanguine personality. I am noisy and gregarious and am liable to drop any solitary task for the pleasure of company. Almost any ordinary incident has a good story in it, and if there's a good story in something stupid I have done, so be it. I love my family, my friends and my work with noisy exuberance. Even clients who have been talking to me about very difficult issues somehow leave feeling they have had a good time. I am greatly reliant on Vernon to remember most things, and when I travel on my own I have to talk seriously and often to myself about exactly where the hotel is and on which floor I am staying. Detail doesn't come naturally to me.

	Diane	
Sanguine **FUN**		

	Vernon	
	Melancholic **PERFECT**	

Vernon's late parents, Marta and Geoffrey, were attracted across the choleric/phlegmatic diagonal. Marta was very controlling, always sure that she was right and that hers was the only way of looking at things, though if you seriously stuck to your guns she might concede a minor point. She was tremendously organised and hard-working and her hospitality and generosity were legendary. When you stayed in her household there was nothing she would not do to make your stay comfortable. She was committed to some favourite charities and her intolerance of different opinions came to the fore when she perceived people as having the means but not the heart to give to others.

Geoffrey's temperament was strongly phlegmatic. Everybody adored his sweet nature and his acceptance of everybody 'just as they were'. He was passionate about medicine, retired at 80 and died soon afterwards. The phlegmatic side of his temperament meant he hated conflict and always looked to mediate disagreements. He had considerable success because no one ever wanted to upset such a lovely man.

Geoffrey

Phlegmatic
PEACE

Marta

Choleric
CONTROL

There is a great lesson to be learned when we look at the interaction between a choleric and a phlegmatic. Because the choleric is strong-willed and forceful in the way they express themselves, they are generally assumed to be 'the boss'. But if you want to understand people's temperaments, it is wise to remember that all temperaments exert their own form of control or *influence* to get their own way.

I am typing this manuscript at Marta and Geoffrey's little one-roomed beach-house, where their spirit continues to be strong. One of the family's delightful memories occurred here many, many times. Marta (choleric) would say, 'Darling, we are going for a walk!' Geoffrey (phlegmatic) would leap to his feet and say, 'Yes, darling,' because, even after 55 years of happy marriage he still wanted to please her — and avoid conflict. However, if he didn't feel like walking, it could take him half an hour to go to the bathroom and put on his walking shoes and socks.

That is how phlegmatics control — through procrastination. They look seriously helpful, busy and earnest about doing what is requested. However, if it is something they don't want to do, they can take an amazingly long time to get there — if ever. This, of course, infuriates the choleric, who needs everything done yesterday, but it is hard to argue with someone who is so earnestly going about doing just what you have asked. So the blood pressure of the choleric quietly rises.

My beloved mother, Sally, was also phlegmatic and everyone loved her for it. She was married to my late father, Emanuel, for 32 years, and then to my late stepfather, Hilel, for 24 years. Both men were strongly choleric in completely different ways.

Emanuel was a lively, dominant, life-and-soul-of-the-party man, and had, although primarily choleric, all the outgoing characteristics of a sanguine. He was also a perfectionist. Hilel was quiet and reserved and carried such power that few people ever attempted to cross him. To his choleric nature he added the quiet precision of the melancholic and was the best listener I have ever encountered. Many people approached him for advice and characteristically he would ask very few questions, but always to the point, listen carefully and patiently until you had talked yourself out. Then he would think silently for what seemed like an enormously long time and deliver some measured advice. The controlling side of his choleric nature meant, once he had delivered his advice, it was almost impossible not to follow it.

There is no doubt that these two men were choleric and appeared to have total control of the relationship. There was also no doubt that my phlegmatic mother was driven by 'anything for peace'. However, when you observed closely you saw that they both adored her so much that she had her own amazingly quiet power. On the rare occasions that she dug her toes in, a choleric was likely to discover that phlegmatics will go along with 95 percent of what you want, but if they seriously decide on a course of action, the choleric doesn't stand a chance because of the phlegmatic's ability to wait things out.

My mother is famous in our family for having said, at 80 years of age, a year after having been widowed for the second time and two happy marriages spanning 56 years, 'I don't think I could ever be bothered to be married again, but a friendship would be nice.'

I consider myself fortunate to have had these five fine parents in my life and am grateful for all their love and care and wisdom, which I carry with me today. I do miss them.

Emanuel

Sanguine FUN	*Choleric* CONTROL
	Melancholic PERFECT

Sally

Sanguine FUN	
Phlegmatic PEACE	

Hilel

	Choleric CONTROL
	Melancholic PERFECT

Across a crowded room

Their eyes meet across a crowded room and two seconds — or two years — later they decide that they will live together for the rest of their lives. What is the nature of this attraction?

- She (sanguine) thinks: 'Isn't he (melancholic) wonderful? He's so gentle and sensitive. He attends to my every need and never forgets important details. He listens so well and seems so enchanted with every smile and move I make. Best audience I've ever had. He's the one for me.'

- He (melancholic) thinks: 'Isn't she (sanguine) amazing. She lights up my life. She brings such energy and fun into my life. Everybody likes her and there is never a dull moment when she is around. She is always thinking up wonderful ideas and always has a smile. I think

I'll keep her.'(Please feel free to change genders according to the combination you are thinking of.)

- She (choleric) thinks: 'My goodness, he (phlegmatic) is just so wonderful. Everyone thinks he is so sweet. He has such a calming influence and is so wonderfully patient. I love his quiet confidence and the way he is happy to do whatever I want. He's the one for me.'
- He (phlegmatic) thinks: 'Isn't she amazing? She seems to know exactly where she's going and what she's doing. She's so goal-focused and motivated. I love the way she is so powerful and "goes for it". That's the woman for me.'

There are, of course, many happy and successful relationships that do not match this pattern of opposites at all, but, if you look around you and think about the personalities of the couples you know, many of them have chosen their diametric opposite to spend the rest of their days with.

After the wedding comes the marriage

Our initial attraction is always to the strengths of the personalities, but after a while we may begin to see the weaknesses as well — and every personality has traits of weakness as well as strength.

I love Florence Littauer's phrase: 'After the wedding comes the marriage.' These days, when there are so many weddings marking a public commitment to stay together, years after a couple have begun to live together and have had children together, you can choose for yourself whether this saying stands as it is, or is just metaphorical. However, there comes a time in every relationship when you become aware that there is another side to your beloved's temperament, which you simply did not see when you were in the flush of first love.

- The spouse of the choleric says: 'I had no idea he would be so bossy.'
- The spouse of the phlegmatic says: 'Well! Everyone else may think she is such a sweetie, but I know just how stubborn she can be.'
- The spouse of the melancholic says: 'I had no idea he would be so fussy.'

- The spouse of the sanguine says: 'She doesn't listen too well and, boy, does she exaggerate.'

After Vernon and I had been married for a while we started to come to grief when I would tell a story about some event the two of us had attended together. I have the natural sanguine tendency to tell only the bits I think make a good story and leave out the boring bits. Vernon has a melancholic tendency to believe that everyone is interested in detail and that my lack of attention to detail can come close to not telling the truth. Sanguines do not see their stories as being enhanced by interruptions to supply boring detail that no one could possibly be interested in.

There is no right or wrong. We both learned that different people like information delivered in different ways. I learned not to interrupt and speed up Vernon's stories. Vernon learned that it is dangerous to correct a sanguine's embellishments in public.

As we got older and a little more 'separable' at parties, I learned that I am to be found in the 'noisy', crowded section and will often come home with a few good jokes or, more likely, remembering who has told good jokes but having entirely forgotten the punch-lines. Vernon, who is an excellent listener and enjoys parties by talking quietly to successive people, one at a time, comes home with heaps of interesting information.

Combination personalities

I have so far spoken as if most people are of one, easily identifiable and precisely defined temperament, but as I mentioned earlier people often have the characteristics of more than one personality.

Sanguine/phlegmatic

My primary personality is undoubtedly sanguine and I also have many characteristics of the phlegmatic. While I love arguing any point just for the fun of it, I don't enjoy arguments and have a basic desire for everyone to get on. I carry a strong element of the peacemaker and spent much of my early parenting life trying to sort out the disputes of our older two children. I am also inclined to give in 'just for peace'. I had the characteristics of the phlegmatic child. They are often described as 'good' and trying to stay out of trouble. The sanguine/phlegmatic lives to play. I am the luckiest woman in the whole world because I have work that I am passionate about and that I can work hard at while playing very seriously.

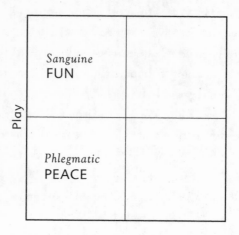

Melancholic/phlegmatic

Vernon has a combination of melancholic and phlegmatic temperaments. This makes for a very sweet disposition in someone who is analytical. He is tremendously helpful but has a very strong idea of the right way to help.

I have already told you that my first blinding insight, when I heard Florence Littauer speak for the first time, was: 'So he's not just doing that to annoy me.' That night, when I drove into the garage, Vernon — as always, bless him — came down to open my car door. I was, as only a sanguine can, bubbling over with stories about my amazing evening and all I had learned and how the whole world needed to know this.

I suddenly remembered Florence talking about the phlegmatic's need for a sense of worth, so I said to Vernon, 'How was your evening?'

Vernon's reply?

'You get two out of four for the back door. You closed it and you turned the key. But you forgot to put on the chain and hide the key.' He then wondered why I flung my arms around his neck and hugged him. It was such a perfect melancholic reply. Only a melancholic could mark you two out of four for closing the back door while opening your car door and kissing you hello!

This story also highlights the sweetness of the melancholic/phlegmatic temperament. No one leaves our house without Vernon accompanying them to their car. He doesn't know that this is unusual. He thinks everyone is this thoughtful.

Phlegmatic
PEACE

Melancholic
PERFECT

Analytical/Sweet

Choleric/melancholic

One day the stork was flying over our house, looked down on the two people living there, said, 'There needs to be a bit of control in that household,' and delivered Robert to us. Since Rob was our first baby we had no idea he was controlling. All we knew was that it was awfully hard to make him happy. He was a tricky toddler because he could switch so quickly from being angry to being upset.

They say, rather rudely, about psychologists and counsellors that they go into their field to solve their own problems. I confess, unashamedly, that I came to the field I am now so passionate about — helping parents to raise their children — largely through my desperate attempts to make Rob happy. Being sanguine, I thought that the whole world should be happy and having fun. I still remember the mornings I would wake up thinking, 'I am going to get it right today, so he doesn't cry.' Sometimes I succeeded. Sometimes it was me who ended up in tears.

Now that I understand personalities so much better I see why a child who is both choleric and melancholic cannot meet his sanguine mother's need for proof of successful parenting.

Robert, as baby, child and teenager, had all the characteristics of the choleric and all the characteristics of the melancholic and his needs switched back and forth. One moment he would be dominating the scene, demanding that everything go his way, and the next moment he would be retreating in tears because people were being insensitive towards him.

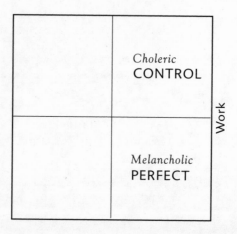

If we can survive this combination through the growing years, if we can find ways of controlling the controller and supporting the melancholic, we will be rewarded with the most splendid adult. This combination gives us the world's great workers. People like Rob have the choleric ability to set great goals, the tenacity to see them through and not let things get in their way, and the melancholic attention to detail to underpin these goals and make them happen.

Rob set himself great goals in the field of judo and became a respected international athlete. We are in awe of his tenacity, focus and sheer capacity for hard and lonely work, and his choleric loyalty to family and friends. Having gone as far as he could go, and having graced our house with many medals and trophies, he is now pursuing a career with equal dedication and ferocity. We are so proud of him.

I continue to be fascinated by the fact that most of the parents who come to see me as a Family Therapist have a child with the choleric/melancholic combination. When I first speak to parents by phone I usually ask, 'What is he or she doing to you?' and I get a few brief examples. My next question is likely to be, 'Is he strong-willed and sensitive?' and the answer is so often, 'Yes. How did you know?'

I don't know why this combination should give parents child-raising difficulties. If I pursue my next observation — 'These children always seem to me as if they would be better off raised on a farm,' — I am met with a description of how, during school holidays, when the child goes to a relative's farm, they are always so contented and no trouble ...

It seems to me that choleric/melancholic children do so well in a rural setting because from a very early age their work is valued and there is also plenty of space: the farm environment perfectly meets these two needs. Because, although these children love to work (and have it appreciated), they also need time alone.

I am not suggesting that all of us who parent a choleric/melancholic child should leave town. But we can help this child's development if we make sure that, after a day in crèche, kindergarten or school, intensively using all his micro-skills, he has some time to be in an open space, on his own, with the opportunity to use all his large-muscle groups.

In Western urban society we have a proliferation of problems with labels: ADD, ADHD, bullying, reading difficulties, low self-esteem and so on. I cannot help but wonder how many of these are a reflection of the fact that our way of life is inappropriate to meet the needs of many of our young people. Those with temperaments that are more able to tolerate intolerable conditions we call 'successful'; those with temperaments that do not have the capacity to manage well under impossible circumstances we label 'troubled'.

Sanguine/choleric

This combination produces our natural leaders. The sanguine part of them is people driven and they like activities that are fun and that involve company and co-operation. The choleric bit of them means that they like to arrange people and situations so that goals can be set and people will pull together to reach those goals, and their sanguine charm makes for willing followers.

I don't think that I fully appreciated the power, charm and natural leadership that comes from this temperament combination until I watched a master at work. Deborah, our youngest, was about five. We were staying at our holiday house. The significance is that, typically of the Kiwi summer holiday, a group of children who don't otherwise meet, form a social group for a short number of weeks.

Lead

Sanguine **FUN**	*Choleric* **CONTROL**

I came around the corner to see Deborah with six children, aged between five and seven lined up in front of her. As I rounded the corner, I heard her say, 'Now each of you will tell me what game you would like to play and, when I've heard what everyone wants to do, we can decide what to play and in which order.' And so, as instructed, each child named the game she wanted to play, Deborah extrapolated a list of preferred games and they all went off happily together to play.

The thing that astounded me was her natural authority and their acceptance of her leadership. No one questioned her, everyone took their turn, everyone co-operated.

The choleric has the ability to set goals and the sanguine has the charm to get everyone to join her. That is natural leadership.

Tanya, too, has the choleric ability to set goals for a group and the charm to persuade them to follow her.

By now, you may have realised all our children have choleric personalities. It makes for a dynamic household and very noisy mealtimes.

8. Interactions Between People

Although our personality is determined before birth, it is not set in concrete. The way I view it is that we are given our children with their personalities firmly set in place and it is our job as parents to rub off the corners to help our children fit more smoothly into the society in which they live.

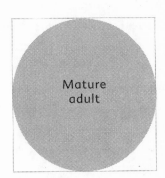

Newborn child

Mature adult

Similarly, as adults, it behoves us not to be entirely temperament-driven, but to moderate our natural impulses to take account of the effect on people around us. 'I am who I am; take it or leave it' is somewhat lacking in grace and sensitivity as an approach to life. At the other extreme, the person who subjugates themselves entirely to the needs of everyone else is not an attractive person to be with either.

Our job is to support our children as they find an appropriate balance.

The masks we wear

Florence Littauer talks about 'masks' in reference to the way in which we adopt different ways of being and interacting according to the situation we find ourselves in. We first learn this as children.

If you find yourself struggling to identify the characteristics of your own personality it is possible you are wearing a mask. The best way I know to recognise a mask is to ask yourself, 'What was required of me in my family of origin?' Did they need me to be cheerful? Did they need me to be good? Did they need someone to take charge? Did they need someone to remember details? If you can answer this it may help you identify the personality you adopted — either to fit in more easily or to keep yourself safe.

Whenever I filled in personality tests in magazines, I would always come up with contradictory responses. Certainly the 'people person' aspect — being sanguine — was consistent, but the rest was a muddle. I wanted things to go my way but I never wanted to antagonise people. I liked things to be done well but I was happy to let people do it their way. I wanted to lead but I was also happy to follow. I sometimes wound up as the leader, but I found it difficult when I had to tell people what to do. I hated confrontation but, when I was convinced my way was the only right way, I would argue ferociously. I spoke up on issues. I wound up as chairperson.

I declared myself to be phlegmatic but if I mentioned to my children that I loved peace they rolled around on the floor laughing and said, 'Don't be ridiculous, Mum. You are a control freak.' When I was a teacher I had a reputation for being strict (choleric), but all I really wanted was for my pupils to get on with their work, love the subject (phlegmatic) and like me (sanguine).

In my mid-thirties I began to reflect upon what had seemed to me like a golden childhood and to understand the great sadness that lay behind it.

My parents and siblings had come to New Zealand in 1939 as refugees from Hitler's Europe. As so many did, they arrived here with the education and culture of Europe, haunting memories and whatever they carried in their suitcases. My father had been a prominent lawyer but was too old and too broken to learn a new language and requalify. My mother became the breadwinner.

When I was born in 1948 the family was just beginning to regroup and, while I was a treasured family member, the care of a baby and child in a situation with no crèches, no extended family and no family benefit was a nightmare for a female breadwinner.

My subconscious decision, at a very early age, was to be a good girl. I put on a phlegmatic mask and did whatever I could to be good and not to cause any trouble. I subdued my choleric tendencies and was pleasant and co-operative — apart from the odd, surprising outburst of temper.

Diane

Sanguine **FUN**	*Choleric* **CONTROL**
Phlegmatic Mask **PEACE**	

In our family we facetiously say that I finally had my adolescent rebellion at 35 and lucky Vernon had to deal with my emergent choleric personality. Twenty years later I still find myself swaying between phlegmatic and choleric. If there is a peaceful solution I will usually give it preference, but in matters of principle I can become pretty forceful. I still find this an uncomfortable mix.

Interestingly, when you look at Vernon's combination of melancholic and phlegmatic, he was likely to choose a wife with sanguine/choleric tendencies, even though, when he met me, I appeared to myself to be sanguine/phlegmatic.

This illustrates something that happens often. Regardless of the masks people are wearing, the attraction between prospective partners usually overrides any mask and involves 'real' personality.

Vernon	
Phlegmatic PEACE	*Melancholic* PERFECT

Likely Choice	
Sanguine FUN	*Choleric* CONTROL

Who's your favourite?

Whenever I ask someone which child they 'prefer' there is always a sharp intake of breath. Whether I am speaking with parents or teachers, they always protest that they like every child in their care equally.

I would like to make a clear distinction between love and compatibility.

I remember the day that the meaning of 'loving your children equally' became clear to me. Robert and Tanya would have been about eight and seven respectively. I have no recollection what the complaint was about, but Rob felt that I had given something to Tanya that he had not received and 'it wasn't fair'.

I remember saying to him, 'If you really want it fair: last week I bought Tanya a pair of pink ballet shoes. I will buy you a pair of pink ballet shoes if you want.' I am not suggesting that this sarcastic parenting response is one you should emulate. Frankly, it was unkind and unnecessary. However, I learned a great deal from it.

I learned that it is impossible to treat children equally — in terms of what you buy for them or what you do for them — in a way that can be measured in cash or possessions or minutes. It would be patently stupid for me to buy ballet shoes for a child who doesn't do ballet. It is foolish to provide all your children with two after-school activities if they have different energy levels. It is crazy to give an irresponsible child the use of your car just because your responsible one can always be relied upon to use the privilege wisely.

I think it is imperative to love our children equally and work equally hard to meet their needs and wants. All of our children deserve all the basics and as many extras as we have the time and inclination to give them. To the best of our ability, we guide them equally toward becoming independent, fully functioning adults, we rejoice equally in their achievements and try equally hard to help them overcome any obstacles they face.

Over and above this, there is no getting away from the fact that some temperaments are more familiar to us and some less so. Some aspects of our children's temperaments we find easy to understand and some are much more mysterious to us. Some children we have a natural compatibility with and others have temperaments we struggle with. It is good to acknowledge this, and also that we love them equally.

It is a two-way process. Our children may find one parent easier to get on with and easier to 'read'. One of the advantages of having two parents — certainly one of the advantages of living in an extended family — is that our children learn to get on with and love a wide variety of people. They learn to appreciate them for the characteristics they enjoy and learn to love them and be loyal to them in spite of — or even because of — their differences.

My late father used to say, 'You love your friends, not in spite of their faults, but with their faults.' He, bless him, was choleric and was bound to see differences as 'faults'. Being more sanguine, I would like to change that to: 'I love my friends, not in spite of their differences, but with their differences.'

Natural attractions

Accepting that we can find some temperaments easier to get along with than others, we can now look at natural attraction within families.

Let's return to our family tree. But first I need to tell you about another mask.

When Tanya was born, she entered a family with a strongly choleric first-born. She was by nature very sanguine and therefore good at reading people and what they wanted. She was sociable and agreeable and possessed the ability from an early age to get on with everyone or to play contentedly alone if that was the only option. She appeared to be sanguine/phlegmatic and, although we knew nothing of personalities then, it was clear that she was easy-going and delightful.

Occasionally we would see a flair of strength in the way she interacted with her friends and there would be lots of jockeying for position, but she was generally willing to concede to the demands of her choleric brother and we were grateful for the resulting peace.

Imagine our amazement when, at about 15, she became strongly assertive and would insist on having her own way. We suddenly discovered that she had a fiery temper when crossed, and set strong goals for herself which she followed through. Towards the end of her schooling it became clear that we had a natural leader (sanguine/choleric) on our hands.

We can draw Tanya's temperament and it may look strangely familiar to you.

Tanya

Sanguine **FUN**	*Choleric* **CONTROL**
Phlegmatic Mask **PEACE**	

When you look at our family tree, it is possible to understand how attractions — by personality — happen in families.

Let's start with Robert. Robert is unlike either parent in temperament. This means that neither parent feels they understand him fully through their own experience. He is our 'Martian'. We adore him and greatly admire him but, until I began to study personalities, I had no idea what made him tick.

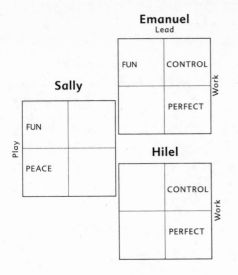

Emanuel — Lead · Sally · Hilel

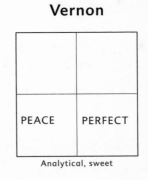

Marta · Geoffrey

Diane — Lead

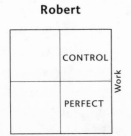

Robert

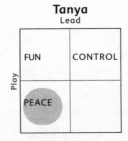

Tanya — Lead

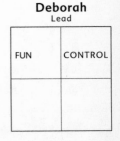

Vernon · Deborah — Lead

Analytical, sweet

I viewed his admirable tenacity as him just trying to be difficult. When he was sensitive I thought, 'What have I done wrong and what can I do to make you happy?' I misinterpreted his need for space as evidence of his not being willing to fit in. It was just as well I loved him to bits!

Knowing what I know now, I can appreciate his goal focus and his need for space. If I were doing it all over again I would guard his space from his gregarious sister, and guard her against his outbursts. Hindsight is a wonderful teacher.

When Rob was four and Tanya three, we went over to visit a friend of mine, Georgina, for an afternoon of play. Knowing that there were going to be four children present, I popped into the local dairy and bought four small packets of Pebbles. Upon arrival at Georgina's, I discovered that there was an extra child.

Since I knew Georgina very well, I went to her kitchen cupboard, took out five little bowls and redistributed the Pebbles. Four children said, 'Thank you, Diane.' My son declared, 'If I can't have my own packet, I don't want any.' I was angry at such seemingly unreasonable behaviour.

Just before I was about to do damage, Georgina said, 'Leave it. I know exactly how he feels. I would have done the same.' I was astounded. To my sanguine need for a social outcome that would keep everybody happy, it was obvious that the Pebbles just needed to be regrouped. Georgina, who is similar in temperament to Robert, perfectly understood that he if couldn't have complete control, he would rather have none.

Although Rob probably suffered from parents who didn't fully understand him — and luckily, loving your child unconditionally makes up for a lot of parental ineptness — he had grandparents who did. First of all, they adored him in the special way only grandparents can. Second, in terms of temperament, he had lots of support from people who didn't find him at all Martian-like.

Rob is very like Vernon's mother, Marta. Being of like temperament they were soulmates who understood each other. Geoffrey, with his peace-loving nature, was also attracted to this grandson who was a temperamental clone of his beloved wife. My mother, Sally, having the diametrically opposite temperament to Rob, appreciated all his qualities, and in later years when we had to leave the country for seven weeks while she was very ill and frail, Rob was a tender and utterly reliable caregiver.

Tanya, as you can see, is a personality clone of her mother. I found her easy to understand and found it easy to meet her needs — particularly while she was in her phlegmatic/sanguine era. When her choleric side began to emerge — and I suspect it happened in parallel with mine — I delighted in her strength, purpose and focus.

Tanya is the child in our family who most resembles the person Vernon chose (me), so they are very close. This is not just father/daughter closeness; it is the closeness you find when a child's personality is identical to that of your partner of choice.

Tanya has chosen to follow her dreams and live in Jerusalem. While I am able to find huge sanguine comfort in all of our phone conversations and emails, Vernon misses her greatly and her absence gives him a lot of pain.

Deborah is also a soulmate for me and an attractive personality to Vernon. She is showing what a natural leader the combination of choleric and sanguine — more or less in equal balance — can be and, having begun with four adults to follow her leadership, will be a force (in the nicest possible way) to be reckoned with in the future.

If you look at the five of us, you will see four cholerics and three sanguines. It is no wonder that our dinner table is a lively place, with four people speaking at once, all with strong opinions. It is just as well there is one melancholic/phlegmatic listening to and supporting us all!

Innate vs learned or 'Am I stuck with it?'

Is there anything we can do to change our personality or are we stuck with it?

Many people say to me, 'But I have all four personalities.' Of course we all do. We have those aspects that come to us naturally and those aspects we have learned because, in order to be a well-rounded individual, there are useful behaviours we can acquire that straddle all temperaments.

While I don't believe we can change our temperaments, it certainly is possible to learn useful behaviours that don't come naturally to us because they fit better into the environment in which we find ourselves. However, there is always a strain being what we are not.

As educated adults, we begin to understand that some aspects of our personalities are less useful in some situations, so we tend to adopt others that are. Professionally, I know that melancholic organisation is a distinct plus in running an organisation smoothly so I work hard at trying to be organised. (Notice the term 'work hard'. When we are operating in harmony with our personality, things come easily to us. When we are behaving in ways that do not necessarily line up easily with our temperament we find them much harder.)

If you came to my home as a client you would be invited into a tidy, organised kitchen and offered a cup of tea or coffee. We would then proceed to a tidy coffee table complete with notepads, tissues, paperclips, business cards, and ballpoints all precisely positioned for maximum efficiency. Ten minutes into our work, the table is somehow strewn with these items — and others — in total disarray as I focus on the needs of the moment and enjoy the interaction. (We won't even mention what the kitchen looks like when I am *not* expecting people.) I can sustain the melancholic approach briefly because I have taught myself to do so, but the sanguine is always poised to override.

This also helps explain why people often have different personae at work and at home. We are, as human beings, infinitely adaptable and most of us have the capacity to fit into the 'culture' of the surroundings we find ourselves in.

This augurs well for us as parents when we contemplate our children's less desirable behaviour. We cannot change their temperament, but we can certainly nudge them into changing some of their behaviours.

Part Three:

The Path to Emotional Independence

9. Meeting a Child's Emotional Needs

Picture the scene

There is a playground with a toddler slide — three steps up and a shallow gradient down. A parent brings a toddler over to the slide. The toddler has not tried this slide before. The parent helps the child up the steps and holds his hand while he sits down and controls the descent. He does this three or four times and they both delight in his achievement.

Now the parent stands right next to the slide while the toddler does it by himself. The toddler is careful, confident and they are both delighted with his newly acquired skill. The parent is free to go and sit on the park bench and supervise from a distance.

The toddler goes up and down, up and down, up and down. He is delighted with his own mastery. Occasionally he glances over to his parent, who calls out, 'What a champ you are.'

The child is enjoying the joys of mastery. The parent is peripheral to his experience.

There are two other children at the playground. One child is glued to his parent. Dad is not allowed to sit on the seat: he has to stand right next to the slide. Alternatively, the child sits with Dad on the seat and won't even look at the slide. Dad tries all his persuasive skills. Dad explains. He threatens. He gets angry. The toddler whines a lot. Eventually Dad gets him to try. It is all hard work. The child has very little time actually on the slide. Dad wonders why he bothered.

We can see the third child vanishing over the horizon. Dad is calling to him to come back. Dad is chasing him, worrying about what is on the other side of the hill. This child spends his time being oppositional. He doesn't spend much time on the slide either.

Both children, the whining, clinging one and the out-of-control one — are missing out on skill development and the joys of mastery. The parents of these children are missing out on the joys of watching their children develop mastery.

If we want our children to spend time in the third strand of development — going from unskilled to skilled — we need to have children who have sufficient emotional independence and self-discipline to enjoy the opportunities available to them.

Learning anew

I remember giving a seminar 10 years ago, called 'Enjoy Your Child: Enjoy Yourself'. It was in a kindergarten setting, which is always a challenge because there are 30 or more parents all sitting on tiny low chairs staring up my nostrils.

A parent had asked me what to do about her three-year-old's tantrums. Back then, I taught behaviour modification. In broad terms: if you like the behaviour, praise it; if you don't like the behaviour, punish it. (If you find the word 'punishment' offensive, read 'negative reinforcement'.)

So I explained that the tantrum was attention-seeking behaviour. The appropriate parental response was to check that the child was safe, then walk away. The child would work out that no one was paying attention and soon stop shouting. I probably added phrases like 'Tantrums need an audience' and 'You can't negotiate with terrorists'.

Another parent asked about head-banging. 'Same thing,' I said glibly. 'Walk away. No child is going to continue banging their head on the floor if no one is there to appreciate it.'

Then another parent said, 'But my toddler bangs his head against the end of his cot when he is all alone in his room. How can I walk away from that?' Clearly, this did not fit my theory. I muttered something and looked around for another question that I *did* know the answer to.

There is a wonderful saying: 'When the pupil is ready, the teacher appears.' That day I was extra lucky — the universe must have decided I was extra needy — because two teachers appeared.

My first teacher

A parent raised her hand. 'The other day my child was really upset and threw herself down on the concrete. She had head-banged before and I just knew she was about to start smashing her head on the concrete. I couldn't bear the thought of that, so I scooped her up in my arms and said, "Don't do that, darling. Mummy loves you and she doesn't want you to hurt your beautiful little face."'

Then she said to me, in a soft and hesitant voice, 'Did I do something terribly wrong?'

Her comment bypassed my brain completely and went straight to my heart. There is a lovely expression in Jewish thought that talks about the Lev Chochem — the wise (or informed) heart. I knew right away that this woman's response was the loving and undoubtedly 'right' approach that no amount of behaviour modification theory could touch. I remember standing there thinking, 'Diane, you stupid idiot. Of course that mother is right. Of course you don't stand by and let a child slam their face into concrete.' I think I said — and if I didn't and could rewrite history I would say — 'I far prefer your response to mine.'

This episode gave me a few sleepless nights because I started to question a lot of what I had believed to be absolute truth — scientifically proven.

My second teacher

At that same class another parent raised his hand and said, 'There's a book you might find interesting. It is about this tribe whose children never cry, let alone tantrum. The parents can leave machetes lying around and the children can pick them up and wave them around without ever hurting themselves or anyone else. Also, the children are very obedient. The book is called The *Continuum Concept*, by Jean Liedloff.

The book is written as a personal account of the time that Jean Liedloff spent living with the Yequana, a tribe of South American Indians who live by one of the tributaries of the upper reaches of the Orinoco River in Venezuela. She had become so entranced with these people that she visited and lived with them several times.

The first thing that attracted her to them was their complete absence of unhappiness, a factor that led her to re-examine the premise that unhappiness is part of the human condition.

Another thing that led her to rethink her previously held ideas was the apparent absence of a word for 'work'. They had words for all the activities that we would include in the concept of work, but no generic term that implied that they viewed these activities as energy-draining or tedious or tiresome. They were activities that were essential for survival and were something that everyone just did.

She was also amazed that she almost never heard a child cry. Yet she observed nothing in their upbringing that showed that any child — or adult for that matter — felt any constraint upon the expression of emotion. She was convinced that the children did not feel a need to cry nor a need to suppress it in the way we call 'being brave'.

Liedloff was also impressed with the children's obedience. A parent only had to ask for something to be done and the child would scurry off, eager to be helpful. How did the children come to behave in these ways?

The lesson: the Yequana

Yequana babies

A Yequana mother carries her baby everywhere until the baby begins crawling. The baby's job is to be a passive observer of all that is going on around him, to sleep when tired and to feed when hungry. He does not have to cry in order to be fed: a mere snuffly grunt means that his mother will offer him her breast. When he has had enough, he stops. This baby does not have to learn to tell the time in order to be fed ('Is it four hours since my last feed and am I supposed to be hungry now?').

When he is tired the Yequana baby falls asleep. When he has had enough sleep he wakes up. The mother makes no attempt to entertain him — she doesn't need to. The baby is with her right at the heart of a busy communal life so there is always plenty to see and hear and passively learn from.

The Yequana community delights in babies. Once a day the women and children will walk down to the river to bathe and the mother delights in playing with her baby. The little girls don't have dolls; they have live babies to play with. Most little girls are expert baby-minders and take them off to play with until they require feeding. The adolescent boys seem to delight in the little ones too, will come back after a day's hunting and find a little child to play 'throwing in the air' with.

The babies thus go from one person to another in a relaxed fashion and seem to be totally trusting of the many people who love and care for them.

Crawlers and toddlers

Once a baby can crawl, he spends as much time with his mother as he wishes and is free to crawl away wherever he likes. The mother, based on her experience, has no concern for his safety and assumes that the crawler knows how to keep himself safe. Liedloff saw no evidence that children were not capable of assessing what was safe or unsafe.

She tells a delightful story about young children playing around a deep pit that had been dug in a central area. She was terrified that the young babies, who crawled over and rolled around near the pit, and sat upright with their backs to the pit, would come to harm. She noticed not only that she was the only person concerned or even watching, but also that although the children were spending a lot of time in close proximity to the pit, none of them ever tipped into it.

Whenever a crawler or toddler felt tired or hungry or uncertain or upset, he returned to his mother and she scooped him up, popped him on her hip and, unless it was a matter of feeding, she carried on with whatever it was that she was doing.

After a short time the child's need for comfort had been met, the child has sorted himself out and wriggled to be let down to toddle off again.

Learned behaviours are hard to shake

I always thought about the young toddler quietly coming over to Mum when he needed her. In our Western way, our children are more likely to stand still and yell, 'Mu-u-u-um!' and we race over to find out what the problem is and how we can solve it. How is it, I thought, that we have children who, instead of using their powerful little legs to rush to us, rely on our tired old legs to struggle over to them?

The best answer I could come up with is that we train them from an early age to yell and we will come to them. The training devices we use are a bassinet or cot and a bedroom. We put our babies down to sleep and we walk way. When our babies need us, they learn to summon us by crying. It's hardly surprising that our toddlers and teens are obedient to their early training and think that what they have to do when they need us is to call 'Mu-u-u-u-um!'

A Yequana baby is carried till he can crawl, and then crawls away only as far as he is comfortable. He is free to return as necessary.

Don't worry: I am not necessarily advocating carrying your baby around all the time. But somehow we are inadvertently training our babies to stay put in one place and yell when they need us or want us.

Here are a couple of stories from the animal world.

The first is about piranhas. They are tiny fish that are voracious feeders and like starring in James Bond movies. If you raise a piranha in a fish tank with a central pane of glass and a tasty victim fish on the other side of the pane, it will initially lunge at the food-fish many times and keep smacking its snout on the glass. Eventually it will give up and stop trying to swim beyond the central pane. It is said that you can then remove the pane and, even though the tasty morsel fish is still there, the piranha won't swim beyond the central point.

The second story concerns the raising and taming of baby elephants. If a baby elephant is regularly tethered with a chain and large iron stake to stop it from running away, even though as an adult it could clearly yank the stake out of the ground and go wherever it wanted, it will not do so. Because of its early training, the elephant assumes it still cannot pull the stake out of the ground.

I didn't know any of this when we had our third child, but because she was the third child I had got over my worries about spoiling babies. I had the luxury of one baby at home while the other two were at school and I was besotted. I would still feed her, change her and put her in her cot to go off to sleep, but often when I heard her beginning to stir at the end of a sleep I would pick her up and sit down in an armchair with her for the pure pleasure of having her wake up in my arms. Is it simply coincidence that she is the only one of my children who doesn't call me from the other end of the house? She is more likely to come and find me.

Letting the child solve the problem

When a toddler rushes back to his Yequana mother she will scoop him up in her arms and carry on with whatever she is doing. She doesn't ask what the problem is. She doesn't try to sort it out. She accepts that her child is upset and needs her support and, given that support, that he will sort the problem out in his own little head and life will go on. Either way, the mother doesn't see it as her problem. Her role is to comfort; the child's role is to problem-solve.

This is in strong contrast to our typically Western response. We pick up our baby with a 'Sweetheart, what's the matter?' We set about distracting our baby from whatever is bothering him. 'Darling, don't cry. Here!' we say, waving and rattling. 'Look at Mummy's car keys. Oh! You don't want those. How about this lovely rattle? Come on. We'll go over to the mirror and Mummy will make funny faces. Dancey, dancey, dancey!'

Usually, by now, our child has stopped crying and we feel we have done our parenting job well. But several such episodes can make for an exhausting day and we are likely to feel that our child has no idea of how to occupy himself happily.

The unconditional, low-energy, wordless support the Yequana mothers give their babies and toddlers appears to breed resourceful and resilient children. Once they have reached what we would call preschool age,

Yequana children are amazingly independent and can tolerate most of the ordinary frustrations and upsets they encounter. If it gets too tough, they return to Mum and their needs for support and comfort are met.

It works for big kids too

It is not only young children who require support. Yequanas of any age are expected to be resilient and resourceful but if there is unbearable pain involved, a display of emotion is accepted as perfectly natural. Two examples follow.

Jean Liedloff was also a 'first aider'. One day a mother brought her very upset 10-year-old along. He was in a lot of pain and needed a rotten tooth removed. Liedloff knew this child well — he had previously elected to accompany her upriver for three months of photography and exploration. In that time he had been entirely self-sufficient and unfailingly helpful and pleasant.

When she did an exploratory prod of the offending tooth it was obviously excruciatingly painful and the boy shrieked. By this time a group of his concerned and curious friends had gathered to watch and Liedloff (still imbued with Western thinking) assumed that he would make at least a token effort at being staunch and brave in front of his peers. She explained to him and his mother that the tooth needed removal and it would be a painful process.

Throughout the procedure the boy shrieked and sobbed but made no attempt to push Liedloff away. His mother held and supported him. The friends watched with concerned interest and clearly thought no less of their friend for his tears. When it was all over, everyone went about their business.

On another occasion Liedloff had to deal with the gangrenous toe of a man in his mid-thirties. Half the village gathered to watch this painful elective surgery. The man brought with him his wife and his mother, who cradled him throughout the procedure.

Since he was a grown man, Liedloff anticipated a staunch, bite-the-bullet response. To her amazement, the moment she began work, the man shrieked with pain. She stopped. Then she noticed that she was the only person who seemed concerned. It wasn't that the 'audience' were unsympathetic. It was just that they accepted the need for the process, knew that it was painful, and knew that their friend had all the support available to him. They also totally accepted that the logical thing to do if one was in a lot of pain was to shout and sob. Clearly no one thought any the less of the patient for expressing the pain he experienced.

Incorporating the new ideas

When I read these accounts I was struck by the naturalness of the Yequana behaviours and the artificiality of our Western ways. We expect people to tolerate the unbearable or, at the very least, not to make a big noise about it. We begin very early with comments like: 'You are *such* a brave boy', 'Big boys don't cry', 'That's such a little scratch', 'It'll be over in a minute', 'Try not to think about it'.

I also started to reflect on how much I intervened in my own children's lives and how much I hovered in case things went wrong. I always explained ahead what could go wrong, so that my children could be prepared ... and I realised that I often had little faith in their ability to learn from their own experiences. They could so much more easily and simply learn from my accumulated wisdom and overview, or so I thought.

My long-held life views were beginning to change.

10. Caring More
and Intervening Less

Shortly after reading Jean Liedloff's *Continuum Concept* and still unclear about its relevance, I was comfortably seated in an armchair enjoying the three-minute respite you get when your child is playing happily next door. Suddenly, Deborah burst through the door crying, 'Mum, Gemma was mean to me!'

Now these perfectly lovely five-year-olds often played together happily and were pretty evenly matched.

I told myself, 'Make like a Yequana mother' and put an arm around my daughter. I understood that a Yequana mother would not say anything to her, but that was too hard for me so I muttered, 'Oh, sweetheart, how awful for you' … and waited … and waited.

Since my response would normally have been wordy and interventionist, Deborah looked up at me with a bewildered expression as if she were thinking, You look like my mother, but you don't sound like my mother. I was frantically wondering what to do next and inwardly muttering, Well it might work in Venezuela but it appears to have little application in New Zealand. We held, frozen in this position for at least 15 seconds. It felt longer.

Then Deborah said, 'Bye, Mum,' and raced back next door to play with Gemma. I sat there in amazement. Somehow it *had worked*. Deborah had been comforted, had worked out a solution and, no longer needing me, raced off to do five-year-old things.

I sat there thinking, Something really important happened then. I had no idea what it was, but I knew it was significant.

The shift in my thinking that began back then has led to a different way of looking at the world of parenting. It has led to my caring more and intervening less. It has led me to help hundreds of parents to liberate themselves from the need to praise every few minutes — and to punish. It has led me to write this book, in the hope of helping you.

A list of don'ts

While I sat there dumbfounded after my encounter with Deborah, I thought about all the things I would normally have said in the situation.

I also thought about her response. She could have rushed next door and hit Gemma, she could have sat on the fence and hurled abuse, she could have stormed off to her room and sulked. Amazingly, she had chosen the pro-social action.

I formulated a list of parental Don'ts.

Don't blame

It is a feature of our Kiwi upbringing to believe in fair play — we are always willing to believe there is another side to every story. Given this, my natural response might have been: 'What did you do to Gemma?'

Often our first impulse is to blame. This, of course, puts the child in a defensive position and makes them feel we care more about what happened to the other child. What we get is a lot of blustering as they try to convince us of the justice of their situation.

Don't criticise

We are inclined to respond to a whined 'Gemma was mean to me', with 'Why can't you just play nicely together?' But any rhetorical question beginning with 'Why can't you just ...' implies that our children's feelings are not important — that they should simply get over it. We are implying that our child is wrong to have such feelings.

Such criticism wounds our more sensitive children and alienates our less sensitive ones. We may think we are giving advice to action — 'Don't think about it. Just don't be so sensitive,' — but in fact we are simply criticising our child's feelings.

I believe *all* feelings are acceptable. How we *act* on our feelings is a different matter.

Don't distract

This is shorthand for 'Don't work hard at distraction'. When a small child comes to us upset we often try terribly hard to get their mind on to something else. We may even insist that they don't think about or talk about whatever is bothering them.

In the context of Deborah and Gemma's spat, distraction would look like: 'Well, don't worry, darling, I am sure Gemma didn't mean to upset you. Let's not think about that. Shall we read a book together?'

Many of us start with our young babies. If they are upset we quickly look for something interesting, noisy or diverting to make them feel better. If the first thing doesn't work, we try something else, and if that doesn't work we try something else.

Please don't misunderstand me. A little bit of light distraction goes a long way. However, if it isn't going to work easily it probably isn't going to work at all, so we should avoid working terribly hard at it. Also, if distraction is your favourite method of getting your child to do as she is told, you are probably working hard at your child's compliance and she is not working at it at all.

Don't explain

My first job was as a teacher so it won't surprise you that, if blaming, crticising and distracting haven't worked, my next tactic was always to launch into an explanation.

'Don't be upset, darling. Maybe you touched some of Gemma's toys that are precious to her.' Or: 'Maybe Gemma is just having a bad day.'

Or: — a fatal error, guaranteed to gets howls of protests out of any self-respecting youngster — 'Maybe you're tired. Remember last night when you mucked about at bedtime?'

When our children are upset, explaining to them the 'enemy's' position or pointing out their own contribution to the problem is likely to result in the child yelling back, 'You *never* listen' or 'You *always* take her side' or 'I'm *not* tired'.

Don't give mini-lectures

The first time I heard the term mini-lecture was when I heard Barbara Colorosa (author of *Kids Are Worth It*) speak.

A mini-lecture is a collection of ideas we have trotted out so frequently and with such consistency that, after the first five words, the child can finish the speech.

In our household, mini-lecture Number 43, saved specially for occasions such as these, would be: 'You don't know how lucky you are to have a little girl next door to play with. When I was your age, I would have given anything to have ...' And so on.

Most of us have a favourite mini-lecture derived from our own experience that we assume will also apply to our children's experience. Not surprisingly, our children neither learn from them nor are comforted by them. More likely they'll interrupt with: 'Yeah, yeah, I know. When you were my age ...'

Don't problem-solve

We may try this first or leave it till last. Either way it is doomed.

Mum: 'How about you go and ride your bikes together?'

Child: 'Naa.'

Mum: (revving up the enthusiasm) 'Well how about you put on your Jellybean make-up together?'

Child: 'Na-aa.'

Mum: (very brightly and with great enthusiasm) 'I know! How about you ring Gemma up and she can come over here. Remember that wonderful jigsaw Grandma gave you last week? Gemma could come over and you both could do it together.'

Child: 'Na-aa-aa.'

Mum: (exhausted and exasperated): 'Well, why don't you just go to your room and sulk?'

What is wrong with this picture? This began as a small problem between two five-year-olds, and here I am working like crazy to come up with solutions. My daughter is standing there quite relaxed, not taking any part in the solution, just saying 'Naa-aa' every now and again to keep me on track!

So what is left to do?

By now at least 10 minutes has elapsed. I am exhausted and frustrated. My daughter is so exasperated that either she has dissolved into tears or has worked herself up into a great rage. Referring you back to the custard diagram on page 60, my daughter had a problem that was perfectly manageable for a five-year-old, she handed it to me — actually I grabbed it off her, I worked very, very hard at it, and now the whole atmosphere has turned to custard.

So if I am not going to:

- Blame
- Criticise
- Distract
- Explain
- Mini-lecture or
- Problem-solve

what is left to do?

Making like a Yequana mother

When I 'made like a Yequana mother', I put my arm around Deborah, muttered something that indicated concern about her feelings, and I waited till she was ready. Was that a one-off, or would it work in other situations?

The answer is that since that moment I have used variations of that response in many, many situations and it works. It works for distressed and angry people of whatever age — with children, with friends and with colleagues. The essential components are:

- Empathy
- A boring cuddle. The "Boring" Hug

Empathy

One way of sharing empathy is to put into words what your child is feeling. Use phrases like:

- How awful for you.
- Oh, you poor thing.
- Wow. I bet that hurts.
- You seem so angry.
- That puzzle is really annoying you, isn't it?

Empathy is about speaking in such a way that the distressed person knows that *you* know how badly they feel. If words fail you, a heartfelt 'O-o-o-o-h' will cover most situations.

Most of us have had the experience of going to a doctor with a *really* sore throat. The doctor looks down your throat, mutters, 'A bit red,' and sits down at his desk to write something. Has he seen how much it is hurting? Does he think you are making a fuss over nothing? Does he even care that you are in agony?

My late brother-in-law, Gordon, was a doctor who would look down your throat and say, 'O-o-o-o-h. I bet that hurts!' He would still sit down at his desk and write something, but you were left feeling understood and cared for.

Similarly, with our children, the intensity of our words must match the intensity of their feelings. We not only use *words* to express how we imagine they are feeling, we use the intensity of our voice.

As Kiwis, I think we are very tough on our children. The standard Kiwi response to a child coming in, crying loudly over a tiny scratch, is: 'Don't cry, darling. It's just a little scratch.'

The child feels that her agony has been underrated and feels compelled to scream, 'It hurts! It hurts! It hurts!' This is very tough on our eardrums.

It is much faster, more efficient and much more supportive to say, 'Oh, those little scratches are often so-o-o-o painful. Would a cuddle help?' If we say it with a great deal of feeling the child will usually settle right down to a soft whimper. (Of course if we overdo the empathy they are likely to say, 'It doesn't hurt *that* much, Mum.')

We have delivered support, and our child — with that support — is able to handle the minor frustration. Most importantly, she has *learned* that she can tolerate a minor frustration.

A *boring cuddle*

Take a baby (with a small baby we tend to pat and pace) or toddler into your arms, put an arm around your child or take her onto your lap, put an arm around an older child or teen or, if that is not appropriate, simply wait patiently and warmly. And what are you waiting for? You are waiting for your child to gain the support she needs and move away when she is ready to solve or leave the problem.

It might take 10 seconds, it might take 10 minutes. Either way, it is easier and much more effective than trying to blame, criticise, explain, lecture or problem-solve.

The reason for the label 'boring' is that you are not setting out to entertain or distract the child with solutions or explanations. You are merely supporting your child until she feels ready to face the world again and solve her own problems, in an age-appropriate way.

In Liedloff's terminology, we are allowing our child to discharge her negative energy into our larger body. This rationale also explains why, when we have been supporting people in great pain, whether physical or emotional, we are likely to feel drained afterwards.

I like the 'cup of water' analogy. If you put a few drops of boiling water into a cup of cold water there will be only a tiny change in the temperature. Similarly, when we comfort an upset child, without getting involved in the problem, we can remain relaxed and give her full support without draining ourselves.

'Aren't we teaching them to be pathetic?'

When I first read about the Yequana Indians, I did worry that their methods would result in weak children who expected support at every turn. Yet Liedloff's book tells us the opposite, and my own experience has been the opposite. If we give unconditional support to upset children, they rapidly become self-sufficient and resourceful.

If we withhold our support they whine for more, become more demanding and may even take to tantrums to get the support they need.

Unconditional support results in children who believe in their own capacity to solve problems, backed by the security of a pair of warm, welcoming arms if they need them.

There are two other concepts I have found useful when thinking about how to support our upset children: 'emotional tanks and parents as the centre of the daisy'.

Emotional tanks

Somewhere, not yet anatomically described, we all have our own emotional tank.

Tank is full. Child is able to solve age-appropriate problem.

Tank is drained. Child is no longer able to handle much.

When our emotional tank is full, we are able to deal with minor irritations, handle ordinary frustrations and solve age-appropriate problems. The boring cuddle I have been talking about is a way of filling our child's emotional tank.

When our emotional tank is drained we lose our resilience and our ability to tolerate frustration. I find this a useful concept when a child who has been pleasant and busy for most of the day suddenly, apparently inexplicably, loses her temper and becomes angry, upset and inconsolable.

It is probably why the time from four to six o'clock carries the wonderful titles of 'Hell Hour' or 'Zoo Hour'. This is the time when our children have run out of steam and become 'fragile'. It is a good time to have things organised and calm and to give them as much 'downtime' as possible. You hope that then, with the last few drops left in their emotional tank, they will make it through to bedtime.

We need to remember that a positively stimulating day is also tank-draining, no matter how much fun it has been. This may be of some small comfort the next time you hear yourself saying, 'I am never taking them for a day at the beach again — they're so ungrateful!'

Plug size

It would appear that — again, in a place not yet anatomically described — there is a plug in the bottom of our emotional tank. The calm and easy-going child has a small plug that fits well. Occasionally it leaks a bit, but it is usually a relatively simple matter to give comfort to this sort of child. Put metaphorically, it is easy to top up the little bit that has drained from her tank.

Then there is the other sort of child. The plug in her emotional tank is large, ill-fitting and inclined to drop right out and roll away.

You wonder how on earth you are ever going to settle her down and get back to a normal existence. It isn't easy to deal with a child who is volatile, easily upset and slow to regain her equilibrium. Sometimes it is hard to remember that this type of behaviour is more about our child's personality and less about her simply trying to be difficult and wreck our day.

Filling a child's emotional tank

Along with empathy and a boring cuddle there are many other things we can do to help our children refill their emotional tanks.

Some children feel much better after they have told you how awful things have been for them; others prefer to have a quiet time on their own to re-establish their equilibrium.

A lot depends on their personality. After a hard morning at kindergarten or school or university your sanguine child may still be bouncing and eager to tell you everything that happened that was fun. However, even the most sanguine child often needs some space at the end of a busy day.

Your controlling child may want to tell you all about what others did wrong or what she did right, or may even go on the prowl to find someone to be mad at after a day of having to be pleasant.

Your melancholic child may need to tell you in great detail all the things that went wrong. Alternatively her need for space may override and she will opt for some quiet time alone.

Your phlegmatic child will just need some peace and will probably crave some quiet time with no demands placed on her.

It may take quite a bit of organisation and diplomacy to meet the needs of both a sanguine preschooler who has just had a nap and is waiting for older siblings to arrive home *and* a tired melancholic schoolchild who has used up all the words she intends to use that day. The most useful rule of thumb is to think in terms of needs and wants. The melancholic child *needs* space and will be very grateful if you say to the sanguine one, 'Jennifer needs a bit of quiet time after a busy day. You come and be with me [thus meeting her sanguine need for company] while she has some space and later on, when she's ready, I am sure she'll come and get you.' This is hard work for a tired parent but a lot less stressful than sorting out the spitting and hissing that goes on when you put a cheerful little sanguine in close proximity to an exhausted melancholic or phlegmatic.

Parent as the centre of the daisy

Another concept that I have found useful is to think of ourselves as the centre of a daisy. As our children start to crawl, they make a small excursion away but, sooner or later, they need to return to us for comfort, support or just to know we are there.

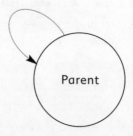

As they get older they are happy to crawl or toddle to the next room, but they tend to keep an eye and ear out for where we are and, if things go wrong, they scuttle back to us.

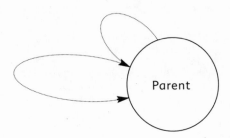

So one way of thinking of our children's growing independence is as an ever-increasing set of excursions out into the real world, always followed by the relief of returning to the comfort of home.

It might be going to the next room, going to kindergarten, going to school, going off to school camp and eventually going overseas. The petals of the daisy get bigger, but the need for a home base (centre) doesn't change.

When our older daughter first travelled overseas we said to her, 'While you are away, there may be times when you're homesick and need to speak to us. There may be times when you need to speak to us every day. That's fine. Ring whenever you need to.' We wanted to make sure that she knew that our support — the centre of the daisy — was always there for her. We hadn't taken into account that *we* would need to hear from her more often than *she* needed to contact us! So we had to change this to: 'We need to hear from you once a week!'

Later, when she went to live overseas permanently, her last words at the airport were, 'Don't protect me from any bad news in the family. I need to hear that even more than the good news.' In order to feel that the centre of the daisy was there for her, she needed to know that we would give her full information so she could stay connected to the family and to New Zealand.

It's not only Mum and Dad

As children grow up, many people can give them the security of that centre of the daisy. Grandparents, siblings, aunties, uncles, caregivers, step-parents, step-family members and teachers all form part of the centre of the daisy that gives our children the security that comes from knowing that there are many people who can give them love and support when they feel bereft.

It is always to that centre that our children return to fill their emotional tanks, to be ready for the next adventure life throws at them.

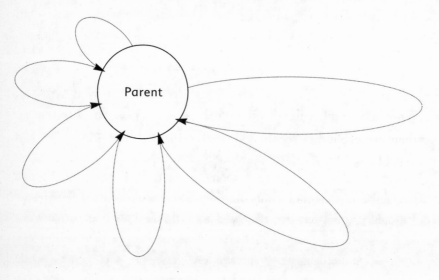

Separation can give our children two daisies

One way of making a parental separation less stressful for our children is to think of their moving from one household where they had two parents to two households, each one the centre of its own daisy. This means that each household has the potential to be a source of support and comfort.

11. Helping Children Deal With Their Frustrations

Having in mind that we will abandon blaming, criticising, explaining, lecturing and problem-solving, how do we apply empathy and boring cuddles in real-life situations?

Babies are not manipulative

When our babies are grizzly and needy, it is highly unlikely they are being manipulative. Now, just before you say to me, 'You haven't met mine!' I would like to distinguish between strong-willed and manipulative. Certainly, there are babies who are strong-willed and need whatever they need *right now*. These are the babies with the strong cries that say, 'Get here right now!' and have you running to comply. However, babies do not *manipulate* to get their own way. Mostly, they cry because they feel uncomfortable. After we have met any obvious physical needs — hunger, tiredness, pain, nappy change — the best thing we can do for our babies is to hold them firmly and either walk and pat or carry on as best we can doing things with one hand. This meets their need for support and comfort.

Don't leap to rescue your toddlers

I believe we should protect our children but I don't believe it is always good to rush to the rescue. As our babies start to learn to walk they are going to need a lot of practice and they are going to make 'mistakes'. But a baby stumbling and falling on the carpet does not have the same impact as an adult falling and need not be leapt up to with the same alarm.

Expect that your child will have many a tumble. Expect that your child will (mostly) pick himself up and carry on. Expect that if he needs you, he will come over to you and you will have a cuddle waiting, just for him.

And what is the difference between protection and rescue? An example from home. We have a square table with rather toddler-dangerous corners. Any time I see a toddler about to walk past one of the corners I am likely to lean over and, without comment, unobtrusively put my hand over the corner. Now if he trips at that moment he won't damage his eyes or teeth. That's protection.

On the other hand, saying, 'Be careful of that corner! Go around the other way! Watch your step! Let me lift you past the corner' is rescuing. You are likely to destroy his focus on toddling and he may well trip with mysterious magnetic force into that very corner.

'We're going for a walk'

Our toddler or preschooler has been rampaging all morning: up the stairs, down the stairs, over the table, under the table. He's tipped all the blocks onto the floor, raced off to another room to find the cat, leapt up onto the couch to look out the window, toddled down the path to look at the people, into the bathroom to see how many flannels he can fit in the toilet.

Desperate, we decide a walk will calm him down — tiring him out ready for his afternoon sleep. We get five minutes down the road and little Mr Lively goes limp and declares, arms uplifted, 'I'm tired. Carry me.' Unwisely, we say, 'Well, just for a little while,' and proceed to zigzag along with one hand on the baby-buggy and an amazingly heavy, limp bundle half over our shoulder. As we struggle we mutter phrases like:

- You weren't tired all morning when you were driving me mad running all over the house. (Blame)
- Why is it that the moment we go for a walk, you get tired and need to be carried? (Criticise)
- Look over there! I think I saw a little mouse behind the tree. Why don't you just take my hand and we can go over there and look. (Distract)

- Mummy will be too tired to make your lunch if she carries you much further. (Explain)
- Now you need to use your legs if you want to grow up to be big and strong like Daddy. (Mini-lecture)
- How about I carry you to that lamp-post over there and then you walk to the next one? (Problem-solve)

It is all very hard work and none of our brilliant ploys work. Our child persists with 'I'm tired. Carry me.'

We may give up and just decide, somewhat resentfully, to carry him. We may regale him with a succession of complaints, growls and threats — while still carrying him. We may put him down and walk off (on the basis that eventually he will follow us), leaving him yelling on the footpath and hoping he doesn't leap onto the road. What set out to be a lovely walk has just turned ugly.

There is an alternative

Pick up your child and stand still. Even better, find a low wall and sit down with him.

Mutter, 'Oh, sweetheart. Are you tired?' (Empathy)

Stay still, without another word and wait. (Boring cuddle)

How long do you suppose your average toddler will last? Ten seconds? I'd say 20 seconds at the outside. As soon as his emotional tank is refilled, he will wriggle to get down and be off.

Your job is to provide the emotional support and soon he will have taken comfort and be ready to walk — probably run. The secret lies in the word 'wait'. Usually we are so keen to 'solve' the problem — a problem that could be solved by a cuddle — that we rush in and turn it into *our* problem.

Helping them do what they don't want to do

We had a family emergency: Our littlest great-nephew came to stay for a week. He hardly knew us and it was a long time since we had had a two-year-old in the house. Pretty soon it became evident that he needed a major nappy change.

'Come on, Jake. Let's get your nappy changed.'

'No!' yelled Jake, and took off down the corridor.

I strolled down after him and, when he had backed himself into a corner where he couldn't get away, picked him up, and cuddled him all the way back to the changing place, muttering, 'You are really, *really* missing your Mummy and you really, *really* don't want me to change your nappy.'

This empathy was at about the same level of intensity as his 'No,' and after the boring cuddle he just lay back and allowed himself to be changed.

It would not have worked if I had launched into an explanation of how much better he would feel when his nappy was changed — particularly since it didn't bother him at all to be in the original one.

Many parents, when given this tip, dismiss it with, 'That wouldn't work for mine. Right away he'd be squirming or yelling.' Well I am suggesting that you try it for children who are upset and/or angry — particularly with children who are not your own.

If this idea, or the ones that follow, have no impact on your child's behaviour, you can be fairly sure that he is being *oppositional* rather than upset. There are lots of useful strategies for this in the next section.

The party

You arrive at the birthday party with your preschooler. He is not old enough to be left, but the arrangement is likely to be that the children will be racing around the garden together, playing a few organised games, watching some sort of organised entertainment while the parents sit inside drinking coffee and chatting.

You watch other parents walk in holding their child's hand until, after a brief settle-in, their child races off to join in the fun.

Not yours. You hobble in with him firmly attached to your leg. Clearly he is planning to stay that way for the afternoon. You show him what fun the others are having and suggest that he should join them. He clings firmly to your thigh. You explain that he will have a much better time if he joins in the fun. He clings firmly to your thigh. You remind him how much he was looking forward to the party and point out that if he doesn't join in, no one will want him to come to their next party. He clings firmly to your thigh. You suggest that he play quietly at the edge of the games and you'll just be inside. He begins to climb your ribs. He demands that you take him to the swing. You spend the rest of the afternoon all alone pushing a child on a swing.

Notice who has been doing all the distracting, explaining and problem-solving. Notice who has been doing all of the resisting. How could empathy and a boring cuddle work in this scenario? Let's try that again.

You hobble in with your child firmly attached to your leg. You offer to take him over to where the fun is and he declines. 'That's fine,' you say warmly. 'Come with me, darling.' You go and get a cup of coffee, sit your child next to you, and carry on talking to adults near you. You place an arm around your child, but otherwise do nothing to entertain him. (Boring cuddle.)

After a while he gets bored. He whines at you to come outside with him. You say, very warmly, arm back around him, 'No, dear. I can't come outside with you because I am talking to the grown-ups, but you are welcome to stay here with me as long as you like.' (I do understand that the more choleric child is likely to treat you to a wobbly at this stage. We will discuss this behaviour in subsequent chapters. For the moment I am assuming that, if you are staying calm and supportive — resisting the urge to solve the problem, the behaviour does not escalate.)

Eventually, totally bored, but confident he can return if necessary, your child wanders off to join his peers. You heave a sigh of relief. Three minutes later he is back. Don't fall into blaming ('What on earth are you doing back so soon?'). Don't criticise ('Why can't you just have a good time like all the other big boys?'). Lift him up onto the chair next to you, put an arm around him and say, 'How nice to see you, darling. You just sit here until you feel like going off again,' and carry on with your adult conversation.

We are revisiting the 'parent as centre of the daisy'. He takes comfort from you, makes an excursion, comes back for reassurance and off he goes again. You give him emotional support and make no effort to solve 'his' problem.

I know that what you want is for your child to be happily in the midst of all the fun and you, proud of his independence and social skills, happily in the midst of your peers. Not all children have that level of confidence, but the strategy that I have just described is the fastest way I know to build confidence in the reserved child.

Dropping them at kindergarten

One of the main areas in which we are advised to distract small children is when we take them to kindergarten or crèche. The general advice we are given is to settle them down to an activity and then, when they are involved, leave. This is wonderful advice for a self-reliant child. They choose the activity they wish to and may even cheerfully instruct you to leave. 'You can go now, Mummy.'

However, many children find it difficult to be left in a relatively strange place with people they don't really know. Even when really familiar with the caregivers and the place, some children find transitions really difficult. Our melancholic children, who do best with a structure in which they know exactly what to do when and what is expected of them, may find the concept of being able to play freely completely at odds with a temperament that is telling them to find out what to do and get it perfectly right.

The 'settle them down and then go' advice is nonsense for the parent of a child who doesn't want you to go. They rapidly work out that the moment they are settled in to an activity, their parent will go, so how can they possibly settle? The sooner they accept your distraction, the sooner you are likely to leave.

For this type of child, you are better off avoiding distracting, explaining, mini-lecturing, etc.

Let's return to the model of the daisy. Your child is about to transfer to another caregiver, who will briefly be the centre of his world and provide any comfort and support he may need. Say, 'I know you really want Mummy to stay (empathy) but I have to go now and I'll be back at mat-time to pick you up. Who would you like to cuddle you while Mummy leaves?' In any care situation, children usually know which caregiver is their best mother-substitute. Let them pick. Then hand him over with a brief, 'James is a bit upset about my going. Can he stay with you for a bit?' Kiss him goodbye and walk away. Wave goodbye at the door and leave.

One more wave at the gateway in case he's watching. Many caregivers hold children while they watch Mum or Dad go out of sight and then begin the settling process.

It feels just terrible leaving a crying child. We spend the next three hours with the image of the woebegone face at the window. We imagine that our child is inconsolable. Our morning is ruined.

However, the odds are high that he has been unsettled for a few minutes, has been comforted by the caregiver and now knows that she is capable of looking after him. If in doubt, phone. Your morning will be much more enjoyable if you know your child is no longer distressed.

After several departures, check with the caregiver for how long he is remaining upset after you leave. It is possible that he may always cry briefly when you leave for quite some time. It is hard on you both but unlikely to be harmful.

On the other hand, if you find that your child is desperately upset when you go and doesn't settle with support from a caregiver, don't continue to upset him to that degree. He has lost his confidence that others can replace your care.

It may be that this confidence can be restored; it may be that he isn't ready to be left; it may be that the environment is not right for him. The best way I know to check this out is to discuss the following plan with the kindergarten teacher and get her co-operation.

You are going to sit quietly and passively in an appropriate spot in the kindergarten. Bring your tapestry/book/letters/laptop so you don't get impatient or bored. Tell your child you will be staying for the duration. Welcome him to bring an activity over to do next to you, and remain supportive yet boring. Don't make his life exciting by suggesting he goes and plays. *Don't* get up and go to an activity with him. ('Sorry, I can't, sweetheart. I have all this work to do, but you are welcome to stay with me as long as you like.') Eventually he will go and join in for a while and then scamper back to you. Be mildly welcoming but don't get involved. Expect that he will make more excursions away but return frequently to check that you are not going to vanish.

If, within three to five such attendances, his confidence hasn't improved considerably, I would start to question whether he is ready for the kindergarten experience, or whether there is something about the situation that is too hard for him to cope with.

The swimming lesson battle

It is a great idea for children to learn to swim, play tennis, learn the violin, do gymnastics, join a singing group or any other of the wonderful after-school and weekend activities that are available. It is only a great idea, however, if you can manage the commitment comfortably and your child has enough energy for it. For the purposes of this example, we will assume that your child has a reasonable quantity of energy, and seems keen enough to go. It is once he gets there that the trouble begins.

You arrive and get to the edge of the pool. Every other child has hopped in and is enjoying the lesson. Your child is glued next to you and doesn't want to get in. The instructor comes over to issue a personal invitation. Your child won't even talk to him. You have visions of your precious dollars dissolving in the pool and you are also concerned that, if your child misses out, it will be difficult to catch up. It also feels pretty humiliating to be the only parent whose child won't hop in the pool.

Resist the temptation to:
- Blame ('You were the one who wanted swimming lessons.')
- Criticise ('Why can't you just hop in like everyone else? Look! There's a child half your age already in there.')
- Explain ('Look — you're going blue. You'll be so much warmer when you are in there swimming around.')
- Mini-lecture ('It is absolutely essential for every child to learn how to swim. We are surrounded by lovely beaches and you want to have a good time when we go there.')
- Problem-solve ('Just get in and hang on to the rail. Once you are in you will really start to have a good time.')
- Problem-solve ('Just listen to your instructor. He'll tell you just what to do so you can have a good time.')
- Fib ('You needn't put your face under.')
- Threaten ('If you don't get in soon we will go straight home and you can go straight to bed.') The danger with this is that some children

respond with 'Okay' — and they really would rather be home in bed than get into the cold water.

- Bribe ('If you get in the water right now, we'll get a huge ice-cream on the way home.')

Try this:

Wrap a towel around him. Pop him on the seat next to you. Say, 'We'll just sit here till you are ready.' Sit and watch the lesson with interest. Make no attempt to entice your child into noticing how fascinating the lesson is or how much he is missing out on.

Be prepared to sit out one whole lesson in this way. I am well aware that it seems like a colossal waste of money but believe me, it is the least work-intensive way to go about getting your child into the pool.

In the next week find an opportunity to get to the pool and see if your child is ready to play there, with you in the pool, and have a good time in the water.

Go to the second lesson prepared to sit it out again — and skip the lecture on the way in. Your child has now had the experience of watching and knows whether it would be better to overcome the boredom by getting into the pool or if it's still too scary. The odds are high that he will choose to join in, either at the beginning or after a few minutes.

If, after two sessions of sitting and watching, your child is not in the pool having a good time, he is not ready. The style of the teacher doesn't suit him, it is not the sort of pool that gives him confidence, or he is simply not ready. There is no point in persisting. Just make sure he never goes near the water without water-wings.

This way of looking at things works well for almost any child joining a group-learning situation. Our first two children were swimmers before they had lessons and then thoroughly enjoyed swimming lessons. Our third child was resistant as a toddler and as a preschooler, but at the end of her first year at school she was ready to hop in the pool and trust the instructor to look after her and to teach her.

'I don't want to go and I'm not going'

Your child's eyes are barely open and he begins the day with 'Is it a school day? Well, I don't want to go and I'm not going!' It is only going to go downhill from here. The first thing to remember and reaffirm, in your own mind, is that this is not a child's decision. It is a parental decision that a child should go to kindergarten, to crèche, to school — and it is not an option for discussion. My reason for saying this is that otherwise you will wind up giving all sorts of rationales, persuasions and mini-lectures, all carefully thought out and with impeccable reasoning, none of which will change your child's mind one bit, because:

(i) He has heard all this before and

(ii) None of the reasons impressed him last time, so why would you expect them to work this time?

You might as well save your breath. In response to 'Is it a school day?' the only necessary reply — unless it is the weekend — is 'Yes'.

The correct response to 'But I don't want to go to school' is not 'Darling! We all have to do things we don't want to.' That is a mini-lecture. The correct response is a warm empathic 'Darling! I know you don't want to go to school. Would a cuddle help?' Very often this is all that is required to top up his little emotional tank and enable him to deal with his frustration.

More determined and stroppy children will launch into, 'I'm not going, you know.' Unless you really like battling or you have a childish need to have the last word, the best response is a non-committal grunt that sits somewhere between 'Ah-ha' and 'Really?' The child does not have a choice.

'How was your day?'

Along with 'Always look on the bright side of life' and 'Let's just think about pleasant things', there is common lore about receiving children after a morning at kindergarten, a day at school, a week at school camp or a day at the office that is counterproductive for many children. It centres on our need to hear only the good stuff.

When Robert was little, and before I understood about the different needs of different personalities, I would pick up my little troupe for carpooling after school and cheerfully say, 'Now, I want everyone to tell me three good things that happened today.' The sanguine children couldn't wait to tell me about all the fun things that had happened. The phlegmatic children were usually happy to humour me. The melancholic part of Robert just needed to get the bad things off his chest and the choleric side of him was angry that I was asking something he couldn't deliver. Things generally deteriorated from there.

'Tell me three good things' is a great opener for cheerful children who have lots of exciting things to tell you. For the child who has had something upsetting happen and has been hanging on all day to tell a supportive adult, this sort of request completely ignores their feelings. This child needs to get the bad things off his chest, gain your support and start to feel better. And the child who is exhausted and has used up all his words is in no shape to oblige you either.

An open-ended question like, 'If you feel like it, tell me about your day' at least respects your child's feelings. You may even like to start with, 'How was your day?' and accept a monosyllabic grunt as an indication that your child needs space more than he needs support right now.

Many of us worry that if we invite our child to tell us about the bad things they will dwell on those and lose sight of the positives. But my experience is that by allowing our children to tell us — if they choose — about the negative things, we enable them to dump them and get on with the next part of the day. With the negatives out of the way, they may even recall that the day wasn't all bad!

It's great for stroppy teenagers too

Your child arrives home. The first grunt, flood of tears or paroxysm of rage tells you that it hasn't been a good day. 'What happened?' you venture tentatively. It all comes gushing out.

(Younger child version) 'The teacher was mean to me and I was only asking for a pencil. I'm never going back to that stupid school.'

(Older child version) 'That stupid teacher. All I was doing was asking James what she said — the silly cow shouldn't mumble so much and I wouldn't have to — and she bawled me out in front of the whole class and then made me stand up and repeat what she had said and I couldn't remember so then she said I wasn't paying attention and gave me a detention and when I told her where she could put her detention she chucked me out of the class and now I have to do a stupid detention on Friday afternoon and the stupid dean is going to ring you.'

This latter example may not faithfully reflect the vocabulary of your child. Both 'cow' and 'stupid' may well be replaced with much stronger expletives in your household. Either way, this is not the time to tell your child to watch his language, nor the time to bring up the famous aphorism about how only people with limited vocabulary use swearwords.

Avoid also falling into the trap of defending the school or the teacher. I am not sure why, but we often feel compelled to support the teacher (whom we have never met) ahead of meeting the needs of our beloved and distressed children.

If we possibly can, we should avoid the trap of:

- Blame ('You always talk when you should be listening.')
- Criticise ('Why can't you just stop talking during class time and do all your talking in the playground? Anyway, if you had been listening carefully enough in the first place, you wouldn't have had to ask James.')
- Explanation ('Maybe the teacher had had a tough lesson before yours and you just copped the flak. Anyway, if she has to stop over every interruption, how do you expect her to get through the class?')
- Mini-lecture (This is a really important year. You've already got a reputation as a bit of a chatterer. At your age your teachers no longer expect to have to tell you how to behave. You really are old enough to keep your focus during a class lesson. Apart from which, it is disrespectful to talk while your teacher is speaking.)
- Problem-solving ('Now you'll just have to do that detention [sigh] and I'll battle the traffic and pick you up later.')
- Problem-solving ('I'll write a note and get you off the detention. I'll explain that picking up papers is bad for your back. Anyway, they shouldn't make you carry so many books home every day.')
- Problem-solving ('Why don't you go to your teacher tomorrow and

ask to be shifted so you don't sit next to someone who gets you into trouble?')

The safest and most supportive response is to say something empathic like, 'What a pain. It must have made the day dreadful,' and follow up with some version of a boring cuddle.

Good mothering foiled
— or — I need you, so please go away

For an older child, just being around and being busy is the safest boring cuddle I know.

It's impossible to recall how many times I did the 'great mothering' bit. When my children came home from school I would have their afternoon-tea plates ready for them on the kitchen table and a cup of coffee for me. The symbolism of the cup of coffee was that it indicated: 'I am available. I am fully focused. I am ready to listen. I am dripping with empathy. Tell me all about it.'

The children would come in, cast a look at the welcoming scene and say, 'Thanks, Mum. Can I take this to my room and read?'

I would sit alone in the kitchen, thinking black thoughts about why I bothered being at home for them after school. I might as well have worked. What difference would it have made?

Eventually I came to understand that we were in 'centre of the daisy' territory. My children needed the warmth and support of having Mum there, but they also needed the space they had lacked in a busy crowded day. With the support of having me there they could retreat, and emerge later from their rooms and get on with their homework. Around the dinner table I could pick up on all the information they might be willing to share by then.

The same principle applies with adolescents in school holidays. They may be away all day. You may wonder what is the point of your being there at all. But somehow our children derive tremendous support from knowing exactly where we are. The centre of their daisy is intact.

For an older child, a boring cuddle is often quite invisible. You just hang about looking sympathetic and concerned till your child wanders off. If he slams out of the kitchen to his room and holes himself up behind closed doors and loud music, remember this is also a boring cuddle if you choose to make it so.

You have the option of baling him up about the decibels and the paint flaking off the door. However, it is unlikely to change his behaviour or help him deal with his frustration and anger. What it will do is result in a lot of yelling and further upset.

Or, you can accept that he is going about getting over the frustration his own way. You can give him support by letting him sort himself out and accepting that he will emerge when he can tolerate the frustration and has solved the problem for himself.

Helping big children handle the big stuff

As our children grow older there is no way we can protect them from all the inevitable hurts and disappointments that go with a full and enriched life. There are bound to be test results that don't measure up, friendships that go awry, romances that crash and burn, and loss of beloved family members.

Often we find ourselves searching for that elusive just right thing to say or do that will make it better. We find ourselves saying things that don't help or that anger or further distress our children.

When I find myself with distressed or angry teenagers my first resort is always to try to listen, to empathise and to stay put until they have sorted themselves out. The boring cuddle may involve wrapping my arms around them. The boring cuddle may involve sitting quietly alongside them. Increasingly, the boring cuddle involves staying on an international phone line until they have talked themselves out. Whatever the situation, I am waiting for those magic words, 'Thanks, Mum. I think I can handle it now.'

Supporting our children to handle their own problems empowers them, makes them more competent and leads to emotional maturity, independence and high self-esteem.

12. Surely a Parent is Entitled to Give Advice?

'But Diane,' I hear you say, 'when do I ever get to give advice? What about all the times I can see my children going about things the wrong way? Surely they could do with a bit of adult wisdom? Are you seriously suggesting that all I do is empathise and support?'

Of course you are right. It is ridiculous to suggest that we should withhold our wisdom, knowledge and experience from those we care about most. On the other hand, we have all had the experience of trying to tell our child a better way of doing things only to have them become hysterical and yell (for a younger child), 'I want to do it by myself!' or (for an older child), 'You are not listening to me!'

However, there are some 'extensions' of emotional support that may prolong our empathic interaction and enable us to support our children without getting our heads bitten off.

Keeping your child talking

Often our children have quite a lot to get off their chests. Stopping at 'Oh-oh-oh' and a boring cuddle seems to make us appear a bit uninvolved. Curious questions for young children keep the dialogue going and enable our children to *tell us all about it*. Phrases like:

- And what happened next?
- How did you handle that?
- Great response. How did he react?
- Did that fix it?

keep your child talking until she has talked the story through. At this point you are information-gathering, so stick with that. Keep away from solutions and problem-solving. These can shut a child down.

With older children — and definitely with teens — you need a light touch. There's a narrow line for them between your being engaged and involved and — a crime my adolescents have often accused me of — interrogating them.

Adolescents also have strong loyalty to their peers and so will often get halfway through their tale of grief, decide they are somehow breaching peer confidentiality and shut down. It is a wise parent who mumbles, 'If you ever feel okay about telling me the rest of the story, I'd love to hear,' and then leaving it alone. (They tell me no one has ever died of curiosity, but I can tell you it has been a close call for me at times.)

Remember that the purpose of your child telling you of her concerns is not for you to be able to hop in and solve the problem. Even more important, don't use the discussion as a way of finding out about the naughty things she has done. The purpose is for her to get it off her chest so she can regain her equilibrium and get on with her day.

Should you comment on inappropriate behaviour or correct bad behaviour?

Your time will come — and it isn't now. Right now your child needs your support to deal with her anger and upset. Now is the time for support and, as a sideline, information-gathering. Remember the content. Later on, when your child is not in a stressed state, you may have an opportunity to reflect with her about what could have been said or done to avoid that situation or — even more important — avoid the same thing happening in future.

Don't leap in with the right answer

A baby or small child needs a sympathetic adult of few words to get them through a crisis and enable them to handle their feelings. Muttering a few soothing sounds helps both parent and child.

The young and mid-aged child needs to tell you her story and it is often in the telling that our children can see their way to a solution. They may even come up with those magic words, 'What do you think I should do, Mum?'

Don't be fooled into thinking she actually wants the benefit of your experience and wants to follow your advice. You are much safer with a delicately put 'Well, I have an idea that you might like to think about.' This leaves you in an excellent position to expand or retreat, depending on her response.

Avoid beginning a sentence with 'Here's what you should do.' Your solution may be good, but you have missed the fact that our children need our support more than they need our solution.

Once your child has poured her heart out, she will more than likely need space before she needs solutions. This would be a good time to let her go out to play, off to her room to read, or blob out in front of TV. Later on, when she appears to have refilled her emotional tank, you might be in a good position to say, 'I've been thinking about the things you told me earlier. Would you like to hear some of my ideas?' Don't be surprised if you get a 'No thanks, Mum. It's okay now.' You have met her needs for sensitivity and space. Her emotional tank is full and she can solve the problem.

Respect a personality difference

Our sanguine children often just need an audience. In telling their story they may see the funny side or their innate sociability may result in their coming up with the most pro-social solution.

Our melancholic children will need to tell us every detail. It is hard for the choleric parent not to leap impatiently to the obvious solution. The sanguine parent will find all the detail tedious and would far prefer to get to the interesting bits. Again, remember that she is not telling you this story for your entertainment. She is upset and needs your support. Happy the child who tells a phlegmatic or melancholic parent their troubles, because those parents are likely to listen well.

Our choleric children are more likely to be enraged and frustrated than upset and it can be quite hard to listen to how mad they are — often with their best friend. Our temptation to leap to the defence of their friend or their teacher is our problem to overcome. It is a wise parent who can allow their children to dissipate some of their anger.

Our phlegmatic children often just need to tell us a brief 'Charlie was so horrible today,' and are content to leave it at that. They have come home and now they need peace. Say, 'I'd love to hear all about it when you have some energy back,' and don't be surprised if that's the last you hear.

Respect the gender difference

In broadest terms — and please take this as a generalised comment — women are more likely to think problems through by talking them through. ('How do I know what I think until I have heard what I've said?') Men are more likely to go off alone and think things through.

Our children's approach may well reflect this gender difference. Whereas my daughters have almost always been susceptible to the 'Let's sit down and talk about it' approach, I have often been snapped at when I have assumed that my son would appreciate the invitation.

I used to be offended. Now I understand that I have offered something completely unsuitable for him. He needs — to use the words of John Grey in *Men Are From Mars, Women Are From Venus*, to go away into his cave and think things through. Beware the cave dragon. If you go too near too soon, the cave dragon will burn you.

Respect age difference

Younger children are much more likely to tell us all about it. They pour their hearts out and then it's all over.

As our children head towards adolescence they are more likely to want time alone to think things through. They like to go to their rooms and brood about a problem. They — especially the girls — like to write their thoughts in their diaries. This is part of getting their thoughts out and then being able to look at them.

Many also like to run problems past their peers rather than their parents. We are inclined to find this difficult. We wonder why we're not good enough and why a child 20 or 30 years our junior is the preferred confidant. We also worry about the sort of advice the peer might be handing out. Can they be relied upon? What hare-brained scheme will they come up with?

It is important to realise that these are *our* concerns, and I strongly recommend not visiting them upon our children. If we ask, it is highly unlikely that we will like the answer.

The telephone and more recently email and text messaging all play a significant part in this process. I could never figure out how my daughters could spend all day at school with their friends, travel home for 45 minutes by bus with them, get in the door and go straight to the phone for a long discussion with the same friend, probably followed up by one or two further 'electronic consultations' during the evening.

Now I think I understand. Some children need to *have* their day, *review* their day, *analyse* their day and *prepare* for the following day. This is the way they use emotional support to solve their problems. The phone companies must be delighted.

Offering advice — delicately

With the right sort of support your child may have moved on and forgotten or overcome the upset of an hour ago. She has got it off her chest but it is now sitting on *your* shoulders. You have been worrying about it. You want to help. A respectful approach is called for.

Respectful? Aren't *they* supposed to respect *our* wisdom?

I think it behoves us as parents to be respectful of our children's ability to problem-solve age-appropriate problems. I never cease to be amazed at how cleverly children can work things out if they are given the support and space they need. So if we are going to approach them with our ideas, I believe it needs to be done respectfully. You may like to try one of these:

- I've been thinking about the situation that was bothering you. Is the moment passed or do you still want to talk about it?
- I have some ideas that you may find useful. Would you like to hear them?
- Do you know how you are going to tackle that problem tomorrow or would you like to talk it through?

Be prepared for your help not to be required. 'No thanks, Dad. I've got it all sorted,' is a cause for rejoicing. It means that your child appreciates your offer, has good manners and can sort out her problem for herself. You have done a good job.

Feel your way

From our teens we await for those magic words: 'What do you think I should do?'

When we get them, we should beware of traps. I am reminded of a saying that the best way to give someone advice is to work out what they want to do and then tell them to do it.

Rob, being my first child, often suffered a parent who naïvely thought that when he said, 'Mum, will you read my essay,' he meant, 'Mum, will you find all the mistakes and point them out to me.' I was a slow learner, but after several episodes of having the essay ripped out of my hand after I had pointed out only four punctuation errors and five spelling mistakes in the first paragraph, I eventually got the message.

Firstly, I learned to gauge his tiredness level — and mine. An essay thrust at me by an exhausted, frazzled child needed an affirming response. I needed to tell him that I enjoyed the essay, that there were several interesting points and that I could see what he was getting at. Then, if that bit had gone well, I might mention that there was the odd spelling or punctuation error. Did he want to know or was he happy for the teacher to deal with that?

Eventually, I learned that I should first deal with the large picture and then work my way down to increasing detail if and when my child could handle it.

When you just can't do it

You may have noticed when I talked about tiredness levels I added 'and mine'. As our children get older they often come to us late at night with worries or needs — too late for us deal with in a civilised fashion. It may be 'I've just remembered that I need three iced cakes for tomorrow' or it may be 'Will you help me with my calculus?' or it may even be 'My best friend just dumped all over me.' You know however hard you try, you are going to be short-tempered and grumpy and it is all going to end in disaster.

If you cannot meet their need at that time of day, you are far better off taking full responsibility for your own feelings and saying, 'I really, really wish I could listen right now, but I am absolutely wiped out and just cannot handle it.' If it is going to take delicacy and patience and you have used your quota up for the day you are much better off to say so.

Emotional support doesn't have to drag on forever

When our children went to bed earlier than I did, I used to sit on their bed for a 10-minute chat before tucking them in and leaving them to read themselves off to sleep.

When Tanya was about eight, she started to come up with three worries at bedtime:

- I'm worried about having a blood test.
- I'm worried about learning to drive.
- I'm worried about having a baby.

Now, being the loving and caring mother that I was, and being a teacher of biology, I handled her concerns with the utmost care. I explained gently and carefully, with lots of reassurance, but she still had these worries every night. I tackled the problems from all directions. Still no success. I stayed patient and kind.

After a while I began to notice that our 10-minute chats had stretched out to 45 minutes. I was becoming impatient and, frankly, couldn't wait to get away.

One day the penny dropped. This was a bright child who usually grasped most concepts the first time, certainly by the third time. If she hadn't got it by now, she was never going to get it.

So what was going on here? I don't think it was a deliberate, manipulative ploy to keep me there. I think it all happened at a subconscious level. She had worked out — subconsciously — that it took an unsolvable problem to keep me fully engaged.

The following night I took a courageous step. I sat down on her bed and said, 'Tanya, darling. Tonight we can talk about any subject but blood tests, learning to drive and having a baby.' And we reverted to 10-minute chats about other things.

You may like to know about the long-terms effects, 20 years later, of my belated refusal to be supportive over these questions. Tanya has managed blood tests without too much trauma. She has driven a car since she was 15. She has not yet had a baby, which is an excellent outcome given that she lives on the other side of the world and is, to date, single.

When we sense something is wrong

Acting in

Often, we know something is wrong but it is hard to get our child to speak about it. All our efforts are rebuffed. Depending on our child's style they may be 'acting in' or 'acting out'.

'Acting in' is easier to live with, but very worrying. Our children become withdrawn and look pale. They spend a lot of time staring into space or holed up in their rooms. They look troubled. Our oft repeated 'What's wrong?' draws in a one-word response: 'Nothing.'

What you want to say is: 'What's wrong with you? There must be something wrong — you've been mooching around for days. You'll never get anywhere just going round and round things in your head. For heaven's sake talk to someone about it. Do you want me to arrange counselling?'

Don't do it. Try this instead.

Knock on your child's door. Say gently, 'May I come in?' Sit next to your child and, without making eye contact say gently and quietly, 'I'm worried about you. You've been quiet and spending lots of time in your room and you seem very troubled. Is there anything I can do to help?' (Notice that you are *not* mind-reading what is going on for your child. You are describing what *you* see and what *you* feel.)

You may get a positive response and your child is willing to talk. You may get the 'Yes, you're right, but I can't talk about it now. Maybe later.' A good response to this is 'Whenever you're ready, I'd love to help.'

You may get a child who bursts into tears and just needs you to hold them until they have cried themselves out. It is sometimes hard to remember that this level of support does not automatically entitle you to the information.

If your child wants to talk about it — fine. If she doesn't, it is hard, but I suggest you respect that and retreat to 'Whenever you are ready.'

Acting out

The concept of our children 'acting out' their feelings is one I found difficult to grasp. When a child is yelling, screaming, hurling abuse or just picking on people, it is hard to tell whether she is just a badly behaved little brat or a child who is worried about something.

If you think it is the latter, avoid: 'You've been in such a stink lately, there's got to be something wrong. For heaven's sake, what is it? You've just been impossible to live with and we are going to have to do something about it.'

The best response includes a fib but a very useful one. This may be a rare case of the end justifying the means.

Try, gently and calmly: 'I've noticed that you have been particularly angry and bitey lately.' [Here comes the fib.] 'That isn't like you. Is there something troubling you? Is there anything I can do to help?'

Since you are dealing with a strong-willed child, expect a negative — possibly explosive — response. Mutter gently, 'Well, if you ever find out ...' give a small hug and wander away. Remember that you have done something positive and useful. Your offer of help has been an emotionally supportive thing to do.

I learned this way by accident. Rob, our strong-willed, sensitive son had been particularly grouchy for a number of days. He was about 18 or 19. He was unkind to his sisters, short with his parents and it was like living with a thundercloud waiting to burst. (None of these behaviours was unheard of in our household, but something this time told me that it might be more than hormones, adolescent rudeness and bad-temper.)

One night he came to our bedroom to kiss us goodnight. (We were already at that stage when children tuck parents in!) I said to him, 'Rob, what's the problem? You have been grouchy and unpleasant for a few days now. That's not like you. Do you want to talk about it?'

'No!' yelled Rob and took off down the corridor. He got to the end of the corridor, turned around, ran back and flung himself down the middle of the bed between us. (Considering that he was six foot tall and 80 kilos of well-trained athletic muscle, it was just as well we had a king-size bed.) 'There is something' he said ... and spent the next half-hour discussing it.

It is hard to tell the difference between rudeness and acting out. My best rule-of-thumb is when you feel there's something not quite right, it is probably acting out.

How adults give and get emotional support

I am privileged to have women friends who meet regularly because we enjoy one another's company and because we provide one another with extraordinary emotional support. Part of the delight and support of being together is that we catch up on what has been happening in the intervening time. I notice that we are all very respectful and listen with empathy.

Since presumably we have all reached emotional independence, whoever is telling their story is given the space and time to talk themselves out. Mostly our relief or entertainment or solution is in the telling. Sometimes we will finish the story with 'What do you think I should do?'

Occasionally, someone will say, 'I'd like to comment on that' or 'Are you aware that you have been in that pickle before?' and I am always in awe of how respectful and gentle we are with one another's worries, notwithstanding our own ability to laugh at ourselves and indeed, with love, at one another. We all value emotional support.

13. When the Solution isn't Obvious

Obviously it is not always as simple as listening and supporting. We may know the best solution to our child's problem; we may not. Even if we do know the answer, many children will not work on *our* solution.

Here is a way to engage your child in generating several options, sifting through to find the best one, making a plan to see it through and reviewing the outcome.

I began developing this module one day when Deborah was about eight and had stormed in shouting, 'I am never going back to that stupid class again.' The teacher in question was highly competent, somewhat abrasive, very warm and caring, admired Deborah's intelligence and passion, and was aware of her lazy streak.

I had offered loads of emotional support on previous similar occasions and it had more or less worked, but this time was different. Deborah was upset and angry and wanted a *solution*, preferably a violent one.

Step one: form a team

At this point you need to be 100 percent on your child's side, forming a team that will come up with an answer.

'Deborah. We've been down this track before and it is obviously really upsetting you. How about we sit down together, with afternoon tea, put our brains together and work out a solution. I'll do all the writing.'

Notice the unabashed use of chocolate biscuits and the apparent offer that all your child has to do is attend and there will be a positive outcome.

Step two: define the problem

The next step is to get the problem down to a single question that requires an answer. Deborah's version of the problem was: 'What to do about stupid Mrs Jones who wants me to do her stupid homework neatly.'

It was really hard for me to write down the problem in that format. My temptation was to get into a discussion about the proper way to speak about teachers, to deliver a lecture on respect and to comment on the need for homework to be legible. I could have done that and felt fully justified. The only problem is that it would have shut down the process completely. It was wiser to swallow my words and allow her to express her anger — after all, if she couldn't let off steam in the privacy of her home, where else?

Use a large piece of paper and draw a circle. Write down the problem to be solved — in your child's words.

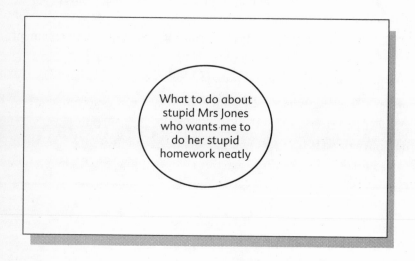

Step three: open the possibility of several solutions

The best way I know of opening our minds to several possible solutions so that we can get to the best one is to set ourselves up for at least 10 options. Draw 10 lines.

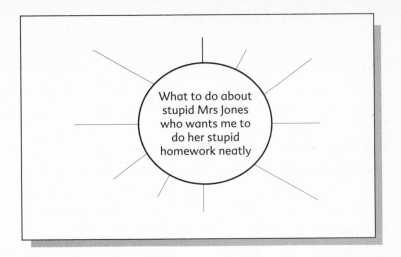

I suggested to Deborah that she should generate the solutions and I would be the scribe. She was still pretty angry so she initially came up with dramatic antisocial ones that, clearly, I could never condone. 'I'll get a gun and shoot her.' 'You go in and beat her up.' It was hard not to comment, 'Don't be so ridiculous,' but somehow I managed. I diligently wrote down 'Shoot her.' 'Mum goes in and beats her up.' I held to my faith that, once her anger was dissipated, she would start to come up with sensible solutions. I also knew that if I started arguing with her at this point we would become diverted and never get to more sensible suggestions.

Deborah, somewhat thrown by my not rising to the bait, carried on:

- Don't go to school any more.
- Go to another school.
- Get Mum to get her fired.
- Keep doing homework badly.
- Don't worry about my writing but make sure I get the right answers.
- Get Mum to go and tell her off.

I couldn't quite keep out of it, so I suggested:

- Alternate neat and untidy.
- Write it out again if caught.

By now Deborah was smiling and she said, 'You can write those down.' I did.

'You'd better put,' she added somewhat scornfully, 'Just do it her stupid way.'

Keep writing till you have both run out of ideas. Add as many extra lines as you need. It is fine to add your own suggestions — just don't rush into 'good child' ones. Let your children come up with those after they have exhausted all the negative ones.

You may find this quite a scary way to go. The reality is that, if you treat your children's angry ideas with reasonable respect, you will be amazed at how fast they start coming up with reasonable solutions.

Your job — and theirs — at this stage is not to process the ideas, just to generate them and get them recorded.

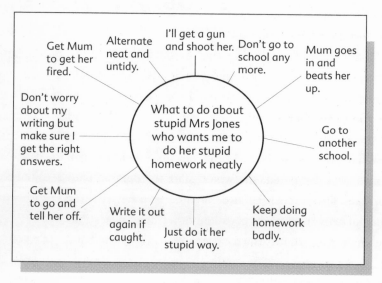

Get Mum to get her fired.

Alternate neat and untidy.

I'll get a gun and shoot her.

Don't go to school any more.

Mum goes in and beats her up.

Don't worry about my writing but make sure I get the right answers.

What to do about stupid Mrs Jones who wants me to do her stupid homework neatly

Go to another school.

Get Mum to go and tell her off.

Write it out again if caught.

Just do it her stupid way.

Keep doing homework badly.

Step four: process the ideas

Tell your child you are going to work through the ideas so she will be left with the best solution. My style is to say, 'We may not be able to come up with an ideal solution, so we'll settle for least worst.' This sets your child up to accept a solution that he may not particularly fancy but that is the best available one.

Start by crossing off the unacceptable and illegal ones. Let your child decide wherever possible.

- ~~I'll get a gun and shoot her.~~
- ~~Mum goes in and beats her up.~~
- ~~Don't go to school any more.~~

That left:

- Go to another school.
- Get Mum to get her fired.
- Keep doing homework badly.
- Don't worry about my writing but make sure I get the right answers.
- Write it out again if caught.
- Get Mum to go and tell her off.
- Alternate neat and untidy.
- Just do it her stupid way.

'It's quite hard to get a teacher fired, and anyway, I don't think I've got that power. We can look into other schools, but that would take some time and you are stuck with her while we sort it out.'

- ~~Go to another school.~~
- ~~Get Mum to get her fired.~~

'I'd have real trouble going in to tell a teacher off for complaining about you scribbling your homework,' I ventured. 'Yeah, and I really like my lunchtimes. That's the best bit about school,' Deb added.

- ~~Get Mum to go and tell her off.~~
- ~~Keep doing homework badly.~~
- ~~Write it out again if caught.~~

That left:

- Don't worry about my writing but make sure I get the right answers.
- Alternate neat and untidy.
- Just do it her stupid way.

'What do you think of those?' I asked. It was really hard not to lead her. I had to remember that this was about giving her a mechanism and the support to come up with the best answer herself. The reality was that these were all solutions that I could live with and that she would learn from.

That day I got lucky and she said, grumbling only mildly, 'Well, I guess I had better do it her way.'

'Good idea,' I muttered, trying to look as neutral as possible.

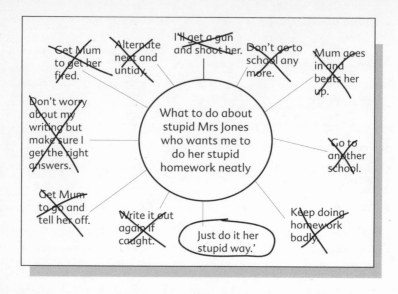

Step five: offer support for the plan

Now it is time to switch to the 'leader as servant' concept. Ask, 'Is there any help you will need to see through that idea?' Helping your child in a good direction is one of the more pleasant aspects of parenting. This is a nice way to show your approval and support. More often than not the response will be: 'No thanks, Mum. I know what I am doing now.'

In our particular example Deborah asked, 'Could you check my homework, please?' Could I ever!

Step six: set a review date

This is the most powerful one to leave in and the easiest to leave out. It is a shame to leave it out because it requires so little effort. It tells your children that you respect their judgement, that you respect the process and that you will follow up.

It also gives them a chance to try out something difficult, knowing it is time-limited and that you will be available to listen to what went right and what went wrong. You are setting yourself up to be their mentor in later years.

A fortnight is usually a good length of time. Write the date on the piece of paper — which has just become a contract. Write it down in your diary, in your child's diary and on the family noticeboard, if these exist.

Be sure to follow through when you have said you will. This may be the end of the matter, or it may have highlighted some other problems to be solved. If so your child is likely to be in a position to generate his own solutions.

'Isn't this a lot of fuss about nothing much?'

I don't think so. You have taken a child from upset and outrage to taking an active part in problem-solving. You have supported your child while guarding the boundaries of decent behaviour. You have shown your child a model that will serve him well for many other problems he will encounter as a teenager and adult. You have shown yourself to be the sort of person your child can turn to in trouble, who will listen but not impose your own solution.

I'd call it a very good use of 20 minutes.

Part Four:
The Path to Self-discipline

14. Getting Children to Do as They are Told

Wouldn't it be wonderful if they did what we asked the first time? Or even without being asked? How many times, from six months to six years, do you think you will have asked your child to let you dress her or to go and get dressed? (Or until she leaves home, for that matter?)

Wouldn't it be great if our child *did what she was told?*

Consider your objectives

When we ask a child to do something we have short-term, medium-term and long-term objectives.

Short-term objective

We may only be aware at the time of the short-term objective, which is to get something done. Usually it is some simple and often-repeated task:

- Let's get you dressed, please.
- Do up your seat-belt, please.
- Go and get your homework, please.
- Pack your bag for tomorrow, please.

Let's deal with 'please' right now. It shouldn't make the least difference to whether or not your child carries out the request, but you are modelling (the most effective way to teach a child, though) good manners and that can never go amiss. Of course you need to be prepared for the fact that no matter how impeccable your manners, your child may not necessarily do what you have asked her to do.

Medium-term objective

Learning to do what they are told as children is an important step on the road to being a self-disciplined adult. If your child spends a lot of energy resisting simple requests, she is using up the time and energy she could better use for learning new skills that are useful to her rather than refining an old skill — resisting compliance — that is ultimately bad for her.

If she has already resisted getting up, getting dressed, cleaning her teeth, packing her bag and making her bed and it is only 7.45 am, what sort of a child do you think you are sending to school? A child who is ready to benefit from the wisdom and experience of the classroom teacher or a child who is ready to resist a new set of requests, such as 'Take out your books,' 'Find your pencil,' 'Stop hitting Jason,' 'Start writing.'?

So our medium-term objective is to have our children do as they are told.

Long-term objective

And long-term? A child who is extremely non-compliant eventually begins to sabotage the relationships in her life. Her parents may be endlessly forgiving but exhausted, her teacher looks forward to weekends and her friends are likely to get sick of her too.

When families approach me worried about their child's progress at school or lack of friends, the first question I am likely to ask is, 'What is her compliance like?' If the response is something like 'Well, she is very strong-willed,' I am likely to recommend that we look first at her compliance at home. If we can improve this, it is amazing how often it flows on to the school and social situation.

If we get improvements at home but not at school, we are in a strong position to go to the school and say, 'We have achieved these changes at home. Can we now look at strategies that may work in the school context?'

A child who learns compliance at home will not only have better relationships with parents, teachers and friends, but is also on the road to becoming a self-disciplined adult. This is our long-term objective.

If we accept that we are on a continuum of development from an undisciplined baby to a self-disciplined adult, then each step needs to be made before our children are ready to move on to the next.

So we can see that, unless our children pass through the 'Doing as told' phase they are going to have trouble further up the ladder.

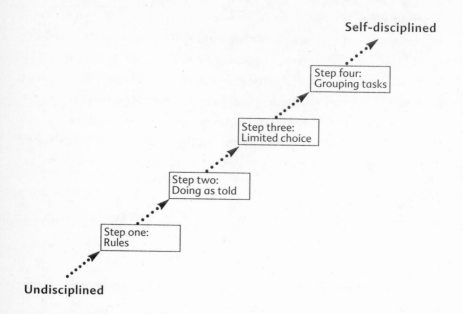

Positive strategies

I brought up my two older children on the 'love them to bits and tell them when they are going wrong' principle. For behaviour I didn't like I used a combination of yelling, growling, explaining and punishing. It was more or less working and they were basically good children except when they were horrible.

I began working at the Leslie Centre (this was Auckland's first Family Therapy Centre and I will always be grateful for the excellent training I received there) and learning and teaching about the use of praise. I would describe what I saw that my children were getting right and give them strong 'I' messages ('I am so pleased that you have set the table so quickly'). I would catch them being good.

When Deborah was born I was determined that, if I could keep reinforcing the good behaviour, I might never have to deal with any bad behaviour. The answer was to catch her being good and to praise her for it.

But what to do about the behaviour I didn't want? Some behaviour needed to be stopped.

She was at that wonderful stage where she found that she could jam the books into the shelves so that no adult could remove them, but a 12-month-old determined set of fingers could winkle out the book of choice.

I hit upon a plan. When I said, quite sharply, 'No, Deborah,' she would heed the tone and briefly stop to look around — presumably to check whether I meant it or not. I would seize the moment and come in with the positive comment: 'Good girl for stopping when Mummy asked.' It would give me enough time to scoop her up and take her off somewhere else.

When she was about 15 months old, we began to see how effective this strategy had been. She was at that stage where you need to rubber-band paired cupboard doorknobs in the kitchen. You could hear her open the door as far as it would go, until the restraint of the rubber band kicked in, say 'No-o-o,' let the door ping shut and then declare, 'Goo-girl, Debbeee.' That gave us a 10-second window of opportunity to get in there.

How could we use this learning as she became a toddler?

It began to dawn on me that when I yelled, 'Don't touch that hot stove,' my child simply heard, 'Touch that hot stove.'

When I yelled, 'Don't throw the plate,' my child simply heard, 'Throw the plate.'

When I yelled, 'Don't tip out all the blocks,' my child simply heard, 'Tip out all the blocks.'

What was a parent to do?

I started to think about positive alternatives to 'No' and 'Don't'. It seemed to me that the best alternative to 'Don't throw the cup' was 'Show Mummy how nicely you can hand her your cup.' The alternative to 'Leave the cat alone,' was 'Show Mummy how gently you can stroke the cat's back.' It seemed the best alternative to 'No' and 'Don't' was 'Show me'.

Crunch time came the day I was picking her up from crèche when she was about 18 months old. She had done many wonderful creations involving runny paint, blocks glued to thin card and pretty cottonwool held on with not enough glue. I was carrying the masterpieces, the kindy bag, the spare nappies, the anorak, the car keys, my handbag, my jacket and the two pages of notices.

(One of my favourite cartoons shows a mother octopus very busily trying to do everything and scowling at the baby octopus saying, 'Can't you see I only have four pairs of hands?')

Suddenly Deborah let go of my hand and ran around the front of the car onto the road. An oncoming car swerved and missed her. I grabbed her, jammed her into her carseat and drove home shaking. I had a very strong urge to smack her and yell, 'Don't you ever run on the road again!' (Actually, a few days earlier I had read an article that said most children who ran into traffic had been smacked within the last few days for the same offence.) I lunched her, put her to bed and sat down to have a good think. What was the 'Show me' alternative? How could I tell her what to do rather than what *not* to do?

The result was that we developed 'Show me' places all over Auckland. 'Show me how you can hang on to that little tree while I get your pushchair out of the car.' 'Show me how you can walk up to that line at the end of the drive and stop.' 'Show me how you can keep your hand on that stripe on the car while I unload the shopping.'

For the next few years I used lots of praise and lots of punishment. Now I find working with a Support-Distance continuum much more useful than the Praise-Punishment one.

Toward the end of the 1990s, I heard Linda and Dan Popov speak about their Virtues Project. Their teaching is that every culture, no matter where it is geographically and historically, subscribes to the development of the same virtues. We all believe that virtues such as caring, courage, excellence, generosity, justice, kindness, loyalty, respect, responsibility and trustworthiness should be developed in our children so they become adults of honour and integrity.

Their work touched me deeply and I greatly warmed to the idea that these virtues are present in every one of us and can be called up if only we notice them in people and affirm them. I am drawn now to the recognition of our children's virtues rather than praising their behaviour.

If we tell our children that we have noticed when they are thoughtful of others, or persistent at difficult tasks, or gentle in the way they take care of their pets, or honest in the way they return property, or humble in the way they receive accolades, we will call up those virtues in them and accelerate their development of virtues, values, ethics and morals.

We will be helping them to become not only independent young adults but, more important, decent human beings.

A star chart that works

Many parents use star charts with great success. They set up clear parameters. They enthuse their children. The children like the idea. The stars are earned.

Many more parents tell me, 'We've tried star charts and they just don't work.' Usually, this happens where the parameters are not clear, when behaviours rather than tasks are involved, when stars are removed for bad behaviour or parents are not prompt in handing out the stars.

Star charts are particularly unsuccessful when used as a means of stopping non-compliance, or with a child who is determined not to be motivated. Because, when all else fails and the parent says, 'If you don't do that, you won't get your star and you won't have enough for your new toy,' the child can always rejoin with, 'I don't want that dumb old toy anyway.'

Is there a successful way of using star charts or should we just abandon the whole idea?

How it started

It was around the time of the 1994 Commonwealth Games and Deborah was about nine. She was struggling with getting ready on time in the morning. I had done all the usual screaming, growling, punishing and nagging.

I said to Deb, 'I know it is awfully hard for you to get up in the morning and get through all your tasks. I also know you hate it when I yell and nag. I have a plan that may help. Chocolate biscuits are involved.' I had her full attention. She was willing to listen. 'It takes 21 days to break a habit,' I said, citing some wisdom I had read somewhere. Every morning I will wake you at 6.45 and set the timer for 7.30. If you are dressed, breakfasted and ready to go by the time the timer goes off, we will hold a medal ceremony.'

I took a packet of chocolate biscuits and wrapped each one in tinfoil. Every time she was ready in time I would announce, 'Deborah Levy, will you please step up to the podium.' I would shake her by the hand and declare, 'For being so competent as to be ready by 7.30 am and in recognition of the enormous effort involved, you are hereby awarded the silver medal.'

Amazingly, it worked easily and well. We suffered the odd tear when she wasn't ready on time, but it was nice and impersonal because the 'judge' was the timer. Once the habit was established it held for many weeks.

When I thought about it, and the factors that made it successful, I realised it could be used in other situations. Out of those reflections I have developed a way of using star charts that works well — although only with a relatively compliant child. It doesn't fix naughtiness.

The contract

Place you and your child on the same side of the problem. Talk to her about one behaviour she is struggling with and offer to help her overcome it. Explain that she will need to get it right 21 times to overcome the difficulty, that there will be stars and Smarties involved, and a celebration when the old habit is overcome and the new one established.

Buy stars or coloured pens and sweets. Draw a simple chart. I am no artist, so all our star charts looked something like this:

Number the bits of the chart in clusters, e.g. Hair 1, 2, 3, 4, 5, 6, 7, Left ear 8, 9, 10 ...

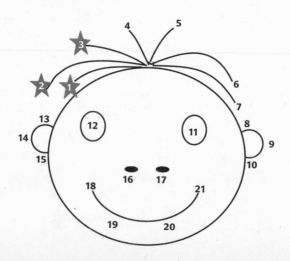

Prolong the recognition

The purpose of the chart, lollies, stars or pens is to prolong the recognition. Your child is doing something she does not find easy. When she has done it, take her to the chart and ask her what number she wants to put the star on. Some children like to start at one and work their way up to 21. Others like to work in 'body blocks'. First they like to do the eyes, then the nose, and so on.

Make success public

Put the chart on the fridge to show trusted people how well your child is doing. This affirms for your child that you value her efforts. It places you both on the success team and invites others to be the cheerleaders.

Support frustrations

If your child has not met the criteria, do not use this as an opportunity to hammer home the lesson. Use empathy. I am sure your child understands what needs to be done.

Celebrate or abandon

When the 21 repetitions have been achieved, celebrate in some appropriate way.

Alternatively, should the chart not be working, don't berate the child or leave the chart peeling and curling in the sun as some sort of ghastly reminder. Reflect upon what caused the lack of success. Almost always it will be because you used it as a compliance substitute or because you chose more than one manageable task.

When praise isn't enough

It would be wonderful to think that we could raise our children entirely through positive strategies. I had always hoped that, if I could keep Deborah being good through lots of recognition of what she was doing right, she would be so busy being good that I wouldn't have to growl, berate or punish. Nice theory. Nice wish. Needless to say, I couldn't get it to work that way.

None of us really likes the process of having to set limits to our children's behaviour. If only my children would just do as I asked them, I would be the loveliest mother in the whole world. Unfortunately, it simply doesn't work that way. Sooner or later — sooner, if you have a strongwilled child; later, if you have a cruisy one — we will need to say 'No' to inappropriate behaviour and insist on their doing as told. Inevitably, our children are going to resist our requests and we are going to have to find ways of insisting.

As part of guiding our children to become self-disciplined young adults, we need to get them to accept imposed discipline — to do as they are told and to accept household rules — before they are ready to make choices, become good planners and ultimately learn to make wise decisions.

Our children need to learn to do as they are told.

Getting action

I am about to describe a swift and powerful way of showing your child that, when you ask for something to be done, that is what will happen next. It involves the following sequence:

ASK — wait 10 seconds — TELL — wait 10 seconds — ACT

Although this looks simple, it will take several pages of rationale and explanation. Bear with me. For parents to be benignly powerful and effective, it helps to have a good rationale and a clear plan. When we are confident about what we are doing, our children sense this confidence and feel safe and protected.

It all starts when we ASK our child to do something.

'Please take those cups and put them in the sink.' Let's assume two cups, one trip. In other words the request is both within your child's capabilities and manageable within a short amount of time.

Now that we have made a request, the next thing that happens in our child's life is that she carries out that request. Otherwise we teach her that if we ask her to do something she does not have to do it.

So, it is important we have this in our own minds before we ask, because once we ASK, we are committed to following through.

Ten percent change: 100 percent improvement

One of the things we parents beat ourselves up about constantly, is that we are not consistent. (If we don't beat ourselves up sufficiently for this, there is always someone else who will.)

My first learning about how to get children to do as they are told was at the Leslie Centre. We did an extremely interesting study. We hired university students to trail around behind parents as they went about their parenting tasks. Every time the parent made a request of a child, the student would note it, plus the response.

Furthermore, we chose families with at least two children where the parents had rung for help with one of them. This meant we had a chance to compare 'good' children with 'naughty' children. (Many people are uncomfortable with those terms and prefer 'compliant' and 'non-compliant'. That's fine too.)

We found that 'good' children did as they were told about 70 percent of the time. This meant that about 30 percent of the time they were not taking any notice or parents were choosing not to follow through. This includes the times we say things like 'Come over here so I can tie your shoelace' and our child doesn't take any notice. Then we remember that she will be having a bath in 10 minutes so it doesn't really matter.

So the 70:30 proportion gives us a child whom we experience as a 'good' child.

The next bit was the one that astounded me. If you had asked me about a 'naughty' child I would have made a broad generalisation like 'She never does as she is told' because that is the way it feels to us as parents.

But the 'naughty' children did as they were told about 60 percent of the time. Amazingly, the difference in compliance between the child who was perceived as 'naughty' and the child who was perceived as 'good,' was only about 10 percent.

So here is the sales pitch for why we should work to increase our children's compliance.

If we can increase our children's compliance by 10 percent, we will feel 100 percent differently about them. Since I strongly believe we should enjoy our children, imagine what a 10 percent difference in compliance would make to our enjoyment of our children's company!

Don't grovel in gratitude

Having asked our child to do something, the next step is for her to do it.

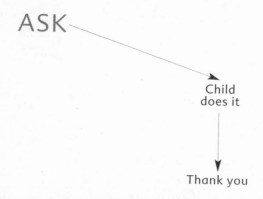

At this point many books recommend that you become effusive in your praise. I have trouble with this idea. I believe it should be natural and expected that, if a parent requests something, the first thought that goes through a child's brain is, 'Yes, that's what I am going to do next.'

If you want your child to learn compliance as an automatic response to a request, then demonstrate that expectation with a simple 'thank you'. If you fall over yourself with gratitude, the message to the child is that you didn't really expect compliance. I cannot emphasise too greatly that *our children meet our expectations*. If we expect compliance, we often get it. If we expect non-compliance, we often get it.

So, with a reasonably compliant child, a simple 'thank you' should more than suffice.

However, many of us have less than compliant children whom we are trying to train to be more compliant. If this is the case, we need to make more of a point of recognising compliance in the hope that it will eventually become the norm — well 70 percent of the time anyway.

Recognition according to temperament

Books on how to praise your child often prescribe the following scenarios:

- Describe what the child has done.
- Be enthusiastic.
- Make an 'I' statement, e.g. 'I am so pleased you did as you were told right away.'
- Get down to the child's level and make eye contact.
- Do it immediately your child does as she is told.
- Do this every time your child does as she is told.

This sounds to me like very hard work — and you need a strong back to make eye contact with short people. This response is also overkill for all but the sanguine child.

If you want your recognition to have maximum impact, deliver it according to the temperament of your child.

For the sanguine, who is driven by the need for audience and approval, enthusiastically say, 'Wow! You did that right away. What a star!'

For the choleric, who needs admiration for what she perceives as real work, try, 'Thank you for your work. I really appreciated your help. What would I do without you?'

With the melancholic, don't go for the full-frontal praise attack. You are likely to encroach on your child's natural need for space. Stand side on, put an arm around her and say quietly, 'I really did appreciate your help.'

With your phlegmatic child, feed her need for a sense of worth and value. Try, quietly, 'Thank you so much for that. What would I do without you?'

Likely responses

Sometimes you will get instant compliance, but often you will not. To a simple request such as 'Take those cups out, please,' non-compliance comes in various guises:

- It's not my turn.
- Why do you always ask me?
- It's too hard.
- I don't want to.

- Will you help me?
- I'll just finish the 500-piece puzzle.
- Those aren't my cups.

And there are the non-verbal responses:

- Moan.
- Grizzle.
- Shrug Mum out of the way.
- Laugh at her.
- Ignore.

Ignoring is a kind of 'mother deafness' and unsuspecting parents often take their non-compliant child for a hearing check!

The three cons

Barbara Colorosa, in *Kids are Worth It*, talks about the three cons that children will come up with when asked to do something they don't want to do.

First, there is the *angry* response: 'It's not fair', 'It's not my turn', 'I'm not going to', 'You can't make me', 'You're not the boss of me'. Any or all of these are delivered in an angry, belligerent tone of voice. Some children can be quite intimidating and respond so aggressively that we go off the idea of asking them. Thus it works for them short term, but of course it is not good for their development of self-discipline.

These are the sorts of children with whom we wind up thinking, 'It's much simpler to do it myself.' That is true. It is much easier to do it yourself, but your children are missing out on essential skills *and* you are teaching them that intimidation works.

Second, there is the *sad* response (delivered in a pathetic whine): 'It's not fair', 'I did it yesterday', 'It's too hard', 'Why do you always ask me?' These children are the masters of guilt induction and we often get side-tracked into wondering if we *do* always pick on them or if the task *is* too hard.

More often than not, parents are fair and distribute tasks more or less evenly and according to ability. It is important to remember this when you are dealing with a child who is expert at 'packing a sad' over issues of compliance. Since your request is no doubt reasonable, you don't have to justify it.

The third style of con is harder to pick up. It involves *distancing*. Your child goes deaf, turns to do something else, looks at you blankly as if you just asked something incomprehensible. Another version of *distancing* is the child who says, 'Sure, Mum' or 'Later, Mum' which, roughly translated, means, 'I have every intention of doing it before the turn of the century.'

Running around in circles

We fall for these cons in a number of ways:

- We explain: 'Sweetheart, I need you to do that now because we are going out soon and we need to leave the house nice and tidy.' Tidiness is rarely on the top of the average four-year-old's or 14-year-old's agenda, compared with carrying on what she is doing.
- We explain: 'We need to get ready fast because Grandma is waiting to see us.' It might work or your child might wonder why, if you are so keen to get to Grandma's, you don't put away the cups yourself.
- We justify: 'You are such a big girl and you could be so helpful to Mum.'
- We justify: 'No, I don't always ask you. I try to be as fair as possible.' And then we get sidetracked into a discussion on our fairness while the two cups sit there staring at us.
- We bargain: 'If you take one, I'll take the other.'
- We cajole: 'Come on, darling. You are such a big, helpful girl. It will only take a minute.'
- We bribe: 'As soon as you've tackled the cups, I am sure we can find a couple of jellybeans.'
- We resort to emotional blackmail: 'You are going to make Mummy very unhappy.'
- We threaten: 'If you don't take those out right now, you're not watching *The Simpsons* tonight.'

Now all of these will work some of the time — often enough to encourage us to try again. But all of these methods have one fatal flaw. *They all indicate that we don't think it is enough to ask a child to do something and have the child do it.* We are showing our children that a parental request isn't serious unless a powerful enough rider accompanies it. Is that really what we want to teach them?

We are also showing our children that *we are ignoring them.* We are ignoring them. You see, when we asked them to pick up the cups, they gave us a very clear message. Whichever reply our child gave us, their response simply meant one thing. It meant 'NO!'

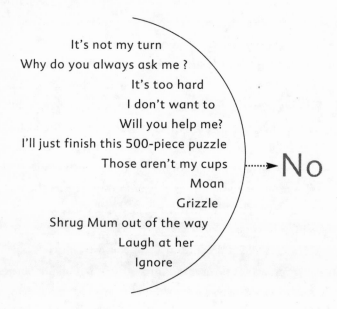

It's not my turn
Why do you always ask me ?
It's too hard
I don't want to
Will you help me?
I'll just finish this 500-piece puzzle
Those aren't my cups ┈┈▶ No
Moan
Grizzle
Shrug Mum out of the way
Laugh at her
Ignore

How long does it take us to understand *no* or, put another way, which part of *no* did we not understand?

Instead, we ignore our child's *no* and get into a meaningless exchange:

Mum (appeasing): 'Look. It's only two simple cups. Just do it quickly and it will all be over.'

Child: 'I don't want to.'

Mum (lecturing and encouraging): 'We all have to do things we don't want. Anyway, as soon as it is done we can go over to Grandma's.'

Child: 'I don't want to go to Grandma's.'

Mum: 'Yes you do.'

Child: 'No I don't.'

Mum (trying emotional blackmail): 'But Grandma loves you so much and she is looking forward to seeing you.'

Child: 'Well I don't want to see her.'

Mum (bribing): 'Maybe Grandma will have some ice-cream for you.'

Child: 'I don't want ice-cream.'

... And so on. We are so carried away with the debate that we fail to notice the cups still staring at us.

If we are to begin on the road to more compliant children, the first thing we have to realise is that all our children's responses (other than compliance) mean only one thing. They mean *no*.

No matter how carefully disguised in reasons and excuses, they all just mean *no*.

Dealing with 'No'

One of the things we have to do, now that our child has declined our simple request, is to make it clear that it wasn't just a casual take-it-or-leave-it request: we meant it. The study I spoke about previously showed that about 20–30 percent of the time we make a casual request, 'I'd like you to ...' it doesn't really matter if the child declines. How do we let our child know we really mean it *this* time?

Let's look at our frequent, if not usual, way of seeking compliance.

We call out to our child from the far reaches of the kitchen, 'Could you take those two cups and put them in the sink?' Our child calls back some feeble excuse and carries on watching TV.

On our way past to do something else, we pause to say, with voice raised, 'I've already asked you once. Will you get up out of that chair and put those cups in the sink?' And we vanish. Out of sight is out of mind and our child carries on watching TV.

Ten minutes elapse. We come through again and see the cups staring at us. This time we scream: 'How many times do I have to tell you to get up now and take those cups to the sink? Don't think Grandma is going to give you an ice-cream when we get there and I tell her how unhelpful you've been.'

Even this does not necessarily mean our child will do as we have asked, of course. We have just screamed unmercifully, completely lost our parental dignity, and our child might feel encouraged to yell back, burst into tears, or continue staring off into space. Even if she does take the cups it has been a 20-minute, drawn-out, ghastly process and what have we taught our child? Possibly that if you really want something, try yelling. Possibly that, if you can withstand parental tantrums, you don't have to do it anyway.

So what is the alternative?

Telling is better than yelling

Ask once, from wherever you are. Wait 10 seconds. By then they'll know you know if the answer is *yes* or *no*.

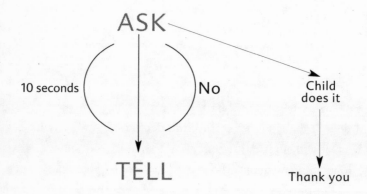

If the answer is *no*, you need to move from ASK to TELL. Move right next to where your child is, stand tall and say firmly, 'I'd like you to take those cups, now' and wait for 10 seconds.

You don't need to shout, you don't need to reason, you don't need to persuade. You have just given your child a very powerful message that you intend her to do as you have asked. Just this action — going close, asking powerfully and waiting — will get you compliance about 80 percent of the time. What you have done is TELL — very, very powerfully.

Telling — powerfully

What are the components that make telling so powerful?

Firstly, you are not calling from a distance. You have invaded your child's space. From the fact that you have taken the trouble to go over your child knows you're serious.

Secondly, you are using your height advantage. In any society, taller people carry more authority. In many societies, when you want to demonstrate someone's power in this way, you set him or her high above the others on a throne. That makes an ordinary mortal appear much more powerful.

This is one more reason why it is easier to get a four-year-old to do as she is told than a 14-year-old. At least with the former, we can guarantee that we will be considerably taller. It may not be so 10 years later. That is one reason to establish 'Mummy Power' or 'Daddy Power' while our children are young.

Most of us still retain respect for our parents when they are elderly. It is unlikely that, if they ask us to pick up a carton of milk on the way over, we would say, 'Oh, I can't be bothered.' 'Mummy Power', established young, holds for the rest of our lives.

Thirdly, you should use strong eye contact. Stare steadily while you say, 'I want you to do that now.' Don't get into an argument along the lines of 'Look at me while I am talking to you'. You divert yourself away from the original request. If you yank her head into a 'looking' position you will have to deal with 'Ow, you're hurting me', which will also divert you both from the original purpose.

Wherever your child happens to be looking, you make strong eye contact. Remember, you are not going for the iris; you are going for the optic nerve — right through the top of their skull!

Fourthly, you should use a quiet voice. If you yell at your child, you are showing her that you are out of control. Although she might find it unpleasant, it is unlikely to make her more compliant or more respectful. It certainly puts you on shaky ground when you say, 'Don't you shout at me. Have some respect.' When you use a quiet voice you are demonstrating that you are in control of *you*, so *you* are far more convincing as the person in control of her.

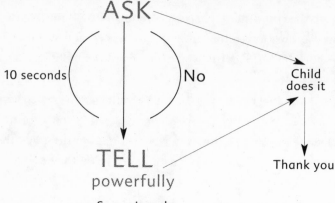

- Space invade
- Use your height advantage
- Strong eye contact
- Quiet, powerful voice

This sequence is very likely to produce compliance to your request.

From 'No' to 'No way'

Some children just don't believe you. They may be very strong-willed or their experience up till now may be that if they put up enough argument or fuss or distance, they won't have to do as they are asked.

If you have ASKED, waited 10 seconds, moved to TELL powerfully, waited 10 seconds, and your child has *not* complied, she has graduated from *no* to *no way*.

However she demonstrated *no* — mad, sad or distancing — you can expect that she will escalate that behaviour. If her initial response was angry, you can be sure her next step will escalate to greater anger. She may well stand, hands on hips, yelling, 'I told you. I'm not doing it.'

Don't divert into 'Don't you talk to your mother like that' or you will have two arguments on your hands — one about her tone of voice and the other about your request. Stick with your request and don't buy into her diversion.

If her initial response was sad, her next step is likely to be an escalation of sadness. She may be so overcome with grief that she collapses in hysterical sobs. She's showing you she is completely incapacitated and far too overcome to carry two cups. This is not a good time to become sympathetic. You haven't asked her to cut off her right arm. With all this emotion bouncing around, it can be hard to remember you asked her to do a simple task, well within her competence. Don't buy into it.

If her initial response was to ignore you, she may now turn away from you, move away from you — though not in the direction of the cups — or even run away. Don't chase her. Don't ask, 'Did you hear what I said?' She did.

Some children even laugh at a parent making a request. This is serious disrespect.

Let me be even more blunt. With a parent who has ASKED and then TOLD, standing right next to her, a child who gets loudly angry or sad or takes no notice or is abusive has moved from *no* to *up yours*.

Your child is being rude and offensive and the time for requests is over. It is time to take action. TIME TO ACT.

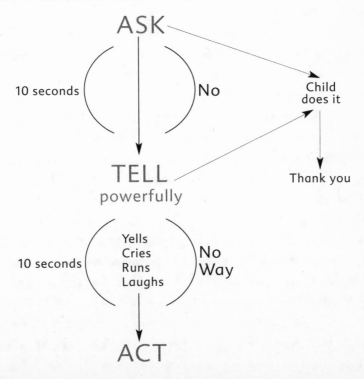

15. Let's Take Time Out to Discuss Time Out

From time immemorial, children have been sent to their rooms when they have misbehaved. This has been seen as a punishment for bad behaviour. Some children have been placed in cupboards, some in coal cellars with spiders, some sent outside in the dark.

Sometimes preceding, during, after and even instead of this banishment, children have been smacked, caned or strapped, and let us not forget the famous cry, 'I'm going to get the wooden spoon.'

The idea was that children would learn, through punishment, that what they did was unacceptable and would feel disinclined to repeat the behaviour. Shades of my dear university friend, my rat. If he got the wrong set of lines he fell into a net. It was unpleasant, he didn't like it, so it was a negative reinforcement: a punishment.

Some 25 years ago, I learned about the concept of Time Out. This was a new idea back then — a new punishment to replace smacking. Parents were coming to see us with non-compliant children. They had used smacking repeatedly and still the children were non-compliant. What else was there to do?

Time Out was different from being sent to your room. It was designed so that, once you had asked your child to do something twice and the child did not comply, you took him to his room for two minutes — or one minute for each year of age. At the end of the time, you opened the door and asked him if he was ready. If he was ready, he came out and did as he was told. If he wasn't ready, you asked him every two minutes until he was. The only way out of the room was to do as he was told.

Better than smacking

This punishment is more effective than smacking.

Let's return to those cups. You ask your child to take them to the sink. He doesn't want to. You offer him a smack. He opts for the smack and then says, 'That didn't hurt.' You produce a smack that does. His eyes water but he holds his ground and says, 'I'm still not going to do it.' You smack once more. He cries, but he is still not going to do it.

At this point one of two things can happen. One, you lose your temper — not surprisingly — and wind up hitting him much harder than you intended. Result: your child is distraught (possibly crying in his room); you are distraught (possibly crying in your room); the cups are doing fine. At the end of an episode like this it is unlikely you will have the heart to insist he takes the cups to the sink.

The other option is that having smacked a couple of times, you don't have the heart to continue. You feel discouraged. Your child may feel unhappy or feel he has won. The cups still sit there. The atmosphere is awful. Your other children are watching and learning interesting things.

Our children see violence day in, day out on television, in computer games and on the big screen. They see endless examples of real-life violence as well. They see violence portrayed as the simplest way to get your own way.

We live in such violent times that it behoves us to model different ways of resolving issues.

Whether we want to or not, we are role-models to our children. They learn their good behaviour and their bad behaviour through watching ours. It is hard these days for them to escape the lesson that if you don't fancy someone's behaviour, the way to deal with it is through physical force.

One of my favourite cartoons shows a father paddling a son while saying, 'That will teach you not to hit other people.'

Yes, I have smacked my children

I smacked before I knew what I know now. I learned that, with 'good' children who usually co-operate, a smack will usually result in their crying for half an hour, sleeping for two hours and then behaving well for the next three months. The only reason they got themselves into that situation in the first place was probably that they were over-tired or over-wrought.

With strong-willed children smacking occasionally works, but more often it does not. It upsets them but it rarely changes their behaviour. More often you get a resentful child who may co-operate briefly with on-the-surface behaviour but is more likely to resort to sneaky sabotage.

The more experienced I have become, both as a parent and as a Family Therapist, the less I have smacked. Our third child is lucky in this respect. Mind you, every time I talk about how she has rarely been smacked, she regales whoever will listen with 'I remember the time Mum nearly strangled me!' Funnily enough, I too remember that episode — when she had been so repeatedly obstructive and difficult that I raised her by her pyjama lapels and yelled, 'Will you just do as you are told!'

Today, I know about so many better ways I could have dealt with such situations.

I learned something else about smacking. Vernon and I were and are loving and caring parents. In 'the smacking days' we probably used smacking about equally. I learned that when I was the one doing the smacking, it felt more or less okay. When I listened to Vernon doing the smacking it felt horrible. Have you ever seen an unknown parent in the supermarket swiping at a child's legs or bottom? It just looks like a larger person hitting a smaller person.

I was particularly fortunate in having parents who never so much as 'flicked' me. They were very strict and I had enormous love and respect for them. I just wish I could remember how they exercised such tremendous control that, most of the time, it never occurred to me to be non-compliant. I was certainly left with the legacy that it is possible to be a strong and loving parent without ever having to strike a child. I wish I had their track record.

A last word about smacking

I will leave the last word to Robert. These events took place when he was about four.

He was guilty of some misdemeanour so I raced into the kitchen yelling,

'I'm going to get the wooden spoon.' When I appeared in his bedroom, waving the said object in a threatening manner, he quietly observed, 'That's not a spoon. It's a spatula.' Undeterred by the precision of his vocabulary, I took a swipe at him. His version is: 'Remember the day you broke the spatula on me?' My defence is that it had been used for stirring breakfast porridge for 10 years, had been wet and dried out hundreds of times. It sheared at the first little pat!

And the second story? At one desperate stage, I stormed at him, 'You're going to get a good hiding.' His response was, 'There is no such thing as a *good* hiding.' He was right, but it probably didn't save him that day!

So, yes, I have smacked and I am not proud of it. I am reminded of a friend and colleague who used to say that it was okay for a teacher to cane a child who misbehaved in class provided that, with each stroke, the teacher intoned, 'I am doing this because I am an inadequate teacher!'

Difficulties with Time Out as a punishment

When we began to teach Time Out as the new effective punishment we came across a few glitches.

Some children, when threatened with impending Time Out if they didn't comply, would amiably say 'Okay' and take themselves off to their rooms. Some would pre-empt the parental instruction and announce that they were going to their room, and some would even refuse to come out when their parents said, 'Time's up', and sometimes even more infuriatingly would add, 'I like it here.' Surely, it couldn't be an effective punishment if a child *liked* it?

I always had another problem with Time Out as a *punishment* for a child under the age of two. There is something rather distasteful about a parent asking, 'How do you *punish* a 15-month-old who just won't leave a pot plant alone?'

At the other end of the scale, it is a strange experience to draw one's parental self up to one's full height and address the neck of our gangly 15-year-old and say, 'Go to your room.'

More and more, I was coming to the conclusion that punishment was inviting a lot of resentment in some children and most teenagers. Choleric children, in particular, often seemed to be very aggrieved at being punished. Sanguines could be heard singing in Time Out. Melancholics enjoyed the time alone and Phlegmatics were often very hurt.

It wasn't only punishment I was having difficulty with. I was also questioning the use of praise. I was, as a parent, beginning to find the 'Find something to praise every 10 minutes' and 'Catch them being good' ethos very wearying. It didn't seem to add up that parental life was supposed to be one long round of praise and stickers.

As I looked around at many children who were compliant, they didn't seem to have parents who raced around all day praising them. Rather, their parents seemed to expect good behaviour and the children delivered it. Inappropriate behaviour was dealt with without fuss, the children seemed keen to rectify their errors and didn't seem to have an overwhelming urge to annoy their parents.

A new concept: emotional distance

As I found that more and more situations of child anger and frustration were being resolved through the use of emotional support, I began to drop praise as a means of changing children's behaviour. I was still finding Time Out effective, but struggled to see how the two were related.

Then someone taught me the expression 'BFO' — Blinding Flash of the Obvious. Well, one day, about eight years ago, I had a BFO. The opposite to emotional support was emotional distance! From time immemorial, people had used emotional distance to show that certain behaviours were displeasing. There is no more powerful force to use on human beings, who have a great need to 'belong' to a social group, than to exclude them. It is not hard to remember back to schoolyard days and recall how hurtful it was when someone said, 'You can't play with us.' We would do almost anything to get back in with the social group.

It began to dawn on me that Time Out is so effective not because children hated their rooms but because of their need for parental support and their need to feel part of the family. We didn't need to use the coal cellar with the spiders or even the perfectly lit but unentertaining room.

Being excluded from the family was powerful enough. The child then had the opportunity to decide to behave in ways appropriate for a family member.

Children, by and large, seek parental approval — and certainly need parental support — so our withdrawal of that emotional support is very meaningful.

When children hit, bite, spit or scratch and we send them to their rooms, we are giving them a clear message that this behaviour is not accepted in this social grouping.

Similarly, when our children refuse to do as they are asked, or refuse to stop doing something they have been asked to desist from, they need to be excluded from the family team until they see it their parents' way.

Remember we are not asking our children to do something difficult or unreasonable. We are talking requests of the order of:

- Put on your socks.
- Leave the cat alone.
- Don't spit.
- Put those two cups on the kitchen sink.

Children need space to struggle with themselves

Thus the purpose of Time Out is not to punish a child. It is to provide a quiet, safe space for a child to wrestle with the issue of wanting to do things his way versus the need to be part of the family. This means it doesn't matter if a child says, 'I like it here.' It simply means he has not yet resolved the issue of whether to do as required and join the family or stay away from the family a bit longer.

This is his issue to resolve and, in the end, because of his social needs, the child will opt for the family. We have given him the space to work it out for himself.

When our child has decided he wishes to be part of the family and that taking two cups to the sink is a pretty fair trade for all the benefits that come with being a family member, he will emerge from his room and do as he is asked. Until he has reached this conclusion, we are wise to keep out of the way.

Think of the daisy

What we have done is briefly shut off our child's access to the centre of the daisy. We have cut off his access to our support until the task is done. You may think of it as a trade; compliance to simple requests for all the benefits of family membership. It seems like a good deal to me. The emotional comforts of home are available again to your child just as soon as he has lifted two cups and placed them in the sink. It doesn't seem like a big ask.

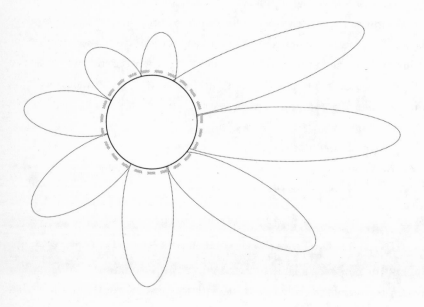

Time Out for tots

The lightest form of Time Out is when you simply get preoccupied and wait.

For example: You tell your 18 month-old it is time to get into his high-chair for afternoon tea. Your little darling says, 'No' and runs to the other side of the kitchen, waiting to play chasey or to struggle and back-arch. You quietly get on with something else, behaving as if you are all alone in the room. Pretty soon you hear a little voice saying, 'Up, up.' Your little one did not fancy the emotional distance and decided to do as you asked.

Slightly stronger is the 'scoop and dump' approach. You ask your two-year-old to hold still while you put his shoes on. He doesn't want his shoes on. (This is not a situation where you can afford to have him learn by experience — it is snowing!) As you approach him he begins kicking and flailing. You risk losing teeth.

Scoop him up and pop him in his cot. Say, 'I'll be back to see if you are ready to have your shoes on' and walk out the door. He doesn't have to get seriously upset. Walk out and wait about 10 to 15 seconds. Go back and ask, 'Are you ready now?' More often than not you have made your point and your child will accept a cuddle on the way down to the ground and then be ready to co-operate. If not, go away for a bit longer, knowing that he is safe and in a position to come to terms with the fact that nothing else is happening in his life until he is willing to do as you have asked.

When is a child old enough?

A child is old enough for Time Out when he is old enough to give you 'the look'. The look that says, 'Do you really mean that?'

Picture the scene. There is a pot plant. Your toddler wanders over to have a look at it. He looks at the front, he looks at the back, he sniffs the leaves, he tests the leaves for taste, bendiness and strength. He runs his fingers through the soil. He is focused on what he is doing.

This is the normal exploratory behaviour of a toddler. He can't tell what the back looks like from the front. Until he has tried, he does not have the experience to know about smell, taste and flexibility simply by looking. He needs to find out for himself through all his senses.

Now picture another scene. Same pot plant. Your toddler wanders over to have a look. Possibly you have told him before, several times on several different occasions, that he is to leave it alone. He goes through the same smell, taste and texture tests. However, while he is doing this, he is keeping a cheekily smiling or a challenging eye on you. The body language says, 'I know I am not supposed to be doing this. What are you going to do about it?' You have just experienced 'the look'.

This child is old enough to be taught that when a parent asks him to do something or to stop doing something, that is what is happening next.

'But, I want him to feel good about his cot'

Choose any spot where he is safe and cannot get out. I favour a cot because it is safe and it is easy on my back. When I put my toddler to *sleep* in his cot, I am warm, soothing and full of emotional support. I am likely to be cooing, 'Come on, sweetheart, it's time for a lovely sleep. Let's say goodnight Daddy, goodnight teddy, goodnight mobile. Tuck you in, darling. Kiss for Mummy. Sleep tight.'

When my toddler is being deliberately obstructive or cheekily defiant, I scoop him up and pop him in his cot. My whole action is one of briefly distancing from his behaviour. Physically it is the same place, but emotionally it might as well be a different planet.

But if you have any concerns about using a cot, or if a cot is not available, a pushchair, a room, a corner, a step — any safe spot will do. Time Out is not a room or a cot. Time Out is an attitude, a state of mind.

Time Out for young children

With slightly older children too, sometimes all you need to do to gain compliance is shut down. You have asked for something to be done. You now go quietly about what you need to do. Your child experiences the emotional distance and decides to comply.

Sometimes your child will need to check to see if you still mean it. 'Mum, do you know if I have swimming this afternoon?' Show him you still have in mind your original request. 'First, please take the cups to the sink. Then we'll discuss swimming.'

Slightly more powerful than shutting down is when you say, 'Go to your room until you are ready,' and your child goes off. He has gone because he finds the room preferable to taking the cups. Once there, he puddles around for a bit, wishes to return to the family and decides to do as asked.

Still more powerful is when you escort your child to his room. There is no way he would go on his own so you need to make sure it happens. You may walk him there, you may lead him there, you may tuck him under your arm and carry him there. Whichever mode of transport you use, once he is there, he stays in his room until he is ready to do whatever he has been asked to do. It may take some time.

A step up from this is when you escort him to his room and close the door. The closed door is a physical reminder to your child that he is separated from his family until he is ready to do as he is asked.

But he keeps coming out

You put your child in Time Out but he keeps coming out (*not* to do as he was asked), destroying things in his room, kicking at the door or climbing out the windows.

It is important to recognise here that you are dealing with serious non-compliance. Your child is not taking any notice of your requests to behave as a civilised family member. He doesn't believe that you mean he must stay in his room.

He is making a monkey of you and you are taking it. You are going to need to demonstrate that when you say, 'Go to your room until you are ready (to do as asked),' you actually do mean it.

You now escort him to his room, close the door and secure it in some way. If you do this swiftly and quietly you are likely to avoid his getting so angry as to be destructive.

You only need to be this powerful when your child has already shown that he has no respect for your instruction to stay in his room.

Holding the door shut is the simplest way to secure it. You need to be silent so that your child believes the door is somehow miraculously jammed. (Many children, mine included, are smart enough to look under the door to see if your feet are there!) If after the first few times he is still struggling with you and pulling on the door, you need to find a way of securing the door that doesn't involve your presence. Otherwise, you are giving your child total control of where you will be — on the other end of the door handle! This is scarcely Time Out from your support.

You can secure a door by tying it to another door or installing a small bolt (sufficiently high up so that *you* cannot be locked in!). Installing it with your child watching is not a bad idea. 'What are you doing, Mum?' 'Oh, just making sure that if the door is shut, it stays shut.'

Major tip: It is no use putting up with dreadful behaviour all day and then at 5.30 pm screaming, 'I've had enough. That's the absolute limit. You go to your room. I don't want to see you,' then expecting your child to go there quietly and come out two minutes later a reformed character. *This is not a last-resort technique.* Start at the beginning of the day, quietly and powerfully insisting that each thing you ask for is done before anything else happens.

Horses for courses

You know your child best. Choose the Time Out spot and the minimum amount of power most likely to work. If you have a sensitive, easily upset child who just needs a place to cry while he decides that he has no option other than to do as you have asked, sending him to his room is likely to be more than enough. If you have a strong-willed repeatedly defiant child, the odds are that you are going to have to use a locked door.

When you think about what you are going to use as a Time Out spot, consider what is safe or what you have to do to make that spot safe. Also, think about proximity. For the child who storms off to his room, slams the door behind him, stays furious for a while and then returns cheerful and willing, it doesn't matter much how far away his room is.

For the child who will be difficult to get to a Time Out spot, you would be ill-advised to try to drag him up two flights of stairs and along a corridor. In two-storey houses it is useful to have a spot on each floor.

'But shouldn't a child like his room?'

Absolutely, and most of the time your children's rooms are places they choose to go to play, to rest, to have time on their own, to contemplate. If you use their room as a Time Out spot they still have all of these available to them — particularly to contemplate the wisdom of doing as a parent has asked. Good thinking can happen in pleasant spots.

It is the same argument when parents choose to use a toilet room as the Time Out spot. It wouldn't be my first choice the same week as I was embarking on toilet training. However, think about the difference.

When I am taking a young child to the toilet my monologue is likely to be along the lines of 'Good girl for telling Mum. I'm so proud of you.

Now let's just undo the buttons on your dungarees. Let's lift you up. Whistle ... Whistle ... Whistle ... Good girl. Now let's pop your pants back on. Up with the dungarees. One button. Two buttons. Now you can flush. Over to the basin. Squirt the soap. Let's get your hands nice and dry. Haven't you done well?'

This is a huge contrast to whisking a child into the same room, saying, 'Let me know when you are ready to carry the cups,' and distancing.

It doesn't have anything to do with the room. It has everything to do with our support or our distance.

What if you are in a hurry?

I don't imagine you would expect a child to learn to swim in five minutes or cook a family meal in ten. Similarly, you cannot teach a non-compliant child to be compliant in the few minutes you have between getting dressed and leaving the house.

I really wish there were smart, quick tricks to getting children to progress up that pathway to self-discipline. I have been watching out for them; I would love to use them on my own children. Until they appear, we are going to be stuck with the fact that teaching these things takes time and persistence. Above all, it takes the knowledge that, when we ask a child to take a couple of cups to the sink, it is not about moving cups, it is about parenting our children.

When you begin on this path, do not ASK unless you have time to see it through. Start at 7 am or 3.30 pm and make sure the first three requests of this time block are going to be seen through. You may be amazed to find how requests four to six are met with much more co-operation.

What if I am out?

Plan ahead what you will do if your child is badly behaved when you are out.

I remember one gorgeous little boy of about three who had an irresistible urge, whenever he saw a baby sitting up, to 'skittle' the said baby. He had a little sister of 'skittle-able' age and his mother was rapidly able to stop the behaviour at home by putting him in Time Out every time he even looked as if he were about to head in her direction.

His mother rang me because they were going out to a playgroup — where there would be rows of 'skittles' — at a private home and she was wondering what to do there. She rang up ahead and discovered that there would be a vacant cot in an upstairs room. We formulated a plan. Unbeknown to us, the little boy had already formulated *his* plan.

As they walked in he looked up at his mother and said, very quietly, 'There's no Time Out here.' I greatly admire the reserve of that mother, who very quietly and lightly said, 'We'll see.' (The reason I admire her is that I would have been unable to avoid saying, 'Actually there is, and I've already planned it ... ')

He caught sight of a few seated babies, took one meaningful step towards them and Mum scooped him up, carried him up two flights of stairs, deposited him in the available cot and walked out without a word. When she returned 15 seconds later, he was glued to the spot, looking absolutely stunned. She put her arms out to him and said, 'Are you ready to go down and behave nicely?' She told me he appeared dazed for a few minutes, but he left all the babies in peace.

Time Out is any space where the action isn't. I have found it effective with my own children simply to excuse ourselves and go to any other room or out the back door. I generally say to the child, 'Your behaviour is unacceptable and we are going to wait here until you are ready to behave well.' Then I don't have anything else to contribute until my child indicates that he is ready. The fact that I am there but unavailable makes it an effective Time Out.

Even with older children, it is very powerful to excuse yourselves and take that child aside to explain that you are not prepared to tolerate that sort of behaviour. You will now wait with him until he is ready to behave.

What if I have visitors?

It is humiliating to have our children behave badly in front of others. When I discuss the options with parents they are always concerned not to harm their children's dignity. I agree that we should preserve our children's dignity wherever possible, but not at the cost of our own.

I have found that the most effective response when children are behaving badly in front of others — whether peers or adults — is to say, 'Would you excuse us, please? I need to deal with this.' This always comes as a great relief to visiting adults because it is unpleasant being around children who are being disrespectful to their parents. I don't believe other children are comfortable when their peers are behaving badly either.

I take my child to his room and go back to the group. Either he comes out relatively quickly because all that was needed was to set a limit on the appropriate behaviour, or my child stays in his room, which is usually a clue that he was finding it all a bit overwhelming and needed the space.

And what about his playmates if he chooses not to return? All you have to do is make sure there is something for them to do. They are unlikely to behave badly.

Time Out for older children and teens

You will notice that I am being very vague about when children are too old to send to their rooms. I am going to stay vague. However, there does come a time when it isn't appropriate and, way before that stage is reached, parents are often saying to me, 'I can handle them now — just — but I am worried about what I am going to do when they are older.'

As our children get older we are still going to ask them to do things or to stop doing things. Luckily, they are still going to need our advice, our support and our services, so the same principle applies. When we ask our child to do something, we still anticipate that the next thing that will happen is whatever it is we have asked for.

It is hard to control what our younger children do. It is impossible to control what our older children do. The only thing we have any real control over is *our own* actions.

We cannot make a 15-year-old move two cups to the sink. But we can decide that we are not going to get involved in his life until the cups are in the sink. It is not necessarily wise to announce it or threaten it. That way we are setting up a challenge. The simplest way, having Asked and

Told, is to get busy with our own things. Sooner or later our child will need something from us. We can say calmly, sweetly and without sarcasm or threat, 'First put the cups in the sink and then I'd be happy to help.'

It may work. It may not. If not, Time Out in your mind still holds. Go about whatever you need to do, quietly powerful in the knowledge that you have asked for something to be done and you are not available until that is done.

Don't expect your child to be thrilled and cheerful. He may have found whining, nagging and tantrums worked in the past. He may be stunned or angered to discover that it isn't working any more. It may take him a while to get used to your calm, uninvolved approach.

Relax and remember that you have asked for a perfectly reasonable and simple task, well within your child's capability. Time Out — meaning cutting off from your emotional support — holds until that simple task is done.

16. Ask — Tell — ACT!

Let's recap. We have asked our child to take two cups and put them in the sink. We have waited for 10 seconds. We have moved over to stand right next to her and we have told her what we expect. We have waited for 10 seconds. Our child has made it clear she has no intention of complying.

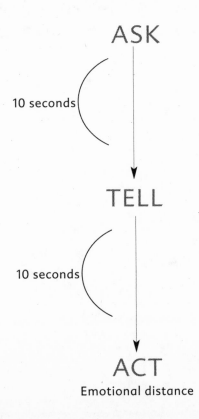

ASK

10 seconds

TELL

10 seconds

ACT

Emotional distance

It is time to act. That action is going to involve distancing ourselves from our child until she changes her mind. We have already planned what level of power we are going to need. For the purposes of this example, let us assume that we have a fairly determined and strong-willed child — older than a tot and younger than a teen. We are going to have to march her to her room and close the door. (I am assuming she is the sort of child who will stay in her room rather than come out and tackle the cups, and will not need to have the door locked.)

As we reach the room we say to her, 'You can come out when you are ready to take the cups.'

Leave her to it

You have done your bit. You have made your expectations clear. Nothing else is happening in her life, in the way of interaction with you, until the cups have been taken. The rest is up to her.

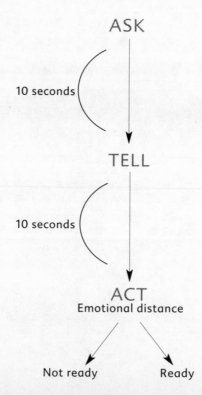

ASK

10 seconds

TELL

10 seconds

ACT
Emotional distance

Not ready   Ready

She is now in her room. There are only two positions she has available to her:

- Ready — in which case she will come out and take the cups.
- Not ready — in which case she will stay in her room.

She looks around for something to do. She finds some Lego blocks to play with. She builds a bit of a structure. She puts it down. She's been in there for a few minutes. It is starting to feel long. She briefly thinks about taking the cups but dismisses it as a silly idea. She picks up a couple of books and leafs through them. She listens to what else is going on in the family. Amazingly, it appears to be going along just fine without her. Two cups seems to be a manageable task, but why should she bother. Her room is just fine. It is getting to be a bit long and a bit boring. What is a child to do?

This is our child's dilemma to solve. We need to leave her to it. Do Not Disturb.

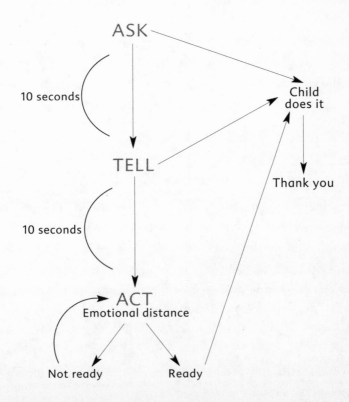

Eventually she will be ready. I don't know how long it will take. You don't know how long it will take. Your child has some thinking to do. We don't know whether she will think quickly or slowly. We don't know how strong her principles ('I am never going to take those cups — they're not even my cups') are. What we do know is that her parent has made a request and that is what she needs to do next.

Sooner or later, she comes out ... but is she ready?

Scenario one: she emerges Ready

When she emerges from her room it is likely that she will take the cups and put them in the sink. In this case you quietly say, 'Thank you for your help. I do appreciate it.' And that's all.

Resist the temptation to launch into a discussion about how long she spent in her room, how much sooner she could have been out if she had done as she was told right away. I would particularly urge you to keep away from explaining to her why you have done this ('I'm sorry Mummy had to put you in your room but ...') and how it is for her own benefit. You have made a simple parental request. She has complied. End of story. Yes, there was a whole lot of learning in this episode, but your child has learned what was to be learned for herself. Anyway, you will need all your energy for the next request!

Scenario two: she emerges Not Ready

She wanders out amiably, looks as if she is heading in the direction of the cups, veers slightly right, picks up anything else and says, 'Mum, will you look at this amazing piece. Why do you suppose it is made like that?' — or any other distraction she may come up with.

Stay calm and stay focused. She seemed ready, she looked ready, but she was not ready. Say calmly, 'Oh sweetheart, you are not ready. You'll need to go back to your room till you are ready to take the cups.'

There are really only two positions: ready, in which case she has done it; or not ready, in which case she is in her room.

What if she changes her mind?

We seem to have an enormous temptation to punish our children for *thinking* about being non-compliant or for not *wanting* to do as they are told. It is fine for our children to not feel like taking a couple of cups to the sink. They are entitled to their *feelings*. Their *behaviour* is another matter. They need to be obedient to simple requests for the sake of their development. They need our boundaries for the sake of their well-being. We are just waiting for them to decide that they need to do it, whether they feel like it or not.

They may decide after we have ASKED.

They may decide after we have TOLD.

They may decide after they have been in their room for a while.

They may decide after they have come out to test whether we have remembered.

They do not require punishment. They require our belief that they know how to make the correct decision and our patience to wait for it. Our task is to set limits on unreasonable behaviour and that is precisely what we are doing.

So if she changes her mind on the way to her room and says, grouchily, 'Okay, I'll do it,' you now know that she is ready and 'thank you' is the appropriate response. Good grace takes a little longer to develop.

What if she does it badly?

What if she takes one cup, or takes two as far as the table instead of the bench, or takes the cups but not the saucers? This is rudeness — and sabotage. Return to the principle of readiness. 'Could you please finish the job or do you need to go back to your room until you are ready?'

Where to start

I suggest you start any time you have the time to see through three requests in a row — perhaps first thing in the morning or straight after kindergarten or school.

Let's start with after school. Probably the first thing you want is for your child to carry her bag in and put her lunchbox in the sink. She wants valet service. Make the request. ASK. 'I'd like you to take your bag over to the sink and put your lunchbox in the sink.' She walks off ahead of you. You have the house key. At the door, TELL. 'I'd like you to take your bag over to the sink and put your lunchbox in the sink.'

If your child is not *ready* to meet this simple, reasonable request it is unlikely that the afternoon is going to get any better so you might as well establish right now who is going to be the boss for the afternoon — and that's you. Say, 'Let me know when you are ready to carry your bag to the sink' and go inside. (I am assuming she is safe in the garage or backyard.)

Look back to the 'custard' diagram on page 60. Your child is trying to hand the problem (she doesn't feel like carrying her bag) to you. You always have the option of taking over the problem and starting to explain, nag, threaten, problem-solve and punish. Far better to keep the problem with her. You have asked her to do something. She works out that that is what is happening next. She does it. She is competent and she has the safety of your boundaries.

Next step: do it all over again

Ask your child for her notices and her homework book. (That way you know what her — and your — commitments are for the rest of the afternoon.) I don't know how long this will take or how much time she will have to spend in her room making up her mind to honour your second simple request; eventually, she will comply.

And again …

You might have had a bit of time by now to prepare her afternoon tea, so a reasonable third request might be to wash her hands before afternoon tea. Having held firm on the first two requests, you are likely to have a child who has worked out that she is dealing with a parent who follows through. She may seem a bit puzzled. You look exactly like the mother she came home to yesterday, but that mother nagged, yelled and eventually gave in. What has happened? Don't explain that things are going to be different around here. Don't give away your game plan. Just change.

Prepare for the revolution

If you are going to begin the revolution and be the boss of the morning, you are going to need a little forethought and preparation. You will have noticed that most generals who lead revolutions do so in full military uniform. They don't try to lead the troops in their underwear.

I always wondered how my children's kindergarten teachers could get them to put away blocks they hadn't played with, wipe down tables they hadn't messed and do puzzles they wouldn't have a bar of at home. I eventually came to the conclusion that it all started at the moment of greeting. The teacher who greeted my child was wide awake, fully clad and groomed. No wonder I didn't stand a chance when I, nighty flapping in my wake, raced into my child's room at 7.30am yelling, 'We've all slept in. Get up.' I would leap into a shower, out again, smallish towel around largish body, and roar in again drippingly: 'I told you five minutes ago to get up and you haven't even moved.' Foray Number 3 probably had me in my underwear, screaming, 'What will it take to get you out of that bed and dressed? We are all going to be late — stop being lazy and inconsiderate!' I was noisy, I was potentially dangerous: I was scarcely the voice or appearance of calm authority that gets things done.

So the best advice I can give you, if you wish to be boss of the morning, is to do your level best to be washed and dressed before you give your first instruction.

The second piece of advice, if you are going to start the day by seeing through each request so that your child begins to develop some respect and belief that what you ask for needs to happen, is not to put yourself under unworkable time pressure.

Pick a weekend, where the only inconvenience will be to your child. (He may be late to soccer and have to explain himself to the coach and team.) If it is a weekday, organise ahead that you may be late. At work, let them know that you need three mornings of arriving a bit late, so that in future you can get there on time and not frazzled out of your brain.

If you are worried about other children in the family, you may be able to arrange for someone else to take them for the first three days. Alternatively, you may be able to use sibling pressure to hurry up your little darling. I used to find it very effective to say to the children I carpooled with, whether it was my own or others, 'Don't worry. I'll take each of you to your teachers and explain why we are late.' Implied and acted on in this statement was that I would take 'the cause' in last and explain her tardiness as well.

Let the revolution begin

You are showered. You are dressed. You are mentally prepared. You go in to your child's room and you ASK, ever so nicely, 'Please get dressed now.' (Or, if you are dealing with a child who is too young or too sleepy to dress herself, 'Hold still while I dress you.') Wait 10 seconds. Say clearly, firmly and quietly, 'You need to get dressed now.' Wait 10 seconds.

You now know your child is ready because dressing is happening. Say, 'Thank you. That will make our morning run a lot more smoothly.' Alternatively, you now know your child is not ready, because dressing is not happening. Say, 'Let me know when you are dressed/ready to be dressed.' Walk away and close the door. You have just handed the problem over to your child. Go and do whatever else needs to be done.

Sooner or later your child will need to show up to see what is going on without her. She will either be ready (i.e. dressed) in which case you will say, 'It's good to see you dressed'; or not started, half-dressed or not fully dressed (i.e. not ready) in which case you will say, 'You're not ready to come out. Please go back to your room until you are ready.'

(With the child who is too young or too sleepy to dress herself, all you need is an indication that she is ready to stand still and passively co-operate.)

The follow-up

If you have had a great performance to get to this stage, the temptation is great to put up with the dreadful and unco-operative behaviour because your child is upset or because she has suffered so much completing one small task. But if you do, you risk undoing all the preparation and hard work you have done up to this point.

It is important that the next two requests have the same expectation — that once you have asked her to do something, that is what is happening next. Make sure they are simple and reasonable requests, such as:

- Please put your lunchbox in your bag.
- Go and brush your hair (short hair).
- Hold still while I brush your hair (long hair!).
- Please make your bed.
- Please put your pyjamas in the washing machine.
- Please put your books back on the shelf.

(You will notice that I have left out 'Eat your breakfast'. I have really strong views on not turning food issues into compliance issues. There will be more about eating in Chapter 23.)

If the three tasks are still in process and you are all ready, quietly tell your child that everyone else is ready to get into the car and wait it out. Tomorrow will not take nearly as long.

Dealing with tots

Most instructions for little children are of the ilk of:

- Hold still while I dress you.
- Let's get into the highchair now.
- Lie down still while I change your nappy.
- Let Daddy clean your teeth.
- Time to get undressed for your bath.

Exactly the same principles apply. Ask, wait 10 seconds, move close and Tell, wait 10 seconds, Act. Scoop your child up and pop her in her cot. Walk out the door. For most children you do not have to wait until she has yelled herself hoarse or stick rigidly with the 'one minute per year age' rule. Mostly, all you will have to do is wait for her sharp intake of breath (prior to yelling), stroll in and say, 'Are you ready now?'

You have made the point that you are not prepared to be messed around with and more often than not your toddler will put her arms up to be lifted out and do whatever you asked.

If she yells at you, swipes at you, arches her back the moment she is in your arms or the moment you approach the changing table/bath/highchair, she is clearly not ready. Pop her back, say, 'I'll pop in soon to see if you are ready,' and leave.

Judge when to go back by your own assessment rather than by the clock. Be aware that when you go back your child may be ready or not ready and be prepared to act accordingly. If she is not ready, it is likely you went back too soon. Give it a bit more time. Eventually, she will be ready. There is no need to make a big fuss over compliance. Just be warm and accepting. 'Good girl. That's much better,' covers most situations.

What if she wants a cuddle?

Many children get upset as they struggle with having to do what they don't want to do. They may well need a cuddle — otherwise known as emotional support — before they can do the task at hand. Just pick them up and hold still. Pat and soothe but don't say anything. Once their emotional tank is full again, you are most likely to get a child who is both ready and able to be compliant. If she is not ready, she may have to wait in

Time Out until she is.

Parents often struggle with the concept of giving a cuddle to a child who has not yet been compliant. They feel they are rewarding non-compliance when they should be punishing it. That is why I would like us to get away from this idea of Time Out as punishment. Time Out is just a way of waiting — for our child to be ready for the task at hand. Provided you make sure you are using a boring cuddle (no talking), you are just helping your child handle her emotions to get ready to do as she is told.

Sometimes your child will, while she is in your arms, mutter, 'Daddy no make Sally have a bath.' This is a great time to practise parental deafness. There is no need to comment. You will know by your child's body language rather than her words whether she is ready or not.

Big kids

As our children get older, the same concept of 'Time Out until the task is done' holds but it is much easier and much more protective of the child's dignity — and ours — to think of it as Time Out from our support and services rather than 'going to your room'.

If you are in the 'training phase' you will need to do a little strategic planning before you begin. Think through what your child needs of you next and ask for compliance when you know you have time to wait it out.

Ask her to put her clothes in the laundry when you are pretty sure that she needs a lift to tennis. Ask for the rubbish bin to be taken out when you know she would like to join the family for dinner in 10 minutes. Ask for help with the dishes half an hour before her favourite TV programme.

Go through the game plan: ASK, wait 10 seconds, move close and TELL, wait 10 seconds, ACT. The ACT is just distancing from her and knowing that when she comes with her request that you will say calmly, 'First you will need to … and then I'll be delighted to …'

Don't expect her to be thrilled. You don't have to stay around to witness bad grace or bad temper. Get distant and get busy. If all else fails, go to the bathroom and shut the door.

Trouble-shooting Time Out problems

'It worked for a bit and now it doesn't'

Changing our parenting habits is a bit like going on a diet or taking up exercise or any other habit change. While you do the things that need to be done, it works. When you stop, it doesn't. But we are always surprised because, having done a fortnight's hard work, we expected it to last.

Initially, when we use Time Out each time our children are non-compliant, they get the message that we mean what we say and they start doing as they are told the first time or after a few minutes of reflection in their room. But being this controlled and consistent is seriously hard work and we may have trouble sustaining it.

Somehow we expect that, having convinced them that we mean what we say, they will *stay* convinced. Regrettably, this hasn't happened in my experience of parenting. We have to either keep holding the boundaries or be prepared to start again when we notice things are slipping or have slipped. Luckily, when we go back to doing what worked, it still works.

When I work with clients I always make notes for them as we go. These notes are for them to take home. When it all starts to fall apart I suggest to parents that they go over the notes. If that isn't enough to get them back on track, I suggest they ring me and we will spend five minutes going over the notes by phone. Usually this is just the booster parents need and they are ready to redo what has worked in the past. All you have to do is remember where you put this book.

'Did I suddenly decide I'd had enough?'

You have let bad behaviour go on for hours or weeks and you suddenly — in the middle of a sentence — decide and yell, 'I've had enough of this. Just get to your room and don't come out until you are ready to behave.' Your child may or may not go. She may be upset or furious. She may race to her room and start being destructive. She may collapse in a fit of tears.

202

It is unlikely that she will turn into a model child just because you have had enough *right this minute*.

Make a calm decision that you are no longer going to tolerate unacceptable behaviour. Decide when you will start to act on this decision — preferably at an initial contact time, say first thing in the morning or after you pick up your child from school or kindergarten. Respond to the first three rule infringements and/or insist on the first three tasks being completed.

You are back in charge. Stay there.

A tantrum of despair or a tantrum of control?

If your child was desperately upset or angry before you asked them to do something, you may get a wobbly completely out of proportion to whatever it is that you asked for. In this case you will need to deal with the upset child before you can insist on compliance. By all means send her to her room, but it is worth asking gently, 'You seem dreadfully upset/angry. Is it about having to pick up three blocks or is there something else that is upsetting you?'

'I seem to be nagging a lot'

It is worth thinking about whether you have forgotten the 10-second recommendations: ASK — wait 10 seconds — move into her space and TELL — wait 10 seconds — Time Out.

If you have spent half an hour explaining, arguing, threatening, warning and nagging, and you have finally yelled, 'I have had it with you. You are going to your room until you are ready to come away from the television and dry the dishes,' don't be surprised if Time Out is ineffective. Your child has already had so much mileage out of the situation that she has shown herself to be the one who is in control.

If you are going to base your actions on the belief that your child does not like to have you being emotionally distant, there is not much point in behaving like a person he would be delighted to keep away from.

'After Time Out she still doesn't comply'

It is worthwhile reflecting on whether you have been using Time Out as an alternative to the child doing as you have asked. Let's return to the two-cups example. Has your child's experience been that, if she can wait it out, have a pleasant time reading on her bed, she can emerge half an hour later to find that the cups have miraculously found their own way to the bench?

For sure, she may have to endure a little lecture about how the moment has passed and it is not fair to expect Mum to do everything around the house, but she is used to these lectures and can easily manage them if it means she doesn't have to do anything other than stand and listen.

Time Out is not a substitute for compliance. It is a time to realise that the task is the next thing on the agenda. Sooner or later it will have to be done.

'She won't come out again'

If we have a timetable of compliance in our head — 'After three minutes she ought to be ready to pick up her toys' — we can find ourselves getting into unwinnable battles. If we say it is time to come out and our child says she is perfectly content to stay, we have reached a stalemate. If we try to go in and get her out, we may risk personal damage. If we haul her out she is likely to be so angry or upset that cup-carrying is out of the question.

Don't try to get a child out of Time Out. The purpose of Time Out is time out from your attention and support so that your child makes up her own mind that she has to do as she has been asked or spend the rest of her life in Time Out.

'She prefers Time Out to doing as she's told'

If we think of Time Out as punishment, we are assuming that our children will prefer the task to the punishment. What happens if they would rather spend two minutes, 10 minutes, half an hour in their room than carry two cups to the sink?

Time Out is not a punishment for not doing as they are told. Time Out is the place a child waits until she has decided to do as she is told.

It is important that, when we make a request of our children, we are not offering alternatives. We mean what we say. After Time Out they must still complete the task.

Of course if your child goes to a space that has a TV, a computer, a library and a CD collection, it is unlikely that she will be devoting an overwhelming amount of time to reflecting upon your request. I suggest you find a less distracting spot.

Where do Time Out and homework intersect?

A lot of homework battles happen because parents take over the responsibility for getting homework done so that their children won't get into trouble with their teacher. Many children need our help and support with homework. They come to it after a busy day and they are often tired and fractious. Even so, we do not have to take any abuse they dish out.

If it is not going well, tell your child, 'This isn't working. Take a break and we'll try again in 10 minutes.' Set a timer. After 10 minutes go and find her and ask if she is ready to accept help and support. You will know by her response, whether she is ready or not ready. If she is not ready, there is no use trying to get work out of an oppositional child. Just let her know the next time that evening you will have time to help with homework.

If your support is not helping, you need to keep the problem with your child. Be prepared to write a note that says, 'My child was not able to settle to do her homework.' Don't tolerate bad behaviour just so that your child gets her homework done and stays out of trouble.

What about really bad behaviour?

I am often asked what is a suitable punishment for the really bad stuff. What if they deliberately spill a glass of milk on the floor? Or shove a door open so the handle makes a hole on the wall? Or push someone over who then needs stitches? What if they destroy someone else's property? Or if they bring home pencils from the teacher's desk? Or what if — as I did once — you walk into her room and discover that your four-year-old has neatly clipped a 10-cm cut in a lovingly handmade quilt?

At moments like this it is hard to remember that punishment is not a good option. The objection I have to punishment is that it takes the problem away from the child. *They* do something dreadful and *you* take over the problem and the solution. Growling, smacking, asking them why they did it, making dire threats you cannot see through, checking out whether they meant to do it or not when you know the answer, TV deprivation and grounding all come into this category. If at all possible, we need to find a way of making the problem theirs.

Is there a way of using Time Out as emotional distance, to respond to these crises? I believe so.

A child deliberately spills a glass of milk on the floor

A lot of parenting books would recommend calmly giving the child a cloth and telling her to clean it up. I think this is an appropriate response to an accident — but not to a deliberate action. It is an admirable approach for saintly people who can stay calm. I am not one of those people.

I prefer to exit the child rather rapidly to her room and say, 'I have a lot of cleaning up to do. You wait here while I do it.' Usually, it takes quite a while for me to clean up the mess and to calm down. It makes the point, it gets the room clean and it saves my child from a very, very angry mother.

In a fit of temper, she shoves a door open so the handle makes a hole on the wall

Clearly this is not something a child can repair. The first step is to send the child to her room with a clear statement: 'I am so angry and upset. That was completely unnecessary. You go to your room until I have calmed down and decided what to do.' Any halfway sensible child would be delighted to get out of this parent's way.

Once you have calmed down, start thinking of ways your child could contribute toward the cost of repairs, *or* think of some tasks she could do to free you up to earn a bit more. If there is any way you can document the child's contribution, however big the gap between contribution and real cost, she can have the experience of making good.

While she is in her room it is also time for you to think about whether this was a moment's impulsiveness or whether it reflects general behaviour that is getting out of control. If the latter, resolve to start dealing with each time your child hits, slams or throws. Chapter 17 will give you some ideas.

She pushes someone over who then needs stitches

Is there any way your child can be of service to the injured party? Do they need help at school? Do they need someone to keep them company indoors for a while? At the very least, your child can find a way of sincerely apologising, in words and in writing, choosing a small gift and giving it directly.

She destroys someone else's property

Take the time you need to think of a plan. Go for a combination of apologising, replacing, reimbursing the person in services.

She brings home pencils from the teacher's desk

It is unlikely that your child would take something from the teacher's desk without a history of bringing home things from other children. There is little point in punishment. Make it your business to notice any time she has anything in her possession that is not hers. If necessary, check her bag and pockets every day. Any time there is anything that is not hers, go with her and make sure she hands it back to the owner at the first opportunity. If she says she doesn't know who the child-owner is, taking it back to the adult in charge of the unknown child-owner's territory will aid in memory loss.

The key to stopping this behaviour is making sure the problem remains with the child.

'What did you do about Deborah's quilt-cutting?'

First, I needed space and time so I wouldn't do serious damage to the child. Several people had lovingly made that quilt as a joint project and it was very important to me. I needed time and space to get calm enough to work out that Deborah had no idea that cutting the quilt was that much worse than cutting any other item, forbidden or otherwise. Secondly, what she had done was beyond the Time Out type of response.

One thing became clear to me. Deborah and scissors could not be in the same room unsupervised. While I was at it, I decided that *felt-tips* needed to be added into the equation. So, for a month, all craft equipment was available for use only under parental supervision at the kitchen table. I mended the quilt as best I could.

Incidentally, one of Deborah's lovely Time Out tricks as a four-year-old was to wet the carpet absolutely deliberately and then greet me with, 'Now look what you've made me do.' It took me a while to work out that the simplest solution was to shift the locus of Time Out to a place without carpet! That worked.

More Time Out tales from home

'That Time Out is so refreshing!'

It pays to be flexible if you have a determined child. Once when Deborah was about five she had been having a wonderful time with papers and scissors and glue. It was dinner time and I needed fairly rapid access to the table. 'Deb, darling, could you please put all the scraps in the bin so that I can set the table?'

'Oh, Mum. I am too tired.'

I knew full well that she *was* tired and, if I sent her to her room she would happily lie on her bed and play quietly. 'Come with me, sweetheart,' I said, looking disarmingly harmless. I gently led her to a little changing area that we have in front of a shower-box. 'You just sit there until you are ready.'

It took about five minutes until Deborah, ever ready to save face, appeared and said cheerfully, 'Mum, you have no idea how refreshing that shower-box is. I'm ready to clean up now.'

Let's take that again

One afternoon Deborah came home in someone else's car. I opened the door ready to be the warm, welcoming earth-mother. 'Hello, darling. How was your day?' She pushed past me, marched to the TV, switched it on and stood staring at it. It was pretty clear that the afternoon could only go downhill from here.

'Come with me, sweetheart,' I said, leading her back to the front door. 'Let's start again when you are ready to knock on the door and say, 'Hello, Mummy. May I come in?' That took about 10 minutes of sitting up a tree and sitting astride a fence, but soon there was a little knock at the door and a pleasant child to come inside.

You may be wondering why I didn't ask what she was upset about. Did she need my support rather than my distance? The reality is that emotional support can only be supportive if it comes from a person who is emotionally bigger and stronger and therefore in a position to provide support.

While our children are disrespectful towards us they can neither accept nor respect what we offer them. First, it was important to put in good boundaries, and then we were ready to start the afternoon.

Big teenage Time Out

Every now and then Tanya would get fed up with us all and announce rather dramatically that she would not be returning home for a while. We had well-established safety rules so she would always tell me — just before she raced out the door for the school bus — 'I'll let you know where I am.' Sometime before bedtime, we would get a call saying, 'I am at Natalie's.' My calm reply would consistently be, 'Thanks for letting me know. We'll look forward to seeing you when you are ready,' and her equally consistent reply would be to growl ominously, 'That will be a long time.'

During school next day I would phone Natalie's mother and thank her for having Tanya. Often the kids had covered beautifully for each other and Natalie's mum had been told that Tanya needed to come and work on a project with Natalie.

I would wait it out. Tanya would ring me every night to explain that she couldn't stand us just yet. I would tell her, with just sufficient regret that she knew that she was missed but not enough pressure to invite rebellion, that we could wait until she was ready. It consistently took three days.

I am very grateful to all the mothers who gave Tanya refuge when she thought we were impossible to live with. I have repaid the universe with an open door to all children who needed a break and sought refuge here. We have one rule: they must tell their family where they are.

This is the teen equivalent of a major 'I'm not doing as you asked. I am going to my room. I like it there.' It doesn't require punishment and it doesn't require scenes. It requires sufficient calm emotional distance until your child is ready. It also requires keeping the problem with the child.

The big teen mistake

Robert had had his licence for a fortnight. In that time he had managed a speeding ticket and an unfortunate U-turn that clipped an unable-to-be-panel-beaten bumper. Four hundred dollars' worth of debt. What is a parent to do? How do you not yell, not punish, not rescue and keep the responsibility with your child?

We paid for both and then we came up with a scheme. He remained responsible for the debt. Every time he got money — he was earning some during the holidays and had grandparents who gave him monetary gifts — he was to give us half. We were the record-keepers.

He honoured his part. Every time he had access to money he would give us half and I would go with him to the notebook and write off the amount. Sometimes after we had done the book-keeping I would have to go off and have a little cry. Eventually, he was debt-free.

In his early twenties he told us this was one of the best bits of parenting we did. I only wish parenting wasn't so hard.

17. Rules of the House

Once we have asked our children to do something, we follow through with telling them and then leaving the problem with them until it is done.

Now we are going to look at stopping those behaviours that our children already know are unacceptable. These are in the realm of hitting, biting, spitting, hurling abuse, pushing, shoving, scratching, pinching, snatching, throwing and so on.

Go straight to ACT

When we see these behaviours, we can skip ASK:

- Why did you hit your little brother?
- Please stop hitting your little brother.
- Don't call your little sister names.
- Please give her the teddy back. She was just cuddling it for a while.
- Please don't throw your plate.

We don't need to make a request for these behaviours to stop. They are a breach of household rules, spoken or unspoken. Think of these as useless behaviours that have no place in your household. They do not contribute to anyone's well-being. They don't add significantly to their learning about positive things. They shouldn't be happening in the first place, so there is little to discuss.

We can also skip TELL:

- How many times have I told you to stop hitting your little brother?
- You really need to stop hitting your little brother *now*.
- You know we don't use those words around here.

- I said give her the teddy back now. It was really unkind to snatch it off her.
- Now look at all that mess I am going to have to clean up.

All that is necessary is to ACT.

When you see a behaviour that both you and your child know has no place in your household he needs to know you will not tolerate it. He needs a rapid exit away from the family until he is ready to behave according to family rules.

'I feel I should explain'

We always seem to think that, if we can hit on the right explanation, our child will understand the gravity of the act, the effect it is having on the other person, why it is not good for him and how it affects us.

I imagine you have gone through this scenario a few times. I imagine you have growled, explained and punished several times. The behaviour is still there.

Often parents ask me if they should have a family meeting to explain the new rules or write them up on a board so that everybody will be clear about them. I don't think this is a good idea. Your children already know that these behaviours are unacceptable. They may not have the wisdom or maturity to understand that the ban on these behaviours is about learning to live in a family, learning to exercise restraint when people annoy you, learning to get along with all sorts of people, learning that bullying is damaging for the recipient and the perpetrator.

They are just behaving badly, and they know they are. They need us to set limits on what they can do and what we will accept or endure. A rule is a rule.

Your child knows it's wrong

Let's assume your child is *18 months* old and I ask him, 'Are you allowed to hit your baby brother?' I imagine he might look a little sheepish and shake his head. I also ask, playfully curious, 'Do you sometimes hit your little brother?' He brightens considerably and nods with a half-grin.

I think we can conclude he knows exactly what is acceptable and what is not. He is just behaving contrary to this knowledge.

Let's assume that your child is *18 years* old and I ask him, 'Are you allowed to call your mother a stupid cow?' I imagine he might look a little sheepish and shake his head. I also ask, curious, 'Do you sometimes call her a stupid cow?' He looks even more sheepish and mumbles, 'Yeah. I guess so.'

I think that we can conclude that he knows exactly what is acceptable and what is not acceptable. He is just behaving contrary to this knowledge.

You don't need a family conference to explain these kinds of rules.

Being consistent is hard work

If a rule is to be a rule, we have to be consistent. That is what makes it a rule.

I hesitated for a long time before I used the word consistent. I have had it used on me as a parent — as a blunt instrument of encouragement and disparagement all rolled into one. How many times have we grizzled about our children to family, friends or professionals only to be assailed with 'You've got to be more consistent.'?

I really rail against this. Good parenting is about flexibility, rapid assessment of myriad factors, balancing support and limit-setting, growling and cuddling, reprimands and hugs, swipes and kisses.

I know I feel differently about a glass of milk spilled on a kitchen floor at 7.00 in the morning when I have had a good night's sleep and a glass of orange cordial spilled on Grandma's white carpet at 4.30 pm on a hellish day. How can I deliver a consistent response?

However, if there is a behaviour we want to get rid of, we are going to have to be clear about its undesirability and we are going to have to respond *every time* we see it. That's the bad news.

The good news is that if we respond swiftly and confidently, in the same way, using emotional distance, *every* time we get a particular behaviour, the odds are that the behaviour will stop. If we prepare ourselves to respond the next 10 times we get that behaviour, the odds are highly likely that the behaviour will have stopped by then.

Don't warn, don't explain: ACT

We see our 18-month-old swiping at the baby *or* the four-year-old. We scoop, send or lead him to the appropriate spot. There is no need to explain. We did the interview in our heads. He knows it is not acceptable.

If we call out, 'You know you are not allowed to hit. That is a bad thing to do. I'm going to have to take you to your room,' it is unlikely he'll stand there patiently waiting for us to finish our speech and walk over.

If we give a longer speech ('Look how much you have upset that baby. Now he won't get to sleep and he's going to be grumpy. What a horrible thing to do to your little brother. It is so important for you two to be friends. One day when you are grown up and Mummy and Daddy are not around, he is going to be the person you will need.') it is likely that our child will have wedged himself into a corner and we will have to drag out a flailing and kicking child who will go starfish-shaped through all the doorways.

The most powerful approach

The most powerful approach is to scoop, send or lead (depending on age, willingness and previous history) the child to the Time Out spot *without saying a word*. Pop him in and walk way.

After a few minutes, he will emerge ready to rejoin the family and behave appropriately. If you do this every time you get that particular behaviour, it soon stops.

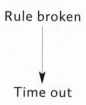

Rule broken

Time out

If you can do it this way, that is what I would recommend. I do, however, feel obliged to put up an alternative, because there is no way I can be that silent and saintly.

The second most powerful approach

The next best approach is to scoop, send or lead the child to the Time Out spot, saying, while on the trot, 'You know you are not allowed to hit/bite/spit/throw/snatch etc.'

When you get to the door you say: (once only!)

- You can come out when you are ready to behave.
- You can come out when you are ready to apologise.
- I'll be back to see if you are ready to join the family.
- Let me know when you are ready.

If the child comes out ready to apologise or ready to be civilised, there is nothing more to be said. (Don't bother going to the door and saying, 'Now why were you sent to Time Out in the first place?' You know why, he knows why — it's not worth a whole new round of aggravation.)

Or the child may come out ready for more trouble. It may be that he is going back to do the same again. It may be that he is coming out planning some other slightly different but equally undesirable behaviour. If so it may happen right way. It may be that he waits for five minutes and then does something provocative. Either way, he is not ready and needs some more time to work out which behaviours get you accepted as a family member and which behaviours get you 'exiled'.

Calmly say, 'Oh, sweetheart, you're not ready,' and return him.

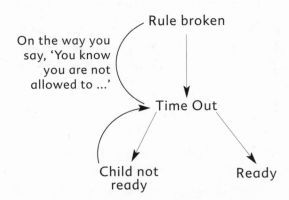

How long must a child stay in Time Out?

My standard answer is 'until he's ready'. However, as a rough rule of thumb for when you will contemplate going back to see if your child is ready to rejoin the family, I say a minute per year of age.

If you go back and find your child playing or sitting happily, the odds are that the behaviour happened because he needed some space. Gently open the door and say, 'I'll leave the door a little bit open. You come out when you are ready.'

If you go back to a child who hurls abuse at you ('Go away. You're a horrible mummy.') he's not ready. Pop back later.

If you go back to a child who needs a cuddle, give him a cuddle and then assess whether he's ready or not ready to rejoin the family.

'My child's too old, and too defiant'

You may have been amazed earlier when I talked about 18-month-olds and 18-year-olds in the same paragraph. It was not a typographical error. Whether a child is 18 months or 18 years, it is not acceptable to break the household rules.

So let's return to the older child who calls you a stupid cow. I am well aware that there are many children from lovely, caring, civilised homes who will use much worse terms — Anglo-Saxon appears to be their second language. 'Stupid cow' may be a mild version but it is quite disrespectful enough for this example.

The response is the same: Time Out — meaning *time out* from your services, supplies and support — until your child is ready to behave like a civilised human being.

Go right up to his space, look him straight in the eye and say, firmly and calmly, 'I don't like being spoken to like that,' and leave the room. Be quietly determined that you will be pleasant to everyone else, but not involved with this child until he has shown that he is ready to be respectful.

What you have done is hand the problem to your child. He has been rude to you. He has lost your goodwill. Along with the goodwill, he has lost your support and your services. Most children — of whatever age — need something from us quite frequently. Expect that your child will appear shortly and ask, 'Mum, do you know where my tennis socks are?' or 'Mum, can I have $10 please?' or 'Mum, can you drive me to Daniel's house?'

But you have been called a stupid cow and you don't like being spoken to like that. An appropriate response could be:

- I'm sorry, stupid cows don't know where socks vanish to.
- I'm sorry, stupid cows do not hand out money.
- I'm sorry, stupid cows don't drive.

If your child has used a ruder name to you, use the same language back. Keep it calm, keep it simple, leave the problem with your child. You have a perfectly competent child. He can work out what to do next. It's not your problem.

Most parents tell me that, particularly if the language has been very rude, their child wanders off in a daze, muttering under his breath, 'You're weird.' That's fine. We are so weird that we are delighted to join the group of parents who are not prepared to tolerate having children who are rude to them.

Should they apologise?

We might say to our child, 'Go to your room until you are ready to apologise,' or, if it is not appropriate to send them we say, 'Let me know when you are ready to apologise,' before we move away.

This is very effective for many children. They think things through — slowly or rapidly — and return with a sincere, 'Sorry, Mum.' If it works, that is great. You have handed the responsibility for his behaviour to your child, he has taken the responsibility and he has solved the problem.

Other children, however, will return and spit out a terse and entirely insincere, 'Well, sor-ry.' That is definitely an indication that they are not ready. I suggest you say, 'That's not an apology. Let me know when you are ready,' and leave them to it.

There is a third category of child who finds it very, very hard to apologise, who rarely thinks they have done anything wrong, and who can always justify their actions as having been caused by someone else's behaviour or attitude. This category of child usually has strong choleric tendencies. Often, you will need to insist on an apology for incidents outside the family. This is a matter of social form and it is wise to insist. Inside the family, however, it may be virtually impossible to get the sincerely spoken words of apology that you are after from this child. But he will let you know he has changed his mind and is ready to enter the family again. His way will be to quietly enter the periphery of family life and try to blend in. He may do or say something nice or something helpful. This is his way of 'apologising' or showing you that he is ready. I suggest you don't revert to a high-minded principle of 'I asked for an apology,' but accept his behaviour as apologetic and ready.

Children who bite

Don't get hooked up into why children bite. I have never managed to find an explanation that made biting acceptable. I have, however, heard many explanations that sound like excuses:

- He's teething.
- He's frustrated.
- He got bitten two years ago at kindergarten and I haven't been able to stop him since.

Why a child bites is irrelevant. Biting is totally socially unacceptable in our society, so we need to teach that to our children.

I get desperate calls from parents whose little biters are about to be expelled from playgroups or crèches. I find they have often tried reasoning with the children about how much it hurts the other child or used phrases like 'Teeth are for eating, not for biting other children'. My favourite response, which was unfortunately ineffective, was when someone handed a two-year-old relative an onion and said, 'Here. Eat this if you feel like biting.' Ever ready to rise to a challenge, the little one grabbed the onion, munched his way through it and then announced, 'Yum. I liked that.' He kept right on biting. Often, he didn't even need to bite. Gnashing his teeth at his cousins sent them screaming in all directions. What amazing power. He wasn't going to give that up lightly.

We hatched a plan. Every time he bit, gnashed or even looked as if he was going to, he was whisked away from the scene. At home it was to his room. At his crèche every teacher was poised to act in the same way. Any gnashing of teeth and he was taken by a teacher to another part of the crèche where there were no children. The teacher would say to him, 'We'll go back and join your friends as soon as you are ready not to bite.' The teacher stayed with him but was not at all involved — in other words, she stayed responsible but not supportive. Time Out. The biting stopped.

The swift and effective response

Whenever the topic of biting comes up in a class situation someone always has a story of the child who bit, the mother who instantly grabbed the child and bit back — and the behaviour never happened again.

I suspect that what happened was that the mother was so prompt in her response — so definite and so sure — that the child got the message instantly that that behaviour would never be tolerated in her family — and gave it up. While biting back has proven to be effective for some parents as a spontaneous response, it is hardly something I can recommend as a planned response.

With any behaviour where parents are crystal clear in their own minds that it is totally unacceptable and they respond swiftly and surely, then the child often decides never again to repeat that behaviour.

Two examples come to mind from our family.

Example one

It was a dark and stormy night about 6.30 pm. Rob was about eight and had already had dinner. Vernon was probably driving home from work.

I have no idea what I did that annoyed Rob, but he turned around and called me a bitch. Now you may well think I lead a sheltered life, but to that stage in my life no one had ever called me that. In our family it was unheard of to swear at a parent.

I was beside myself with rage and outrage. I put him outside the front door, saying, none too quietly, 'I have no idea what I am going to do with you. You never speak to me like that. You'd better stay out there.' I slammed the door and went back inside.

About 15 minutes later, I had simmered down enough to realise that it was a winter evening and that if he got pneumonia the suffering would be worse for me than for him. I tossed him an anorak. I was still too angry to have him in the house.

After about another 15 minutes, Vernon arrived home, saw Rob and had enough sense to smell the danger. He stepped around Rob and came in to ask me what was going on. I was still in 'He's not going to be able to live here' mode. Vernon suggested, 'How about I let him in out of the cold and at least let him go to his room.'

'If you must,' I ungraciously agreed.

Vernon opened the door enough to allow a skinny eight-year-old to scuttle to his room. We didn't see him again that night. In the morning normal life was resumed and Rob has never sworn at me since.

Example two

Deborah was about 18 months old and we went over to my parents' house. Again, I have no idea what I did to annoy her but she took a swipe at me which connected. I was outraged.

I scooped her up, plonked her in my mother's laundry and stalked out, yelling, 'Don't you ever, ever, ever hit a mummy.' A very few minutes later, much calmer, I remembered that in the laundry also was Grandma's cactus collection and Grandma's bleach. I also remembered that I was a Family Therapist who gave lectures about the need for a Time Out spot to be safe.

When I went back Deborah hadn't moved. She was standing frozen to the spot. I scooped her up and took her out to rejoin the family. She has never hit me again.

These are two examples of when a swift, sure, one-off response did work. To be that powerful, I suspect it cannot be planned that way. It has to have the power of outrage and surprise on the part of the parent.

But most of the totally unacceptable behaviours in our family have had to be changed by the slow, hard ways I have already described. The best way to stop biting is to respond with Time Out every time.

Hitting: no way

No child is ever allowed to hit another child. I cannot think of one good reason why they should. I can think of lots of excuses why one child may *wish* to hit another, but I cannot think of a good reason why it would be appropriate for a child to resolve a dispute or express annoyance in this way.

Once we get this principle clear in our own minds, it is possible to act on it. Until we are clear, I seem to hear so many justifications (excuses):

- When he was a baby, she kept taking his toys. It is lovely to see him getting his own back now.
- Boys will be boys. What do you expect in a household of boys? It's just testosterone, you know.
- She's just got to learn she can't have everything she wants.
- I don't care who has the remote. You kids just sort it out between you and for heaven's sake shut up.

In each of the above examples we have inadvertently abrogated our parenting responsibilities and allowed one child to hit another. We have made one child take responsibility for the bad behaviour of another.

When he was a baby, she kept taking his toys ...

It's not up to the little one to get big enough to discipline the older one. It is up to us to teach our children not to take toys off babies.

Boys will be boys ...

Yes, boys are boys. Yes, testosterone is a hormone that promotes masculine characteristics. Yes, children need a lot of activity to use up and enjoy their energy. Yes, little boys — and quite big boys — and girls as well, like to roll around on the ground and tussle with each other. But, it is not essential or acceptable for any person, of whatever gender, to have fun or to release energy or to express their feelings by hitting others.

She's just got to learn that she can't have everything she wants

True, but it should not be a sibling teaching her that. It is a parent's job to support their children as they struggle with the frustrations of life.

I don't care who has the remote ...

One remote, four children. It is a parent's job to teach children how to set up systems for sharing and taking turns. 'Might is right' is not an appropriate system.

So if you find you have children who hit, don't focus on the reason. Focus on the undesirable behaviour. Make it clear to your children that hitting is not going to be accepted in your family. Every time you see hitting, exit the 'hitter' to his room. Invite him to rejoin the family when he is ready not to hit.

The same decisions and techniques are good for spitting, pinching, scratching, tripping and any other behaviour that you decide has no place in your family.

'Leave that baby alone'

In the interests of not making an older child jealous we sometimes tolerate unkind if not downright cruel behaviour towards our babies. But one of the things that is sure to make older siblings think there is something to be feared from the presence of a baby or toddler is if we allow him to carry out behaviours we wouldn't otherwise tolerate.

If I asked you questions like:

- Is it okay for someone to put a large metal toy truck into a baby's bassinet — with the baby still in there?
- Is it okay for someone to play chasey around a sleeping baby's bassinet?
- Is it okay for a five-year-old to get the baby up because he has decided he wants to?
- Is it okay to push the baby high in the swing-seat, just because he's there?

- Is it okay to push your face right in front of the baby and startle him?

I imagine that your answer would be, 'Of course not.' However, these are the sorts of behaviours we tolerate because we don't want our child to be 'negative' about the baby.

The reality is that if one sibling is being unkind to another, there is *not* a good relationship going on. A baby is entitled to lie in his bassinet without having a small roomful of soft toys heaped on top of him. We don't need to mistake this for kindness. One soft toy may be an act of generosity, though not if it is dropped on the baby's head while he is asleep. Several soft toys is likely to be a form of non-compliance.

When we tell a child to leave the baby to sleep or to have a quiet time in a bassinet it is out and out naughty for him to go in and shake the bassinet or shout next to the baby.

I think it is reasonable to have a rule that no one (of the short variety) goes into the baby's room without checking with you. If you are as clear about rules around the baby as you are about all other household rules, you will enhance your child's security in your love.

Go back to the concept of the imaginary interview. If I asked your child, 'Are you allowed to shake the baby's bassinet while he is asleep?' what would the answer be? Your child knows the behaviour is unacceptable. Your child does know the rule. Now it is up to you to enforce the rule each time it occurs. Any attempt to break household rules will need to be dealt with through Time Out.

'He always plays up when I am feeding the baby'

When you consider how many times you will be feeding your baby you really don't want to have to re-establish your authority with each feed.

Before you start, set up a situation so that your older child can be near you, playing with something appropriate, coming backwards and forwards while you feed, doing appropriate things. If your child misbehaves while you are feeding, there should be immediate Time Out. The easiest way is if you have another adult present who is prepared to deal with your child while you continue feeding. However, sooner or later, your child will need to know that the same rules apply even if Mum is the only adult present.

Promise yourself that you will hold firm for three feeds, however much of a nuisance this is. Every time your child misbehaves, you will respond. You will put him in Time Out and then go back to your baby and complete the feed. I realise that this may disrupt your baby and even wreck a feed but, long term, you are doing this for everyone's well-being.

Your baby will lead a much safer life with an older sibling who knows to respect boundaries. Your child will lead a much better life being kept doing socially appropriate things and knowing that the family rules protect all members from being hurt. You will enjoy the feeds so much more knowing that the household is safe from a marauding child, and you will enjoy your child's company so much more when he behaves in a civilised fashion.

See, want, have

Your toddler is sitting playing quietly with a small toy, turning it over and over in her hand. She is completely preoccupied with what she is doing. Peace reigns. Her brother races past, snatches the toy and runs off with it. You growl and say it is unkind and that he should give it back. He gives the toddler something else. She doesn't seem to mind, or if she does, a quick cuddle and substitute toy settles her fast. Peace reigns until the next time.

The question is: Does it matter? I believe it does. Your toddler is entitled to sit and turn over and over the toy of her choice. Her sibling needs to be able to see that the toddler has something he may fancy, yet resist the temptation to snatch it away and keep on walking. This is important behaviour for your child to learn. It is not good for a child to grow up thinking, 'I see it, I want to have it, someone else has it, I will grab it off them.' It is irrelevant whether the toddler minds or not.

Unkind words are also hurtful

Sticks and stones may break my bones
But words will never hurt me
This oft-quoted poem is nonsense and damaging nonsense at that. The

words people use to us and about us can be really hurtful and we can carry those hurtful messages for a long time.

Sometimes we manage to raise children who do not hit or shove one another but will use viciously nasty language. Often, just after they have said something particularly nasty, they will follow up with a quick 'Just teasing', as if that means that the hurt doesn't count.

Our households will be a lot more peaceful if we have children who are not deliberately unkind to each other — restraining their language as well as their fists.

I think that deliberate unkindness should be labelled when it happens — 'That's terribly unkind' — and the perpetrator be asked to leave the room until they are ready to be kind.

Throwing is an outdoor sport

There is a wonderful game a child in a highchair learns very early. I drop stuff, Mum growls and picks it up. I drop more, Mum growls more — and picks it up. As long as I can withstand the growling, I can play this game for a very long time.

As our baby gets older, this game progresses to food, drinks, plates and cups. The game is more fun if the plates and food are in combination.

Having mastered the art of dropping, a talented child can progress to throwing. Young children have little ability to distinguish fragile from sturdy except by their parent's response. We tend to yell more when things are fragile.

It is unwise to have a confusing range of rules about throwing: e.g. It is okay to throw sponge balls in the hall at the end where there are no pictures but it is not okay to throw plastic balls at the other end. Far too complicated. Just go for a 'no throwing indoors' rule. Anyone who violates it goes to his room until the urge has passed.

Harming pets

I absolutely cringe when parents tell me they are pleased when they see their pet getting their own back on a child. 'He just picked up the cat one time too often and the cat had had enough and scratched him. He cried a lot but I didn't feel any sympathy. He had it coming to him.'

What is wrong with this picture? In the first place, the parent is leaving the disciplining of the child to the cat. Though I happen to believe most female cats are excellent at raising kittens, I have some doubts about their ability to raise humans.

In the second place, the parent has clearly been allowing the child to torment the cat over quite a period. It is not good for children to be allowed to be cruel to animals — and I don't imagine it is much good for the cat either.

Thirdly, no matter how intelligent and self-controlled your family pet may be, it is a big ask to expect a feline or canine to exercise judgement when it comes to deciding how big a bite or scratch is appropriate — that nipping an arm is okay but scratching eyes is not.

Many animals are extraordinarily tolerant and patient. My favourite pet story from our family is about Shari, a cute and bright little white French poodle. She belonged to my sister's family and the one and only time she was ever known to bite was when my young nephew held on to her tongue for too long!

I think we should train children to leave sleeping and eating animals alone, to avoid picking them up and carrying them around like teddy bears, and to be gentle and kind at all times. The rough and tumble that children enjoy with larger animals can be quite delightful, but it is our job to protect both pet and child.

As with babies, I believe that children always know when they are stepping over the line from kind to unkind. They may not have the self-discipline to stop themselves and this is where we come in.

Use Time Out and allow the child back when he is ready to be kind or to leave the pet alone. Repeat as often as necessary, whether it is two minutes or two days later.

'Swearing: shouldn't you just ignore it?'

I would have thought so too on the basis of all the parenting books I have read. They seem to tell me that if I don't make a fuss and 'draw attention' to the swearing, the phase will pass. Sounds great in theory but it has rarely worked in our house.

My experience has always been that it is necessary to have a household rule that there will be no obscenities, and when they do occur there is a rapid Time Out. Of course, what was obscene yesterday is likely to be adjectival tomorrow. Certain TV ads have put some parents on shaky ground!

These days parents need to focus on the *intention* of the word rather than simple usage.

I remember an occasion when Deborah had just started school. It was a formal family dinner and there were the five of us including Rob (18) and Tanya (16), and four grandparents.

At a lull in the conversation Deborah innocently asked, 'Mummy, what's a fucking bitch?' I got such a fright I asked, 'What did you say?' and Deborah, obligingly, repeated the question. The two older children did not help by falling off their chairs laughing. The grandparents with perfect hearing were doing their level best to maintain bland, hard of hearing looks although the shaking shoulders were a giveaway.

It turned out she had heard it in the playground and genuinely wanted to know. I told her we would discuss it later and I followed up by taking her away privately and explaining briefly about the words and how rude the phrase was. I have maintained the policy of telling children the literal meaning of rude words because I would rather they got the truth from me than believed playground interpretations.

Where swearing is semi-accidental and not focused, I tend to growl, accept a 'Sorry, Mum,' and expect there to be a very long interval before the word is used again in front of me.

Where swearwords are used abusively to anyone, adult or child, by a child of any age, a household rule (no verbal abuse) has been violated and Time Out (for younger children) is the appropriate response. For older children I tend to choose a version of 'That is unacceptable. Please go away,' or 'You know I don't like to be spoken to like that. Let me know when you are ready to apologise,' and I distance myself from them.

Children are capable of learning and unlearning the use of words. Every summer holidays our children went on youth camps. Somewhat naïvely I always hoped this would improve their knowledge of spoken Hebrew. In practice they always came back with an increased fluency in Anglo-Saxon expletives. The first two days home seemed to be peppered with 'Sorry, Mum. Sorry, Dad.' After that, they seemed to revert to the household standards — until the next time.

Having misgivings?

'But won't he be spending all his time in Time Out?'

Our big fear, when we contemplate stopping these child behaviours, is that, if we tackle them all at once, our child will live in his room.

I want to give you some reassurance. You do not need to 'knock off' every behaviour one by one. The important thing is that you, as a parent, are going to take responsibility for setting boundaries around the behaviour of your children. You are not going to tolerate unacceptable behaviour and you are going to hand the responsibility to your children.

They can behave according to the rules and values of their family and be entitled to all the benefits or supports of that family. If they choose *not* to uphold the family rules and values, they will be spending time *without* all the supports and benefits. They can change their minds slowly or quickly. The sooner they change their minds, the sooner they have access to lovely parents.

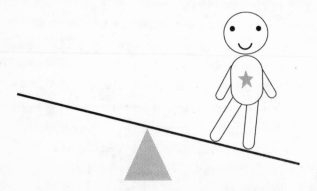

Once you make it clear that the basics, like doing as they are told and not hitting, are being monitored and followed through, it is amazing how many other behaviours fall into line. It is rather like walking up a seesaw. You may remember doing this in childhood.

You have to put in the effort walking up one side and then there is the balance point. But once the seesaw has tipped the other way, it all becomes much easier.

Most parents tell me that once their child has understood that they will follow through, they give in remarkably quickly on all manner of issues.

'But won't he be terribly unhappy?'

I would imagine that if I were 'meaner' to my children they would become unhappy. That if I gave them anything they wanted and let them get away with everything, they would be very happy. But it doesn't appear to work that way.

Amazingly, when parents come to see me about children who are behaving badly, their biggest worry is that the child seems to be unhappy. These are children who have everything and yet they appear disgruntled, ungrateful and miserable.

As parents we need to realise that our children live in paradise. Does your child have at least one parent who is absolutely crazy about them? Does your child have enough food to eat? Does he have enough clothes to wear? Does he have the odd toy to play with? Does the roof over his head keep him dry? Does he have access to excellent education? Does he live in a democracy?

Your child is better off than 90 percent of the children of the world. He is definitely living in paradise.

You are not asking him to pull out his toenails and give them to you — even though the way he fusses may look like it. You are insisting on a little bit of civilised behaviour such as not hitting, not being unkind and doing simple tasks when asked. He is not going to suffer.

He may be suffering currently however. Children who live without adequate boundaries to their behaviour are unhappy. Children who are permitted to behave badly are often unhappy. Children who are not useful contributing members of their families are often unhappy.

One of the things that continues to delight me when parents return a fortnight after we have set up some changes in their parental behaviour is what they say about their children. After we have discussed how much better the children are behaving, almost always one parent will stop, look bemused, and say something like, 'I don't quite understand it, but ever since we have tightened up on his behaviour he seems much happier. He's also become more loving.'

Clearer boundaries make for happier children.

'But I don't want to crush his spirit'

And neither do I. The last thing we want is to create a little robot that does everything we say automatically, without feeling and without question. We want children who are curious and playful and observe and comment. We want them to think about things and not obey out of fear.

All this is true. We want children who can think through issues, who can debate, who can tell right from wrong, who can make grand plans, who can dream and who can follow their dreams.

But we do not need their debating skills exercised over whether they should pick up their socks or stop hitting their sister.

18. Helping Children to Choose and Plan

The last few chapters have been devoted to taking our children from being undisciplined to obeying family rules and accepting imposed discipline (doing as they are told). These are essential developmental steps for the first three years and will often be revisited in the 17 or so years that follow.

However, it is not good for children to keep doing as they are told until they leave home. If we seal their development at that stage, if we insist that they do as they are told and never question our ideas or our ways of doing things, we will have raised children who cannot think for themselves. They will, in adolescence, go one of two ways: toward submission or rebellion. Neither of these positions leads to the development of self-discipline. Submission involves watching for what someone else thinks we should do without engaging our own brain. Rebellion involves doing the opposite of what someone else wants us to do without engaging our own brain.

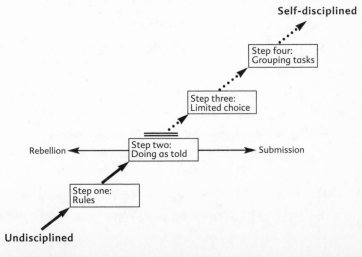

What we need to be able to do is assess situations and exercise wise choices.

In order for our children to become fully self-disciplined, they need to develop the ability to make limited choices and the ability to order their thinking so that they can carry through several tasks in the correct sequence. We need to develop their planning skills. Only when we have good planners able to make wise decisions will we have truly self-disciplined young adults.

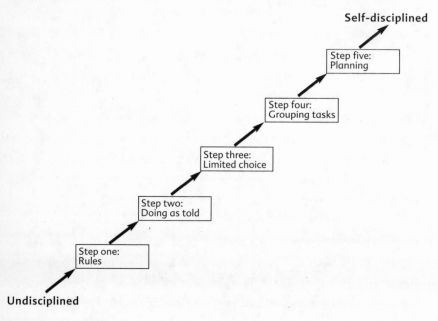

Limited choice: red or green?

A lot of books tell you to offer your child a choice as a way of getting her to do as she is told. The system goes like this. Your child doesn't want to get dressed so you say to her, 'Do you want to wear your red sweatshirt or your green sweatshirt?' Your child is so bemused by having been offered a choice — or is so involved in making the choice — that she forgets that a few minutes ago she was insisting that she didn't want to wear a sweatshirt at all.

This works often enough that we are encouraged to use it as an easy way of getting things done. And let me say straight off if you have a system that works for you, please don't let me talk you out of it. In fact, don't let

Helping Children to Choose and Plan

anyone, no matter how expert they may appear, talk you out of a system that works well for you.

However, if you have a strong-willed or non-compliant child you may have discovered that she sees right through your ruse and declares either that she is not going to get dressed or that, even though it is snowing, she intends to wear a T-shirt.

Furthermore, if your child sets out to be difficult and you are trying to be placatory, you may wind up offering three more choices, all of which your child rejects. Or you may wind up in the situation of having your child try on five or six different items of clothing and leaving you with a floor strewn with clothes.

Some parents get into a similar pickle over food. They say to their child, 'What would you like for breakfast?' This works fine for a child who loves her food and knows what she wants. However, if you offer this choice to a fussy child, don't be surprised if you wind up making three or four different breakfasts only to be strung along with various versions of, 'Well that wasn't quite what I had in mind, but if you make me something else I just might deign to sniff it and possibly have two mouthfuls.'

Once our child has got the hang of doing as she is told, the next important stage — on the way to developing self-discipline — is learning to make a wise choice of two or more preferred options. When she is confronted with a choice, it is not just which one your child wants to choose. It is also that, if she chooses, for example, the red sweatshirt, she has to give up the green one.

Some children find it easy to make choices. Others find it very difficult. That is why they need the opportunity to practise. I remember a dreadful scene that arose because I had no idea of the importance of limited choice or the difference in my children's decision-making abilities. When Rob and Tanya were respectively about six and seven, I — thinking I was being a wonderfully kind parent — took them into a large children's bookshop and told them they could each choose two books. At this age and stage Tanya was a wonderfully decisive child. She walked up and down all the shelves, chose about five books, sat down on the floor, leafed through them, chose two and found me to tell me of her choice.

Rob was our sensitive, perfectionist child. Unbeknown to me at the

233

time, this was an overwhelming choice for him. He had an entire bookshop and he could have only two books so they had to be the best — the most perfect choice. At the end of half an hour it was hard to tell who was the most upset: Rob, who was lying on the floor having hysterics, or me, who was wondering why I had reared such an ungrateful child.

Where had it all gone so horribly wrong?

The problem was that I was offering Rob *unlimited* choice. He was at a stage where he could quite satisfactorily have chosen between four or five books, but an entire bookshop was overwhelming.

You may well be wondering how come Tanya could manage so easily and differently. She was a different child with a different temperament. Not being a perfectionist melancholic, she was not so concerned about making a perfect choice. Being sanguine, she also had an interest in pleasing me and so a Mum who said, 'Good idea,' affirmed her choice. I would have been perfectly happy to affirm Robert's choice — if only he had made one!

Now I know a lot more about how to handle a child who finds choice difficult. First, make sure that you are dealing with a reasonably compliant child. She needs to have mastered doing as she is told. Second, begin with choices of only two items. Third, be prepared to say, 'Not an option' to unsuitable choices. Fourthly, be prepared to be a little bit flexible about wise choices that hadn't occurred to you.

Our aim is to work through the following steps:

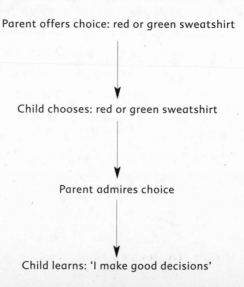

Parent offers choice: red or green sweatshirt

↓

Child chooses: red or green sweatshirt

↓

Parent admires choice

↓

Child learns: 'I make good decisions'

'Yellow, please'

We also have to deal with the child who, on a freezing cold day, responds to 'Are you going to wear your red or your green sweatshirt?' with 'I am going to wear a T-shirt.' The simplest way is to say, 'That's not an option. Are you going to wear the red or the green sweatshirt?' Remember, we are offering *limited* choice.

The other stumbling block we may encounter is the child who says, 'I want to wear my yellow sweatshirt.' There are two possibilities here. It may be a perfectly reasonable suggestion, in which case we affirm their choice: 'Good idea. I hadn't thought of that one.' Or it is not a good idea, in which case it is 'not an option' and we return to the choice of red or green.

Once your child is two and a half to three is a good time to be offering simple two-item choices of the 'this or that' nature. As she becomes able to handle this choice, you can start adding in a greater range.

When she is having difficulty in choosing, your job is to provide the emotional support to help her deal with her frustration at herself for not being able to let go of 'the other choices'. Stay near, put an arm around her, say, 'It's sometimes very hard to choose when you want both.' Offer to talk through the options and then be prepared to warmly wait. Try really hard not to get impatient with the child who cannot choose or the child who, having chosen, finds it necessary to rethink her choice or worry about the opportunity missed. Avoid the blame, criticise, explain, distract and mini-lecture options and stick with empathy and being available.

Too much choice

We of the 'corner dairy' era owe a great debt to the patient men and women who waited while we made agonising choices between five winegums and three jelly aeroplanes. It used to be easier for parents and children when there weren't entire shops devoted to selling lollies, when the range of goods was much smaller, when you simply had to say 'No' because you didn't have the cash and there was no hole-in-the-wall, and when our children were not bombarded with TV ads that gave them overwhelming choice and the belief that they were entitled to everything — on credit if necessary.

The reality is that we live in an era where there are wonderful choices available to us, and the skill we all have to learn is to exercise choice wisely. The red/green choices of the three-year-old will translate into our 10-year-old's choices about academic, sporting and social commitments. And we all want our teens to make wise and healthy choices between the demands of their peers and the needs of their well-being when it comes to decisions about sex, alcohol, drugs and driving.

This is an important developmental step for our children on the way to becoming good planners.

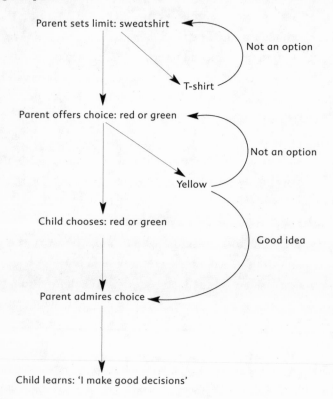

Grouping tasks

As our children get older and can handle limited choice, it is time to move on to the next step towards self-discipline. Our children need to be able to break down the steps involved in any project, order the steps correctly and maintain the motivation to see the project through.

What constitutes a 'project'? For a five-year-old, it may be of the 'Go and get ready' variety. This project may involve three or four steps such as:

- Clean your teeth.
- Have your hair done.
- Put your lunchbox in your backpack.
- Put on your shoes and socks.

For an older child, it may be a school project that requires some days of sustained planning and doing, or fitting several commitments into a weekend.

Ultimately, the ability to plan and effect is one of the most important attributes our children need to be successful adults.

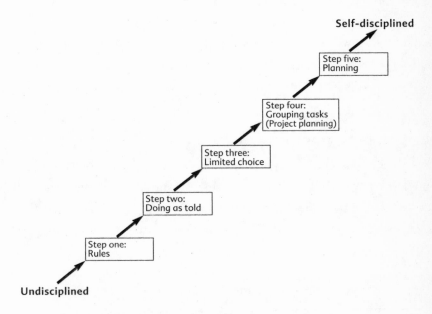

Checklists are great

When Deborah was first at school, she always seemed to be leaving something behind. She left behind gym gear, swimming gear, homework, lunch, music — anything I hadn't remembered to remind her of and then checked on.

Eventually I tired of being her memory — and a failing one at that. I made a checklist for what had to go into her bag every day and a second list for what was special to each day, and stuck them to her mirror. This meant my tired old memory just had to cope with reminding her to check her daily checklist. Back then I considered it was up to me to know which day of the week it was (sometimes a challenge!) so I could call out, 'Have you done your Thursday checklist?'

If you find your child is relying on your memory rather than her own, I recommend documenting what needs to be done. Then all you have to remember is to say, 'Have you checked your list?'

This will work just as well to remind a child of the five steps she needs to do to be ready in the morning. If your child is just edging into reading, write the words and put a little picture next to it.

Remember to be specific. Writing 'togs' may not mean 'and towel' to the child who is used to using Mum's memory and hasn't exercised her own.

This system requires some work to set up — particularly the day-specific lists — but it will save you lots of shouting, reprimanding and arguing.

Of course this won't work for a child of any age who is still stuck at a two-year-old level of refusing to do as she is told.

Developing planning skills

It is said there are no new ideas — simply rearrangements of old ones. My ideas about helping quite young children develop their planning skills came about with the intersection of four ideas.

Idea one

Vernon and I went to a business planning seminar run by Andrew Smith. His organisation was APT (Accelerated Planning Technique) and he worked on the basis that, no matter how big a project was, it could always be broken down into manageable bites.

A manageable bite was any task that could be written down on a piece of memo cube paper and handed to a person so that, if you asked that person, 'Bill, can you do this?' Bill could look at the piece of paper and say, 'Yes, I can do that.'

Idea two

Our two older children were in their mid to late teens. When they went out at night, Vernon would often leave them a note on their pillow saying,

'Hope you had a lovely time last night. Love Dad.' This was a lovely way to communicate when adults were keeping civilised hours and teens were keeping 'bat hours'.

Idea three

At the same time, I was experiencing struggles getting the same children to get tasks done. It wasn't that they were completely unco-operative; it was simply that, on occasion, I just couldn't face their faces. These are the faces that mothers encounter when they ask a child to empty a dishwasher. It is the face that, even while your child is actually preparing herself to do as requested, says, 'I really don't want to and that is a horrible thing to ask me to do and I will do it but I am going to have to grumble a lot.'

There are some days when it is easier to do the job yourself than to face that sort of face.

Mindful of Vernon's lovely notes, I started leaving notes of my own for the children. These were notes that said things like, 'Dear Rob, I hope you had a lovely time last night. When you get up, could you please empty the dishwasher and hang out the washing. Thank you so much. Love Mum.' Now I knew that, as he looked at the note, Rob no doubt had the face I couldn't face, and was muttering under his breath, but since I didn't have to see the face, I could cope a lot better. These notes were effective with Rob, who was a proactive teen. With Tanya, who was an expert procrastinator, I learned to add 'by 10.30 am' to any note.

Idea four

One day when Deborah was a little over five I had to counsel a client at 4.30 pm. (I worked from home and rarely saw clients outside school hours.) I perched Deborah on my bed in front of TV and said, 'Don't move till I come and get you.' All the children knew not to interrupt any counselling session and to be very quiet while there were clients in the house.

An additional piece of information you need is that we live in an old wooden house on clay soil and the previous owner was something of a home handyman. When a door would stick, as the clay became drier or wetter, he would whip it off the hinges and plane it. Consequently, all our doors had quite large gaps at the top and bottom.

My client and I had been together about half an hour when we heard a rustling sound at the door. As we looked over, two slices of plastic-wrapped cheese were pushed through the gap at the bottom of the door, followed by a piece of memo cube paper. On the paper Deb had carefully written 'Yes' and 'No' and had thoughtfully drawn tick-boxes for me.

With the intersection of these four ideas I began to form a way of helping children to plan the tasks they need to do. The first experimental victim was Deborah.

'For heaven's sake tidy your room'

One day I walked into Deborah's room and the entire carpet area seemed to be a sea of books, clothing and possessions. I was about to do my usual yelling about tidying up and quickly, when it occurred to me that it was a completely unmanageable task for a five-year-old. Each separate task on its own was completely manageable — putting books on shelves, shoes in pairs, pencils in pencil boxes — but to do it all was completely insurmountable for her and looked a very unattractive proposition for me.

'Deb, darling,' I said, 'this room needs a lot of tidying and that looks like a very big job for you. How about we find a way of making it simple?' We sat down together and looked around the room to see what needed to be done. I was the scribe and 'we' wrote the tasks down in manageable bites:

- Pair shoes and put in cupboard.
- Clothes in drawer.
- Hang up dresses.
- Blocks in block box.
- Rubbish in bin.
- Felt-tips in pencil box.
- Books on shelf.

Deborah was too young to read and remember, so I did a very inadequate sketch next to each line. I then put squares in front of each item and said she could tick them off when they were done:

This seemed to work well and out of that day I developed a slightly more elaborate system that seems to clarify the task at hand and provide built-in encouragement and reinforcement.

The beauty of this system is that it avoids parents having to remember everything themselves. It encourages children to be involved in the planning stages and that makes them participants in the process, rather than having something imposed upon them. It keeps the responsibility with the child and places the parent in a facilitating position rather than being the one who is giving orders.

Best of all, it teaches our children how to break tasks down into manageable bites and to take responsibility, not only for each step, but also for the entirety of the project.

Let's take as our example helping our child to get through her responsibilities on a school afternoon.

Planning an afternoon

Write in the 'fun stuff'

Collect pen and paper and afternoon tea and say to your child, 'I've got some ideas about how we could make your afternoon simpler.' Start to list what she needs to do between now and dinner time. Begin with all the

things that are likely to appeal to her:
- Afternoon tea
- 15-minute break
- 15-minute break
- Half-hour favourite TV programme

This will appear to be a fairly attractive set of options and by now you should have her full attention.

Help her own her responsibilities

Ask her, 'What are your homework responsibilities?' and add those in. Try to break them down into tasks that can be done in about 10- to 15-minute blocks. Then add the household responsibilities.

In having her help you to construct the list, you give her ownership of the responsibilities. Now give her the power to choose the order in which she wishes to do things. Add a list of squares on the left-hand side and tell her these are squares for her to write in the order in which she wishes to do the tasks.

- Afternoon tea
- 15-minute break
- 15-minute break
- Half-hour favourite TV programme
- Learn 4x tables
- Spelling list
- Write five sentences
- Reading
- Set the table
- Feed the dog

We always worry that our children will choose all the fun stuff first and then moan and groan about the 'work' ones. I think we underestimate their intelligence. Within a few days you will find your child will organise herself a sensible alternating plan of work and play activities.

Give her recognition

Lastly, add a set of squares on the right-hand side and tell her these are for ticking off the tasks that are completed. Ask her whether she would like to call you and show you when each task is done, or take you on an 'inspection tour' at the end. Some children need your support and recognition every step of the way. Being briefly involved every 10 minutes and being lavish in your admiration for what has been achieved is a small price to pay for diligence. Other children like to do everything and then show it to you at the end. Both ways are equally valid. Let your child choose.

☐ Afternoon tea	☐
☐ 15-minute break	☐
☐ 15-minute break	☐
☐ Half-hour favourite TV programme	☐
☐ Learn 4x tables	☐
☐ Spelling list	☐
☐ Write five sentences	☐
☐ Reading	☐
☐ Set the table	☐
☐ Feed the dog	☐

Leader as Servant

There is a lovely concept used in the business world called 'Leader as Servant'. It implies that one of the best ways we can lead people is to be of service to them. When we have sat with our children and made up a list of tasks for them to do, a lovely way of supporting and encouraging them is to offer, 'Which one would you like me to do for you?' (In the case of homework the equivalent would be, 'Which one do you need my help for?')

They feel tremendously empowered being able to order us around! For our part, doing one task in order to get seven others done easily and smoothly is a small price to pay.

Premature closure

Stay alert to the child who says, 'Everything's done, Mum. I'm just going next door to play.' Smile brightly and say, 'That's lovely, darling. Show me.' You will be amazed at how often this leads to 'Oh! Just wait a minute! I'll just …' and she vanishes to complete something or even several things.

It's not magic

This is definitely not magic. It will not turn a surly, unco-operative child into a helpful charmer. It is, however, useful for the child who is moderately willing but keeps forgetting what she was there for in the first place. It is also useful for the child who has a lot on and has trouble ordering it in her head, and it is definitely useful for the tired mum who is fed up with trying to keep three children on track.

Parents say to me, 'But surely you don't expect me to do this every afternoon for each child?' No. Once you have taught your children this way of thinking they will start developing their own systems and making their own lists. Our experience was that our children would ask for help to make a list when things felt overwhelming and muddled. As they have grown older, they have developed the habit of writing plans so they won't have to hold all the information in their heads.

Packing for overnights, weekends, holidays

Since I was the sort of dependent child whose mother packed her bag to go on honeymoon (I was only 19, but I don't think that was a good excuse!), I was keen to raise children who were more independent. I was also aware that one of the important parts of parenting is to allow our children to make safe mistakes, thus learning not to repeat those mistakes.

One safe way for our children to learn planning is to pack their own gear when they go away overnight. This way, anything forgotten will not be too much of a disaster, but will sharpen them up to think things through next time.

Our children went to summer youth camps from the time they were 10.

Usually there were lists in the camp brochure. The system we developed was that our children would take things they thought they needed out of their bedroom and place them in arranged piles in the living room. When everything was assembled they would call us to go through the checklist.

When they were younger we would do the initial pack — always making sure that they had night gear and the following morning's gear on top. Pretty soon they did their own packing.

It was/is amazing to see that, even as adults — while they were still living at home — they would always seek permission to use the living room as a packing station and would still often say, 'Mum, can you please run your eye over the piles and see if I have forgotten anything.'

Great preparation for hare-brained teen plans

I have found that this scheme — of making lists of ordered manageable bites — has saved a lot of hassles as the teens planned outings. I remember a time — about 15 years ago now — when they always wanted to go to a particular teen-type nightclub. Robert was at the younger edge of this group and my instinct was to say no right from the start.

My friend Valerie gave me excellent advice. Don't say no right from the start. Mutter something rather non-committal like, 'Well, let's see what the arrangements are,' and leave it to the kids to keep working on the arrangements. More often than not, by the time we got to the weekend, the plan had not quite got off the ground and we didn't even have to use the 'N' word.

At the early teen stage their ability to plan to get an entire group to be at the same place at the same time, with transport in place and all the parents aligned was not so well developed. When they were in the 13 to 15 age group, they seemed to spend most of their week trying to get Saturday night off the ground. But most of the time we never even had to deal with refusing permission because they simply couldn't get their act together. Just because we have helped them develop good planning skills, it doesn't mean they can plan for all their mates as well!

But lists and planning did come in handy for when our children were in their mid-teens. We developed a predictable checklist (verbal rather than written) when confronted any time with 'Can I go to ... ?'

- What time does it start?
- What time does it finish?
- How are you getting there?
- How are you getting home?
- Does whoever is driving you have a full licence?
- Who is the adult in charge?
- What is their name and phone number?
- What is the situation with alcohol?
- What help do you need from us?

Since the list of questions was predictable and permission to go predicated on the suitability of the answers, our children learned to do their research first and to come to us with a list of answers before we even asked the questions. Children with this degree of planning ability and responsibility are more likely to have plans that will give them fun and keep them safe.

Good planning leads to self-discipline

As our children become better at planning, they are developing the life skills that they will need to become self-disciplined young adults. They are developing the ability to delay gratification, to order their thoughts, to think through the benefits and pitfalls of their actions and focus their behaviour towards longer-term outcomes.

All of these — and the learnings that come from making mistakes along the way — will help our children toward keeping themselves safe as they struggle with issues around sex, alcohol, driving and drugs, as they balance the tensions between the opinions of their peers and those of their parents and as they plan social and career paths.

The more practised their planning and problem-solving skills are, the greater their chances of making wise decisions about how they choose to live their lives as young adults.

Part Five:
Pitfalls and Problem Areas

19. Knowing Which Way to Jump

Often we are not sure whether we should be supporting or distancing. Take tantrums, for instance. I used to think most tantrums could be fixed by walking away. That was called planned ignoring. The alternative was to say, 'Stop that yelling,' and, if the child persisted, to punish him by putting him in Time Out until he had calmed down.

Once I had grasped the idea of using support or distance, rather than praise or punishment, I was still left in a quandary about tantrums. Was the child in need of my support or was he simply being unreasonable or naughty?

Nowadays I understand that there are two sorts of tantrums. There are tantrums of despair, where the child is distraught and upset because he is frustrated or hurt or offended. And there are tantrums of control, where the child is furious or angry because he cannot have his own way.

Tantrums of despair require our emotional support until our child has regained his equilibrium and can try again or leave it alone. Tantrums of control require us to distance emotionally from our child (Time Out) until he has worked out that he is not going to get his own way on this one.

How do you know which one is which?

Tantrums of despair and tantrums of control look much the same. Just think of watching an unknown child having a tantrum in a supermarket. Some of us think, 'Oh, that poor child. He's probably been out for too long and is exhausted.' Others think, 'Why doesn't the mother do something with that noisy little brat? He's just having her on.' The reality is that, just by looking at the situation, we have no idea what preceded it or what the intention of the child is.

If you are the parent of the child having a tantrum, or being difficult, or being non-compliant, or hitting out at someone or any other of myriad unpleasant behaviours, you may have a better idea of whether the issue is control or despair. However, if you are still not sure which way to jump, I suggest you check your feelings. Are your feelings 'Poor little thing'? In this case the poor little thing (of whatever age) probably needs your emotional support. Or do you feel 'You little … '

When I am working with parents I leave this blank for them to fill in. They usually stick to a small range of nouns: toad, rat, rascal or … you little shit — where children are being particularly trying! For the purposes of my printed diagram, I will go with the amphibian.

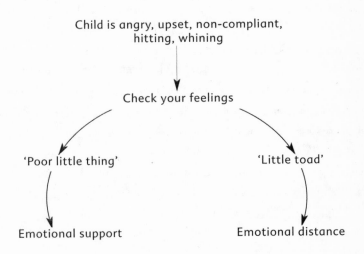

Child is angry, upset, non-compliant, hitting, whining

Check your feelings

'Poor little thing'   'Little toad'

Emotional support   Emotional distance

Different path, same outcome

In either case, what we are after ultimately is that our child solves his problem and comes up with his own pro-social solution. It may be to stop yelling and get on with the rest of his day, it may be to let his little brother have the block, it may be to leave the puzzle alone and find a more co-operative toy to play with, it may be to do what Mum has asked.

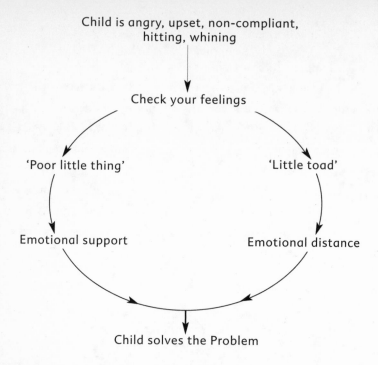

Child is angry, upset, non-compliant, hitting, whining

Check your feelings

'Poor little thing'

'Little toad'

Emotional support

Emotional distance

Child solves the Problem

With emotional support our child feels comforted and understood and can calm down and think of a way to go about solving the problem.

Or, from a position of emotional distance, our child can decide that his current behaviour is getting him nowhere and he needs to behave differently.

Either way we have kept the problem with the child; we have not moved to rescue or persecute. Our child has solved the problem and is demonstrating age-appropriate competence.

'My child whines a lot'

Let's use whining as another example. Whining, whingeing children are very, very irritating. On the other hand, we may have some sympathy for them. For example, our child has asked for a biscuit and it is five minutes before dinner time. We explained why we were saying no and he is still going on about how unfair it is.

Practise now, because the same child is likely in a few years to be whining about why he cannot stay out until 4.30 am or why it is not fair that he cannot drive after 10 pm on a restricted licence. The strategy is identical.

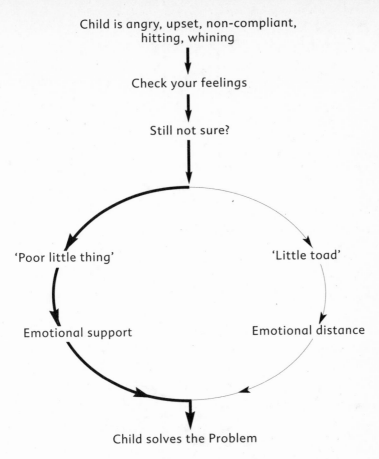

Child is angry, upset, non-compliant, hitting, whining

Check your feelings

Still not sure?

'Poor little thing'

'Little toad'

Emotional support

Emotional distance

Child solves the Problem

Always start with emotional support. Put into words what he is feeling. 'Sweetheart, I know you really, *really* want a biscuit. But it's too close to dinnertime.' Offer physical comfort. 'Would a cuddle help?' That may be all that is needed.

A stroppy, strong-willed child is likely to shout, 'No. Go away. I hate you.' You are welcome to get into a discussion about how we don't use words like that and how he doesn't really mean that he hates his mother — but it is not helpful. Some parents even like to respond with 'Well, I love you', which will send an angry child who is struggling for control right through the roof.

Far far better is to accept that this child needs space to handle his feelings and let him storm off. All that has happened is that you pitched in the wrong direction. This particular child will not get over his frustration this time with support. He is going to need space. Give it to him.

251

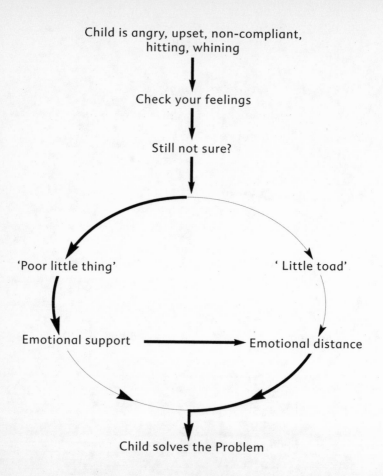

Child is angry, upset, non-compliant, hitting, whining

↓

Check your feelings

↓

Still not sure?

'Poor little thing'   'Little toad'

Emotional support → Emotional distance

Child solves the Problem

Hand the choice to your child

This is a great challenge to those parents who feel they should control their children's feelings. Don't. Please *do* limit their behaviour, but *don't* tell them that they should not or do not feel what they feel.

If you are dealing with an angry or upset child, a safe and respectful way to go is to ask him, 'Do you need a cuddle or do you need space?' Then respect your child's choice. I find it hard to back off from an upset child, as I am so keen to help. But trying to cuddle a child who needs space is dangerous and you risk your teeth or your ribs. They may want a cuddle *and* space. They can choose the order. A nice way to go, if you can be this gracious, is to say to the child who opts for space, 'Take as much time as you need. I'll keep the cuddle warm for you.' Then when he returns, it is easy to give him a big, wordless cuddle and the problem is over.

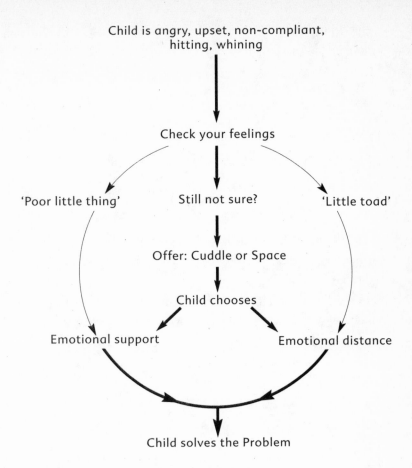

Child is angry, upset, non-compliant, hitting, whining

Check your feelings

'Poor little thing' Still not sure? 'Little toad'

Offer: Cuddle or Space

Child chooses

Emotional support Emotional distance

Child solves the Problem

It's okay to change your mind

Occasionally you will want to change your mind. Your child has behaved badly and you have sent him off to his room until he can mend his ways. You hear the sound of a broken-hearted child. Probably something went wrong during the day, he held himself together until he came home and then — at the first request — let go and behaved badly.

You don't need to hesitate. Support does not look like weakness. Go in. Pat his back. Wait for the upset to subside. It is likely that, once he knows you are available for support, the whole story will come out. Listen with warmth and empathy.

The odds are high that, having regained his equanimity, he'll volunteer to do whatever it was you asked. My strong-willed ones would, under these circumstances, regain both equanimity *and* control before they rejoined the family. 'Thanks, Mum. I'll be fine now. You can go now and I'll come out and dry the dishes in a little while.'

Shy children

Helping our children to overcome shyness is a wonderful example of how we can first use emotional support and, if this is not powerful enough, move to emotional distance.

Our first impulse with a shy child is to protect him. There is something endearing about shy children. They appear vulnerable and we move to protect them. In a world of loud, boisterous children who take off in carparks when we least expect it, it is a relief to have one who will stay near us, hold our hand and speak softly.

But then we worry about them. If they cannot even say hello to their teacher, how on earth are they going to be able to find a group of children to join in with to play? If they cannot meet their beloved Grandma's eye and smile, what about the less familiar adults whom they encounter — and what about their peers?

We notice that adults generally begin by being caring and patient with our shy child. They crouch down to his level and try hard to engage him. They try every guaranteed child-conversation-opener they know. However, if it isn't working, we also notice that they give up and move away to another child who will appreciate their efforts more.

Shyness or rudeness?

Finally, we become exasperated. It is awkward to have visiting parents say to their children, 'I'm sure Jo will be out soon.' It is embarrassing to have your child grab the gift and be unable to say thank you. It is inappropriate to have him march right past his smiling, welcoming teacher.

We start to get that 'Here we go again' feeling. Is this shyness or is it tipping into rudeness? At first we thought, 'Poor little thing'. Now we are not so sure.

We notice that our child is getting selective in his ability to meet and greet and farewell. Some days, he races out to say hello, sometimes he will only come out when he is ready or the presents look interesting. We are starting to get fed up with saying, 'Please excuse him, he's shy, you know.'

Kind people can be a problem

Kind people sometimes help them to stay shy. When we try to insist that they say hello or thank you or 'I'd like the orange one, please,' kind people — just as we are trying to hold firm — say 'Oh, don't worry, I understand.'

It is best if you can cue Grandma or the teacher beforehand. Enlist their help. Tell them you are trying to teach your child to be courteous and you need their help. When they greet your child, could they please wait until they get a response and not excuse the child. The adults then are a team who is helping a child learn appropriate behaviour.

So, what is okay? A certain amount of natural reserve is attractive. Many people hold back a little till they find out if you are going to treat them well or badly. Many people are great listeners and do not need to give you every piece of information about themselves before you have even had time to phrase an enquiry.

However, there comes a point where reserve tips into rudeness. It is simple courtesy to greet people when they greet you, to answer reasonable questions, to thank someone for a gift or for a service or for inviting you.

Unless a child is normally unable to utter words, it is reasonable to expect him to be able to say, 'Nice to see you', 'Thank you for the ride', 'Thank you for a lovely party', in a normal voice, at an appropriate time, with a reasonable degree of enthusiasm and sincerity. If children are capable of civilised interaction when it suits them, it would be hard not to come to the conclusion that, in matters of courtesy, they have shifted from 'I can't' to 'I won't'.

Offer support twice

My first move would always be to give your child support and time to be able to say what needs to be said. Before you arrive, remind him about how pleased Grandma would be to be greeted nicely. When you get to the door, put a supportive arm around his shoulders or hold his hand and prompt his behaviour. Say, 'Darling, say, "Hello, Grandma. Nice to see you."'

Wait. Keep your supportive arm there, but don't rush in to rescue your child. He has a minor tension to overcome. He has to struggle between *I don't want to do that because I find it hard* and *It is necessary for me to say a few appropriate words, nicely*. Sorting out the struggle in his mind may take a few seconds, which may feel like half an hour. Stand patiently and wait. Let your child solve the problem.

If you are this clear about your expectations and this generous in your support and your child is still tearful or has a tantrum, the odds are high that you are being challenged by a child who is both sensitive and strong-willed. It is time to move to 'little toad' mode.

Say, 'I need you to say, "Hello, Grandma" and we are not going in until you are ready to do that.' (If it is at home, quietly insist that he stays in his room until he is ready to greet Grandma politely.) If he declines to get out of the car, wait quietly with him. 'That's okay. We'll wait till you are ready.' If he declines at the door, take him back to the car. 'That's okay. We'll wait till you are ready.' And wait quietly. You are showing your child that ordinary courtesy is not negotiable and, as long as you don't make it exciting by persuading, threatening or punishing, your child will be ready quite soon.

I have often, somewhat facetiously, recommended to parents that they take a thermos and a book. You may never get to drink your coffee, but your child will understand that you mean what you say.

Responding to the greeting of a kindergarten teacher is an important social skill for our children to master. If they are capable but repeatedly reluctant, we may have to take a strong stand. Tell your child he is not going into kindergarten until he is prepared to greet the teacher in a nice voice. Be prepared to go back to the car and wait quietly until he is ready.

Occasionally, I have known a really determined child to hold out for a whole morning. Invariably, he has been ready to greet his teacher the next time he goes to kindergarten. It is a battle worth winning, for your child's sake.

When you are in the middle of any parenting struggle, it is worth remembering why you are doing this. It may seem harsh, but remember that courtesy is a behaviour and a habit that *can be learned*. People who are reasonably outgoing and genuinely polite tend to have much easier and more pleasant interactions with others — and are better liked. People respond well to reasonable behaviour and tend to give up on boorish behaviour.

Protect your child's natural reserve, support him to overcome shyness, and insist that he is courteous.

'He won't take "No" for an answer'

Some children are just delightful as long as everything is going their way. They can even be relatively compliant to requests. But the moment you have to decline a request, they become upset or angry or both.

Begin with emotional support. Tell them you have heard what they want, you know they really want it, but regrettably, they cannot have it. Be prepared to give a brief reason. I have found it useful under these circumstances to say that I will think about it. Almost always, when I think about it, the answer is still 'No' but I am prepared to give my child the courtesy of rethinking the issue.

If the child persists, use low-grade emotional distance. Be a bit preoccupied and distracted. Get on with something else or move off to another space.

If this is not successful, your child is clearly not going to accept any explanation. Don't feel obliged to keep thinking up different reasons until he finds one acceptable. The odds are that nothing except your compliance is going to be acceptable, so save your breath.

Persistent questioning when he knows the answer, or getting abusive about it, is unacceptable behaviour. He has to get over it somehow. It is his problem. He can probably best solve it in his room.

'My child can't take a telling off'

I am not sure that he needs to be able to! For sure, when our children have done something wrong we feel a need — or a want! — to berate them. Strong-willed children do not take to this kindly. They argue back. If you are yelling, they yell louder. If you get upset, they can get more upset.

All of my children seem to have perfected the technique I developed when I was in high school. Back in the good old days we were expected to take a telling off. We were supposed to stand there submissively while a teacher roared out all our misdeeds and character faults. I never felt particularly submissive, but it was in the days where you answered back at your peril. I developed the art of staring my teachers right in the eyes. I was thinking, 'You silly old bat,' while I looked as if I was paying attention to every word.

For my sins, my children seem to have inherited this behaviour. The problem is, I recognise it when it is done to me and tend to get the giggles, which somewhat undermines a good telling off.

Lecturing children about their misdeeds is not an effective way to have them learn how to behave. Telling them what you expect, reminding them once if necessary, insisting on appropriate behaviour, distancing them from the scene or distancing you from them is much more effective.

Learning to be a good sport

Some children are excellent at taking turns, accepting losses with good grace and being gracious winners. Others find the frustration of the give and take of play very difficult to manage.

If you are involved in a game with a group of children and someone is struggling with their own lack of competence, first try emotional support. Put an arm around them — if it is appropriate — and say, 'Sometimes it is really hard when you can't make the ball go in the direction you want.'

It may be that this amount of empathy is all that is needed for the child to regain his equanimity. But if he is still upset or frustrated, call for a 10-minute breather and do something non-competitive for a while. It may even be afternoon-tea time.

If his behaviour gets worse, it is time to move to emotional distance. Tell him to go off for a while and that he is welcome to return when he is ready.

If at all possible, avoid the situation whereby you lose your temper and announce that the game is over because he is spoiling it for everyone. That qualifies as a grown-up tantrum. Besides, it doesn't give him a chance to collect himself and come back and try again — and that is the best learning experience.

Summary

When you are not certain whether the situation calls for support or distance, think about support first. If you are still not sure, ask the child. 'Do you need a cuddle or do you need space?'

If you head off in the wrong direction, and hear a deeply distressed child sobbing in their room, it is not too late. Go the other way. Offer support. The outcome you are after is that your child tolerates the frustration and solves the problem.

20. Sibling Mayhem

'Sibling rivalry' is a most unhelpful term

I intensely dislike the term 'sibling rivalry' used to describe the sort of irritations, scrapping and downright battles that go on between brothers and sisters. The term 'rivalry' implies rivalry for their parents' attention and that, in turn, implies that the child may not be getting enough attention from her parents. If this is so, then presumably we should be giving that child more attention. But mostly, that is the last thing our children need. This generation of children tends to get loads and loads of attention.

Furthermore, it implies that we somehow have to 'quantify' the attention each child gets, so they are all getting their 'fair share'. If they are all getting the same amount of attention, surely they won't have to be rivals? However, if you get the quantity the same, there will always be someone who will berate you over the quality.

And none of this takes into account that, according to their temperament, some children crave attention and some need much more space.

Sibling mayhem or sibling 'stuff'

I far prefer the term 'sibling mayhem' to describe the scraps that break out between children. First of all, the term 'mayhem' hints at the sort of running around, noisy, boisterous, somewhat out-of-control things that happen when siblings behave badly. Secondly, 'mayhem' has a touch of humour about it and, although I believe we should stop our children from fighting, we shouldn't take their fights too seriously. The moment we take them too seriously and begin to get involved, we are tipping into Karpman's Triangle and soon we will be rescuing, persecuting or feeling ourselves to be the victim.

Leaving them to sort things out for themselves

There are several reasons why I don't like the 'let them sort it out for themselves' approach. First, there is a lovely concept in Judaism called 'shalom bayit' — 'the peace of the household'. We are all responsible for having a home that is a pleasant oasis rather than a war zone. Of course there will be disagreements, but it is important that home is a place where everyone feels valued and secure. Lots of fights between siblings makes for a very unpleasant household.

Secondly, most fights involve someone of greater power and someone of lesser power, someone being tormented and someone being the tormentor, someone who just wants to play quietly and someone who just wants to disrupt. In these situations it is an adult's responsibility to stop the unpleasant behaviour from continuing.

Thirdly, I am keen that we don't let disputes between children become our problem. I would like to suggest ways you can keep the problem with the children in such a way that they solve their differences.

Wading in to help

We have all had the experience. We hear the children arguing and fighting. We go in to find out what is wrong. The first child tells us her tale of woe. The second one gives us her perspective. The first one disagrees with that version. The yelling and recriminations start. We find ourselves as counsel for the prosecution, counsel for the defence, judge and jury. Each child hopes we will also be the executioner — of the other sibling, of course.

This is a no-win situation. If we leave them to sort it out, it may not happen. If we go in to sort it out, there are no guarantees that it will work. Is there another way?

Keep the problem with them

There is a way we can keep the problem with our children, so they become more skilled at the sort of self-control and compromise necessary to have pleasant relationships with each other. There are three positions we may find ourselves in:

- We see bad behaviour happening in front of us.
- One child or more comes to us upset.
- We hear the situation heating up.

We need to find a way of responding to each of these situations that means the problem stays with the child.

You see it happening

When you see inappropriate behaviour happening in front of you, stop it. No hitting, no biting, no nasty comments, no shrieking, no shoving, and no grabbing of toys someone else is playing with. It doesn't matter who started it. Don't even try to find out. The best answer to 'Who started it?' (meaning sibling rivalry) that I know is 'Cain and Abel'.

Send the child to her room until she is ready to behave in a more co-operative way. You are making it clear that 'Who started it' is irrelevant. You will not allow these behaviours in your household.

Someone comes to you

Give lots of emotional support. Don't move to solve the problem. Don't go and sort the other child out. By listening carefully, you will get amazing information.

If you learn, in your listening, that the other child is being unfair, don't roar in and growl or punish. Resolve that, the next time the children are playing together, you will make a point of hanging around more so you can see the unfair behaviour and stop it.

The other reason why you don't want to follow up by growling and reprimanding is that while you are giving your child emotional support, she is learning a valuable lesson. There are times when the most sensible thing to do if things become unpleasant is to move away. Once equanimity is restored, she can decide whether to go back or find something else to do.

You hear the temperature rising

The temptation, when we hear our children getting annoyed with each other, is to bury ourselves deeper in whatever we are doing, and hope it will all go away. This is known as the triumph of hope over experience. Generally, it doesn't go away and sooner or later there is a crash, a scream and, if we are seriously unlucky, blood.

I would like to suggest that you go in early. Sometimes it just takes a diversion or shift of scene to solve the problem. 'Morning tea's ready' is an elegant solution to an amazing number of potential problems. If you don't like the chocolate biscuit approach, going in with a chore for each child, phrased as 'Darling, I desperately need your help with ... right now,' works nearly as well but somehow isn't quite as popular with the children.

The easiest solution, which involves very little effort on your part, is to go in and utter Diane's famous no-blame phrase, 'This isn't working.' If challenged, you are confident that it is not working for you! Then split the children up. 'You go to *your* room. You go to *your* room. I'll set the timer.' At the end of 10 minutes, you go to each room and say, 'You are welcome out whenever you are ready.'

They may choose to play together again. They may choose to continue with a solitary activity. Either way, peace reigns.

Your children may learn something surprising

If you do this each time they fight, your children will learn one of two things:

- They will learn not to fight, or
- They will learn to fight very quietly.

Either sounds pretty acceptable to me.

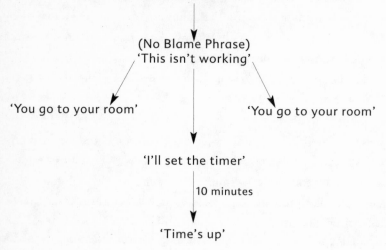

1. You see it happening
Inappropriate behaviour ⟶ Go to your room (Emotional distance)

2. Someone comes to you ⟶ 'Oh, oh, oh' (Emotional support)

3. You hear the temperature rising

(No Blame Phrase)
'This isn't working'

'You go to your room'   'You go to your room'

'I'll set the timer'

10 minutes

'Time's up'

Two more tactics

Blame the toy

If you walk into a dispute about a toy, blame the toy. 'I can see that truck (or TV remote) is causing a lot of trouble. I'll just take it away so it stops annoying you.'

Take it away. Set the timer. At the end of 10 minutes, without drawing any attention to the fact, you may quietly put the disgraced object back. No doubt they will have moved on.

Approach heavy-footed

Once your children have had the experience a few times that, if the volume or intensity is such that you get involved and put a stop to their play, they will conspire together to keep playing. You hear the sound of rising tension, you approach heavy-footed. By the time you walk in your two children are standing side by side beaming angelically. They've ganged up on you by being nice to each other. I think we can cope with that.

'Deliberate irritating'

Sometimes it's not open warfare. One child is busy drawing; the other walks past and whips the paper away. It's not the end of the world, but it is irritating another person for no good reason. It is unkind and it is unnecessary.

One child is playing happily; another walks up and puts in a quick shove on the way past, or takes away a puzzle piece and puts it just out of reach. One child is busy watching television and another sits down to play his guitar in the same room. For some reason it has to be this room. And the space between the couch and the TV is the best musical spot in the house. Again, it's not the end of the world, but it is irritating, unkind and unnecessary.

It is not that any of the actions described above are so terrible. They are just a few steps beyond teasing. However, they tend to result in one child being picked on and tolerating it, or, if the child is not so tolerant, these behaviours tend to lead to a lot of shouting and screaming.

I recommend that one of the rules you have in your household bans is 'deliberate irritating' and that each time it occurs you exit the irritator. Your child will learn a lot about reining herself in. This is good both for her ability to develop self-discipline and for promoting her ability to tolerate frustration — an absolute requirement if our children are to progress from being emotionally dependent to emotionally independent.

21. Bullying: Zero Tolerance

This is another area of childhood where emotional support and a boring cuddle are sometimes not enough.

Most of us have the schoolyard words 'I'm telling on you' and 'Don't tell tales' still ringing in our ears. If you are of my vintage, you will remember this nasty little schoolyard ditty:

Tell-tale tit
Your tongue will split
And all the little puppy-dogs
Will have a little bit.

We often had to cope with difficult choices.

On the one hand we could go to a teacher and tell them our woes. This choice risked being called a tell-tale by our peers and it could lead to our exclusion from 'the group'. It may have offered us a degree of comfort and protection, it may have given us an adult who tried to sort things out, it may have got the others into trouble, or the adult might have said, 'Don't tell tales,' and left us feeling bereft and deserted.

Another option was to 'put up and shut up'. Sometimes this was seen as being a 'good sport' and led to our acceptance by the group. Sometimes it led to further exclusion, taunting and bullying.

Sometimes we had the opportunity to move on to find more pleasant companions. Sometimes we sought the safety of loneliness.

Kiwi culture: 'Don't tell tales'

Very often, when I talk to parents or teachers about emotional support, their response is: 'But surely you are just encouraging them to tell tales.' It is still common today for a child to go to a parent or teacher because they are being tormented by another child only to be rebuffed with 'Don't tell tales.'

Not good enough. You shut your child down without getting the information necessary for you to distinguish between a child who needs support to solve his own problem and a child who has a problem he cannot solve for himself and needs adult intervention.

Kiwi culture: 'You've got to learn to take a tease'

Accepting mild teasing with good grace is part of learning to tolerate the ordinary frustrations of life. Some children have the sort of humour and resilience that means it is never an issue. They can give as good as they get and they can even enjoy it when the joke is on them.

Other children are much more sensitive and take mild hassling rather badly. They go red in the face and are easily moved to tears. They need our comfort and support, but not our rescuing. If they come to us upset, we need to find out what happened, put an arm around them, gently suggest that it was 'just a tease' and, when they are ready to move on, leave it up to them to decide whether they want to rejoin the group or go off and do something else. More often than not, with their emotional tanks topped up, they can go back and join in where they left off.

At home, whether with only our own children or with our children plus playmates, we need to keep an eye and an ear open for how the interactions are progressing. When we see or hear a child beginning to suffer — even though the others do not appear to be acting out of turn — it is time for us to go over and say, 'This is getting too hard for Chris. You are beginning to be unkind. Lighten up.' The majority of children in the majority of situations just want to have fun and don't want to be unkind. This gentle reminder may be all that is needed. You are making it clear that there is no fun to be had at the expense of someone else's well-being.

Behaviour that crosses the line

There is a fine line between teasing and taunting. Parents and teachers need to watch that childish play does not go over that line. We have a lot of clichéd sayings that excuse unacceptable and often cruel behaviour.

- 'They are just having fun. They didn't mean to hurt you.' Any behaviour that hurts or upsets one person while the others are having a good time is likely to have crossed the line between mild teasing and taunting.

- 'Two's company, three's a crowd.' This cruel little aphorism only becomes true if we let it. It is far better to have a culture of inclusion. If an activity or game is suitable for only two children and there are three present, the socially responsible solution is for the children to find another game rather than exclude a child. Insist on it.

- 'She's *my* friend. You can't come in.' We can do a lot at home to teach our children about inclusion and to teach them not to be unkind. Parents often tell me how badly they feel when one child has a friend over and the other doesn't. 'He just keeps going in and annoying them. I just tell them to shut the door. He'll just have to learn.' We may be teaching our children to be unkind.

There is no magic answer to this one and we need to employ a variety of tactics. For some of the time it is perfectly appropriate to insist on inclusion. We can insist that they accommodate a child who is close in age. We can insist that they are protective towards a younger child. We can also make sure an older child does not take over and dominate the play. Equally, there are times when it is appropriate to let the friends get on with their activities and take the other child with us. Make it explicit. 'You've had a lot of time together. Now the girls need to have some time to themselves. Come and give me a hand with what I am doing.'

The important thing is to model and teach our children consideration for others' feelings, flexibility that all groupings are equally acceptable, and imagination to find a way that accommodates and includes everyone.

I remember the first time I went on a counselling training live-in weekend. I was almost moved to tears at how considerate and inclusive people were. They made sure no one was at a dining table alone, and if going for a walk someone would always call out, 'We're going for a walk.

Anyone care to join us?' I suspect my tears were a flashback to schoolyard days of 'You can't play with us. Go away.'

Zero tolerance at home

What can we, as ordinary parents, do to stop bullying?

Our first step is to deal with what we see happening in front of us. Refuse to tolerate unkindness, physical or verbal. Name it and stop it.

- 'That is an unkind thing to say. Stop it.'
- 'This is a no-hitting zone. Go to your room till you are ready to play peacefully.'
- 'I won't accept you talking to your brother like that. Go away.'
- 'That toy is clearly causing fights. I'll put it away for a while, so it won't annoy you both.'

This policy is good for everyone. The little thug learns not to be a little thug.

Listen and learn

Ask your child, 'How was your day?' and listen for the answer. If you want good information from her answers, don't put her off. If she complains about being hassled:

- Don't blame ('Well what did you do to him?')
- Don't criticise ('Why can't you just laugh it off?')
- Don't contradict ('But he seems such a nice boy.')
- Don't lecture ('You have to get on with all sorts of people.')
- Don't explain ('He's probably just jealous of you.')
- Don't problem-solve ('Well, next time just find someone nicer to play with.')

Listen with empathy. When he tells you about something that was unpleasant for him, reflect his feelings and respond with a similar intensity:

- 'How awful for you.'
- 'What a nasty thing to do.'
- 'That is just a dreadful thing to have happen to you.'
- 'How unkind.'

As Kiwi parents we always think we have to be fair and consider the other side. But at this point you are information-gathering. Place yourself on your child's side. (If you are not on his side, who will be?)

Girl or boy bullying?

Boys tend to bully by picking on differences, teasing with words, jostling and outright scrapping. Girl bullying is much more subtle but even more damaging. They are the masters — or maybe mistresses — of the tongue-click accompanied by the eye-roll, the note-passing, the snide remark and horrible exclusion.

Helping them to help themselves

Avoid wading in to sort things out at the early stages. Often, your child, having gained emotional support from you, will go back to join the group, or go and play elsewhere. Many things can be resolved this easily.

There have been many times with my own children that focused empathy has been all that was needed to resolve the problem. I tell them I can see that this has been bothering them for some time. I am taking it seriously and I want to be able to help them.

'So here's the plan,' I might say. 'Every afternoon after school I am going to ask you how your day was and I'm going to take notes because what you say is important to me.' Then I do that for a fortnight. Each day I listen with empathy, I am sympathetic, I may ask for more details, and I write down key reminders.

After a week or so, your child may not have anything bad to report — they are back to being best of friends. The careful listening you have done has enabled your child to solve the problem himself. The fact of your writing things down made him realise you really cared and that you were safe to talk to. And, if you do need to go to the school, you have a fully documented set of incidents to discuss.

With any luck, while you were busy listening and note-taking you were too busy to blame, criticise, lecture and problem-solve!

Give them skills

Often, once we have enough information to understand the problem, we can give our children the skills to handle socially uncomfortable situations. The important thing is to keep them out of that 'triangle' as the victim. Role-plays are a good way of showing our children that there are alternative responses to going red in the face and crying, or slinking off to the library at lunchtime to pretend they have somewhere to go and something to do.

Role-plays are particularly helpful in dealing with the sort of verbal insults that are directed at the child or his possessions. Let's assume the class big-mouth bully has told your child: 'That's a stupid lunchbox' (hair-tie, football, pair of glasses …). Skip the 'sticks and stones' lecture. Your child *is* hurt by the words. He needs a response that will empower him.

Introduce the idea of a role-play so that, together, you can work out smart responses that will help him disempower the bully.

Firstly, find out how he responds to a comment like that. Does he hang his head and look deep into his lunchbox? Does he sidle away hoping the bully won't follow with a few friends prepared to join in with the taunting? Your first role-play should be him showing you what he does.

Now reverse roles. Let him be the bully and let him experience how his feeble response makes the bully feel powerful. Let him come up to you and say, 'That's a stupid lunchbox.' You gaze intently into the lunchbox or look at your shoes and mutter, 'Got to go,' and sidle off. By now your child should have some idea of how his behaviour is making the bully feel big and strong.

Now try out lots of alternative smart replies. Any reply will do, as long as it is delivered with confidence. (Humour helps.) Here are some of my favourites:
- 'You're right. It is an ugly lunchbox.'
- 'It's okay that you think it's stupid. I like it.'
- 'Yes it is. Will you write a note to my mother telling her I shouldn't bring it to school again?'
- 'Really (in mock horror)? I didn't realise. Thank you so much for pointing it out.'
- 'I know it looks strange. I chose it because it turns into chocolate after 10 days.'

It doesn't matter much what the reply is. What matters is that your child now has options other than to be hurt and defensive. He is able to show that he has the situation under control.

Once you have a few comments prepared, ask him which one he would like to try first in a role-play. You be the child and he can be the bully. Let him start with 'That's a stupid lunchbox' and try out the first idea. Work through the rest. He will know which of them most disempowered him as the role-play bully. Now reverse roles.

By now he has a clear idea of how he is going to tackle the next episode of verbal bullying. Remember to ask how it worked.

And if this is not enough?

If focused empathy, zero tolerance at home and role-plays don't stop the problem — for a short time, anyway — you know this problem is too hard for your child to solve on his own and adult intervention is going to be needed.

Remember that bullying is bad for your child and bad for the bully. You are well justified in seeking help. You need to broaden the number of adults who can help keep your child safe. It is time to go to your child's school and alert them to the bullying problem they have.

Approaching the school

Make an appointment with the classroom teacher and go with an approach that says, essentially, 'This is what is happening, this is what we've tried, my child is distressed, I need your help.' Often, the details you are able to bring will enable your child's teacher to know what to watch for and when. The more specific you are, the more difficult it is for your concerns to be brushed aside.

Respect the fact that classroom teachers are very busy people who cannot watch everything in the playground and ask her what it would be possible to do to keep your child feeling safe at school.

If you get the 'Well, we can't be watching them all the time' treatment, go back to quietly stating, 'My child is terribly unhappy and worried. What do you suggest I do?' and leave a good long pause so the problem stays with the teacher.

It is a teacher's role to be responsible for your child's safety — *in loco parentis* (in place of the parent) — and the school has an obligation under law to watch out for your child's safety.

If you get nowhere, make an appointment to see the principal or, failing that, the chairperson of the Board of Trustees.

Follow-up

If the strategy (whatever it is) is working, the teacher needs to know. Dealing with bullying at school is hard work; your child's teacher needs your support and feedback. Make an appointment to discuss what has worked so that it can be repeated if necessary. Show gratitude.

If it is not working the teacher also needs to know. Don't wait until it all goes horribly wrong. Discuss with the teacher that you and she may need the power of someone higher up in the hierarchy. Maybe you can go together as a team.

It may break out again

Once may not be enough. Often peace will reign for a few weeks and then it all starts up again.

Many parents come to me about bullying, saying, 'I went to the teacher about a year ago and things got better for a while and then it started up again.' When I ask them why they haven't gone back to the person who was helpful, they say it had never occurred to them.

This is quite understandable. It is often not easy for us to go in to bat for our child and we assume that once it's done it's done. But real life doesn't work that way. We need to go back to our empathic listening, then our focused listening and note-taking.

When you go back to the school, try to find the person who was the most helpful to you last time. Start with 'Last time you were able to work such wonders and we need your help again.'

Remember, it is never helpful to attack people or accuse them of not doing their job properly. Stick with the important facts:

- My child is unhappy.
- Someone (or several someones) is/are being unkind to him.
- I need your help.

When the bully is a teacher

This doesn't happen often, but when it does it is very damaging for the child.

The majority of teachers are wonderful, caring people who treat our children as if they were their own and in whom we can have great confidence. They are heroes who, day after day, go into rooms filled with 30 or so short people. Personally I have enough trouble managing three.

However, there is the occasional exception. Most of us can remember a teacher who made our lives miserable — or that of one of our friends.

Children are mostly defenceless against a bullying teacher. The misery that is heaped upon children by a cruel teacher may result in a child who is tearful, frightened, unable to learn, or reluctant to go to school. Our children may show symptoms of high anxiety with headaches, stomach-aches or nausea on school mornings.

Sometimes our child may be a direct target. The teacher may single him out, denigrate his work or his ideas in front of peers, mete out unreasonable punishments or pick on him with sarcastic, humiliating comments.

Sometimes our children may be an indirect target. There are the good and diligent children who do not put a foot wrong but find themselves in a state of continuous anxiety in case they inadvertently incur the wrath of this teacher and wind up in the sort of trouble they see their peers experience. Often these children have no awareness of what the problem is but they show anxiety symptoms on school days and not during holidays.

If you suspect such a thing is happening to your child:

- Listen to what he says.
- Talk to other parents and pupils.
- Take notes.
- Go to see the teacher.
- If nothing changes, go higher up.

- Follow up.
- Be prepared to go back.

If you are rebuffed

Any time I have approached a principal about a bullying teacher their first explanation is always that this teacher is 'strict but fair — in fact one of my best teachers'. Bullying teachers usually pick on only a small number of pupils and it is perfectly possible for many other pupils to be happy and not notice. This does not mean it is not a serious problem, or that it will go away by itself.

Don't be discouraged. Stick with the important facts:

- My child is unhappy.
- His teacher is being unkind.
- I need your help.

We can make a difference

Bullying is a serious problem and we need to protect our children from this form of abuse. Some bullying is obvious and some bullying is subtle and hard to prove. Dealing with it is a difficult but essential part of parenting.

Unkindness and bullying are unpleasant and damaging to both the perpetrator and the recipient. As parents we have the opportunity to effect change that is good for all children at home, at school and in their adult lives.

22. Overcoming Sleeping Problems

Sleeping is such a basic bodily function, why should I need to write about it?

The reality is that it is common to have problems getting children to go to sleep or stay asleep. Given enough incentive, our children are quite capable of overriding their need to sleep, so parents need to be armed and prepared. The key, as ever, is to keep any problem with the child.

Here are three basic methods of getting your child to sleep on her own at night and to stay asleep through the night:

- Go in at increasing intervals
- Leave them to cry it out
- Diane's pop-in method

There are many, many sleep books available, so I will briefly comment on the two most common methods and then tell you about one that I devised and have found useful.

Go in at increasing intervals

The idea here is that you go in and reassure your distressed child that you are in the house and that you love her. You settle her down quickly and leave the room. If she is still upset, go in five minutes later, reassure her, settle her down and leave. Now leave a five-minute interval and, if necessary, repeat the settling process. Increase the interval by five minutes until your child is asleep.

If this method is going to work, you will have a considerable improvement after three nights, and within a week most of your sleeping problems will be over.

The advantage of this method is that it gives you the opportunity to go in and reassure the child, which is nice for you and nice for her. The theory is that your child is reassured that you love her and you are there for her, so she can go off to sleep feeling secure and reassured.

When I ask a room full of parents how many people have used this method — some people refer to it as 'controlled crying' — almost everyone puts up their hand. When I ask for how many it has worked, about a third of the class raise their hands. It sounds a perfectly reasonable method, so why doesn't it work for the other two-thirds of parents?

I believe the successful third (of children) interpret their parents' actions just as described above. However, the other two-thirds of children interpret their parents' behaviour quite differently. I believe their interpretation is: 'So I just have to keep on crying and sooner or later they come back. As long as I keep on crying.' So for these children, we are inadvertently teaching them to cry for longer.

Leave them to cry it out

This is a well-proven method with lots of documented evidence that it does work and it is not harmful. At bedtime we tell our child we will not be returning until morning and that she should go off to sleep on her own. She may cry herself off to sleep, but eventually she goes to sleep on her own. It is not an easy method because it goes against the way we are programmed — to go to see upset children and comfort them.

We used this method for Robert when he was about 10 months. I know we did, because Vernon is an honest man and he tells me we did. I presume I found it so ghastly that I have blocked it out. We needed to do it for about a week and we did not have sleeping problems with Robert after that.

He was a child who never went off to sleep easily and I had a fairly strict code about bedtime. There came a time each day when I had had enough parenting. I worked on the basis that, between the hours of 7 am and 7 pm, I was a lovely mother. Between the hours of 7 pm and 7 am, I was not particularly interested. (The exception was for an ill child. Of course, I was willing to look after any child when it was a 'need' rather than a 'want'.)

So, after about seven o'clock he was in his bed. I remember he used to read and play in his bed for a long time, before going off to sleep.

Tanya was an excellent sleeper.

By the time we had Deborah I had probably worked through the Leslie Centre Sleep Programme, which was of the 'cold turkey' variety, with more than 200 families. But with her, we had to carry out the method several times. She would just be settling into a nice pattern of sleeping through when she would get a cold or a tooth or mumps and would need my care during the night. I would look after her the first night and the second night and the third night. By the fourth night I would be a little suspicious. By the fifth night I knew that I was being 'had' and would refuse to go in to her. We would have two unpleasant nights and then she would be sleeping through until the next time.

I learned from Deborah that, if a child has a tendency to night-wake, you need to be prepared to train and retrain them. It is not possible to do a sleep programme once and expect it to hold for the rest of your child's life.

Diane's pop-in method

When I was a young mother of two tiny children I was very tough with sleep routines. If I went out for lunch during the day I would travel with a portable cot so that my children could have their daytime sleeps regardless of where we were. By the time I had Deborah, I was considerably older and not prepared to drag around quite so much gear. Deborah's daytime behaviour was getting very, very grumpy.

I was interested in finding a way of encouraging her to have a daytime sleep, but was puzzled as to how one could give recognition to a young child for going to sleep. It didn't seem reasonable to wake a child who had just gone off to sleep to tell them how good they had been. And by the time she had woken up, the moment was long past.

I decided I would recognise and admire the behaviour of staying in bed, rather than the sleep itself.

You're going to sleep in Jan's bed

We were going around to Jan's place so I told Deborah (about 14 months old) that she was going to have a special treat — she was going to sleep in Jan's big bed. I resolved that I would go in and 'catch her being good'. I tucked her in and said I would pop in very soon to see how good she was being.

I popped back after 30 seconds — really, I timed it — and kissed her and told her she was wonderful. I repeated it after one minute, two minutes, three minutes and four minutes. By the time I went back after a six-minute interval, she was fast asleep with a half-smile on her face.

It requires a lot of parental self-discipline to do it this way. The aim is to stay ahead of your child's frustration at not having you there. Although it is hard work, it is pleasant because you are not dealing with a crying child.

What about the anxious child?

Many parents are relieved to know that there is a way of teaching children to go off to sleep on their own without having to leave them to cry themselves to sleep. However, some tell me their child clings and won't let them leave the room.

If this is the case, your method should be the same, but say slightly different things for a start. Begin with 'I just have to go to the toilet and then I'll pop straight back.' I choose this one because it is hard for your child to argue with this need! Go back and reassure her and then say, 'I just need to go and put the kettle on.' Stay away for about a minute. Keep generating reasonable excuses, popping back very briefly but reliably at increasing intervals.

If this is more than your child can tolerate, then either she is exceptionally needy or you are being had.

The child who keeps coming out

First, you need to decide at what time of night your parenting services finish. After this time you are no longer prepared to entertain your child. This means you are not prepared to entertain her by growling, lecturing, yelling or supplying drinks or food.

You are, however, prepared to pop in to a child who is being good, and you are prepared to leave the door open for a quiet child who is in his bed. The majority of children like to stay connected with the family by having their door open.

If your child comes out or is making a lot of noise, tell her that the family is being disturbed. She has a choice. Either she stays quietly in her room or the door will be shut for five minutes.

She comes out again. March her back without a word and plonk her into bed. Say, 'I'll be back in five minutes to see if you are ready to stay in bed and have the door open.'

At the end of five minutes, go back and open the door. Tell her that if she is quiet, you will leave the door open and pop in to see how good she is being. If she is noisy or begins arguing or bargaining, she has rejected your generous offer. Tell her she will have another chance in five minutes and close the door.

It shouldn't take more than one round to discover whether your child chooses to have the door open or the door shut. Respect her choice.

Life becomes so much simpler

Once a child is content to stay in her room, with the door open, while adult family life goes on, your evening will be much more pleasant. You will be free to go in just to give your child a hug or just because you have some socks to put away in her drawer.

I used to love it when my children slept so well that, after a night when we were out and had a baby-sitter, we could pop in to tuck them goodnight. With a good sleeper you can have the pleasure of kissing them, tucking them in and saying, 'We're home now. Say "Goodnight, Mummy,"' and having a little voice murmur back, 'Night, Mummy. I love you,' and then drift back to sleep.

A last word about popping in

Years later, even now when she is getting beyond her mid-teens, Deborah still says goodnight the same way. In one of those rare times when she is in bed before us and we go in to say goodnight to a sleepy child, the last thing she will often say is 'Goodnight, Mum. Goodnight, Dad. I love you. Pop in.'

Young habits die hard

Children go through several sleep cycles throughout the night. They go from shallow sleep to light sleep and down to deep sleep, then resurface about once every hour or so depending on their age. When they come to the surface during the night, they may need the same circumstances to get back to sleep as they had early evening.

If they cannot get off to sleep at bedtime without a parent lying next to them, they will need that when they wake in the middle of the night. If they cannot get off to sleep without a dummy, they will need it each time they wake in the night. If they are in the habit of getting off to sleep with a bottle in their mouth, they will need that to get off to sleep in the middle of the night.

None of these things matters with a good sleeper. If your child goes off to sleep with a parent present, a bottle, a dummy, a 10-piece orchestra — it isn't a problem if they sleep through. But if you are having night-waking problems, you will need to teach your child how to go off to sleep unaided so that she can do the same in the middle of the night.

Begin at evening bedtime

If you decide your child is going to have to go off to sleep without props, begin the process at bedtime. Don't decide in the middle of the night that you have had enough and change the rules on an hysterical child.

If your child is used to your lying there, begin by taking in an armchair and sitting next to her bed instead. As the days go by, move your chair further towards the door. Give the process a week. Then begin to pop in.

If your child likes a bedtime bottle, give it to her in the living room, clean her teeth, take her to bed and begin popping in.

If your child is used to going to sleep with a dummy and that is leading to your getting up to put it back several times a night, you need to decide whether you are prepared to keep doing that. If you are, that is absolutely fine.

If you are not prepared to do it in the middle of the night, it is time to teach your child to manage without. I don't know any way other than having a few horrible nights of putting up with crying until your child gets used to taking herself off to sleep. I wish I did.

Safety first

If ever you have a concern about your child's safety, of course you go in and check. If you are greeted by a child who stops crying, beams at you — still with a tear halfway down her cheek — and says, 'Hello, Mummy,' you know you've been had. Kiss her goodnight, say, 'You're just fine, darling,' and walk out. Expect her to be outraged.

Will she ever stop crying?

If we are going to leave our child to cry herself to sleep, our big fear is that she is incapable of stopping.

I suggest you listen to the cry. Often our child will cry full bore for about 10 minutes and then stop to catch her breath. There is a tiny break in the cry and then she starts up again. She works herself up into a fury and then it begins to subside. She stops for a few seconds and then starts up again. The next time she is quiet for a little bit longer. She seems to be listening to see if anyone is taking any notice. They're not, so she starts up again.

If you are getting this on-and-off crying you can reassure yourself that your child does indeed know how to stop. It is within her capability. She may take a while to make the decision.

Perfect night vision

There was a time when Deborah had begun night-waking. I awoke one night to find her standing beside my bed. Being inherently lazy, I opened one eyelid and said in my most sinister tone, 'You know that if I have to get up I will be very, very cross.' She scuttled away and I went back to sleep well satisfied at my assertive parenting.

In the morning Rob (at 15, he was now calling himself 'Rob') appeared, looking absolutely dreadful. Deborah had made her way down two flights of stairs, told Rob to move over so she could be on the wall side and not risk falling out, and climbed in. She had made herself comfortable and went off to sleep in a starfish position. Rob had spent a miserable night clinging to the edge of his bed.

From this I learned that children have excellent night vision and we do not need to be worried that they cannot find their way around in the dark.

An afterthought

When parents phone me with a sleep problem, they are often surprised that my first question is about daytime behaviour. When children are relatively compliant during the day, the idea of your popping in is very appealing to them and will usually ensure that they can read themselves off or simply drift off to sleep.

If a child is non-compliant during the day, there is no particular reason — other than total exhaustion — why a child should suddenly become the model of co-operation just because the moon is visible. One of the best things you can do to help your child sleep at night is to get better compliance during the day.

23. Food Wars

When your child is a good eater and sturdily built, you feel like a successful mother. The food you offer is eaten with gusto. At weigh-ins you are praised. The line shoots up on the graph. Your baby nurse, your doctor and the grandparents can see you are doing a good job.

But what if your child is naturally slight? What if your child has little interest in food? And what if, in addition, your child does not have excellent health? Under these circumstances the pressure on mothers is enormous. Everyone, it seems, feels free to offer advice, usually unsolicited.

- I'd give him a tonic.
- What about her iron?
- Don't let her eat in front of TV.
- Maybe if he ate in front of TV, he'd eat better.

Some children are not overly interested in food

Deborah was our first child to be uninterested in food. Robert and Tanya were both keen on food, interested in food, entertained by food. Deborah was a revelation. Sometimes, when she was hungry, she would eat voraciously and demand more. Other times she would have a few mouthfuls and that would be it. Not another speck of food would pass her lips. 'Just one more spoon for Mummy' had no effect whatsoever. She appeared not to understand my emotional need to nurture her by feeding, but paid attention to her own body signals. What a strange child!

Remember the grasshopper

Most of us feel responsible for how much of which food our children eat. We worry about whether they have eaten enough to sustain them till the next meal. We worry that if they didn't eat enough (in our view) at 6 pm, they will be starving at 2 am. We worry that if they don't eat vegetables, they will not get adequate minerals. We worry that if we cannot persuade our teenagers to have a healthy breakfast at 7.30 am, their inability to do algebra at 2 pm will be our fault. We worry that if we worry, or if we don't worry, our child may be anorexic.

Even a grasshopper has the brains to eat the right food in the right quantities. So if a grasshopper can manage to get it right, how come we have no faith in our child, who surely has considerably more mental capacity?

Mileage in refusing to eat

We all start with a genetic blueprint designed to see our nutritional needs met. If you've ever struggled with a child's eating problems someone has no doubt said to you, 'Don't worry. No child ever starved surrounded by plenty of food.'

While I do generally agree with this I want to add a rider. 'No child ever starved surrounded by plenty of food … unless there was greater mileage in not eating.'

If our children get a lot of attention when they are refusing to eat, if food refusal alters the atmosphere in the household, if they hear the adults around them discussing food as if eating were an unnatural pastime that requires discipline and training, if *not* eating can worry Mum and eating can please Granddad, if our child can make us — his parent — prepare different food just because he thinks some perfectly wholesome food is 'Yuck', then we are setting ourselves up for feeding battles because there is more mileage for the child in the battle than there is in the natural satisfaction of eating.

How not to get a child to eat

Deborah was about two when I learned to understand the futility of food battles. It was morning-tea time and I had put in front of her a plate of mandarin segments, toast cubes and cheese cubes. These were all foods Deborah enjoyed.

She scoffed down the mandarin and some of the toast and cheese and then asked to get down from her high-chair.

I don't know what motivated me that day, but I decided she was not going to get another mouthful of anything until that food had been eaten. Every mealtime she was going to be offered that food until it was gone. I was not going to raise a child who wasted food. I was not going to raise a child who was picky. I was not running a restaurant. Deborah was just going to have to learn to eat what was put in front of her.

But if mother was made of stern stuff, daughter was made of sterner stuff. She wouldn't have a bar of it and just drank water. Robert (15) and Tanya (13) both came to me privately and said, 'Are you sure you know what you are doing?' I would go off and cry in the bedroom. But it was a matter of principle. Deborah was going to learn to eat what and when I said.

I couldn't bear it to have her eat dried-out old toast that was set like concrete and cheese that was so dry it had split, so whenever she was asleep or not looking I would replace them with fresh cubes.

Deborah held out for 36 hours on water only. Then she ate. I had won ... but it was a hollow victory. And at what cost?

I had learned a lesson. I resolved that I would never again engage in a food battle.

Messages from the society we live in

Many of us come from a 'family meal' background, where every meal operated under more or less the same conditions. Here's what the rules may have looked like:

- The family eats together at predictable times.
- Everyone has designated seats.
- Mum dishes up the food.
- You eat what is on your plate.
- You use cutlery correctly.
- If you have finished what is on your plate, you may have dessert.

- You may not leave the table until you have emptied your plate.
- Children should not speak when they are eating.

For the children who came to the table hungry, who enjoyed the food offered, whose appetites and tastes matched what was presented to them, and where the atmosphere around the table was harmonious, this was an excellent system.

However, you may have less-than-pleasant memories of family meals. You may have disliked the foods. (My favourite trick to deal with cooked vegetables as a child was to add huge quantities of salt. For me, the taste of salt was infinitely preferable to the taste of vegetables. We won't even think about what that has done to my arteries!)

You may have memories of moving your food round and round your plate in the hope that it would somehow disappear. You may remember being alone at the table after everyone had left and you were still staring at a pile of cold silverbeet. You may remember a lot of tension around the table as adults argued or siblings fought. (My brother's favourite trick was to open a mouthful of half-chewed food. He'd do this very cleverly, so that only I could see it. I would let out a loud shriek, by which time he had his mouth firmly shut and a look of complete innocence on his face. Guess who copped it?)

You may have wonderful memories of family meals. You may remember fun and laughter and discussions, good food and a feeling of love and security.

All these memories will affect how you raise your children and shape their attitudes toward food and mealtimes.

Today we eat in many different ways

Families today tend to have several different ways of having meals during any one week:

- We eat as a whole family, at the table, using cutlery.
- We eat out at a restaurant.
- We eat at a fast-food place using no cutlery.
- We eat around the TV.
- Young children eat at a special low table earlier than the adults.

- We eat finger-foods at the table.
- We eat in the car.

For each of these ways of eating we have different rules of conduct and our children are quite capable of learning these provided the rules are clear. Notice that our young children will not only learn the rules as early as preschool age, but will display different tastes at different places. How many of us have a child who won't touch baked beans at home but loves them at daycare, when everyone else is eating them?

My mother used to love telling this story from the early 1930s.

She was a young newlywed and in the apartment next door lived another young woman with a four-year-old son, Frederick. Frederick was a terrible eater; every meal was a struggle. So Frederick's mother and my mother hatched a plan. My mother would invite the four-year-old to come and have dinner with her. This would be a big treat for him. Unbeknown to him, his mother had prepared his usual meal and sneaked it over.

Frederick duly arrived, feeling like a very grown-up guest. He not only ate everything on his plate, he went home and berated his mother for not preparing him nice meals like Mrs Hift did.

What are meals for?

In our society, our meals often are multi-purpose, meeting several needs at once:

- Nutrition
- Sociability
- Family unity
- Celebration
- Mixing generations
- Peer-group bonding
- Reinforcing family rules of behaviour

When you are deciding whether you need to do something about your children's eating habits, keep in mind the purpose or purposes of that particular meal. The purpose of the meal dictates what set of rules will prevail. Are you clear about the rules of acceptable behaviour at this meal? Because if you are not, there is no way your child can be clear about your expectations.

So what are reasonable expectations?

I expect my children to know how to behave in several situations. I expect them to know how to eat finger-foods on a tablecloth (or a bath-towel!) on the ground, and how to use crockery and cutlery in a formal setting. I expect young children to stay at the table as long as they are eating. When they have lost interest in food they are more than welcome to stay and enjoy the company or leave the table. The same rules of reasonably good, socially acceptable behaviour and courtesy apply at mealtimes as they do at all other times.

And nothing gives me more pleasure than being around a table with three generations, enjoying good food and company, with children contributing their ideas. But this conviviality doesn't happen by magic. To be able to enjoy mealtimes you need children with reasonably fuss-free ways of eating, reasonably good manners and a reasonable level of discipline.

Setting up your own programme

What can you do, if your child is already a feeding nightmare? If every meal is torment for everyone in your house, if you dread the question 'What will your child eat for lunch at my house?', if you fear going into the doctor's surgery in case she decides to weigh your child — it is definitely time to do something different.

It is not helpful for parents to be told:

- Just put the food in front of her and forget about it.
- Wait till he asks for food.
- Why don't you try making the food more attractive?
- No dessert until he has at least tried one mouthful of each sort of food.
- If he goes to bed hungry, he'll know better next time.

Instead, I would like to offer you a way of thinking and behaving around food that:

- respects your need to nurture.
- gives your child regular access to food.
- respects your child's boundaries of his own body.
- stops you trying to make your child eat.

- gives you a break.
- reduces friction around food.
- offers opportunities to your child to have healthy food without pressure.

(I was already using this programme by the time Barbara Colorosa's excellent book *Kids Are Worth It* came onto the market in New Zealand. Our thinking on this subject is almost identical.)

Some useful thoughts before you start

Begin with very small quantities. Should he ask for more, you will find a way to cope.

- It is your responsibility to offer your child access to reasonable quantities of healthy food that he 'sort of' likes five times a day. What he does with these opportunities is his business.
- Avoid foods touching each other. Particularly avoid an undesirable food touching a desirable food. Apparently the contamination renders all the good stuff uneatable. If I were dealing with a really fussy eater today I would contemplate buying a Japanese bento box.
- Juice and milk are liquid foods. If our children get a substantial proportion of their calories from liquid foods, we shouldn't be surprised that they have little appetite for solid foods. Water quenches thirst.
- You are not running a smorgasbord.
- Don't put up with appalling or even halfway bad behaviour just so your child will eat. If you allow him to loll out of his chair, eat off the tablecloth, mix it all together to make food soup that he won't eat anyway, walk around with food, gaze at the TV while you spoon food into an absent-minded mouth, you are giving your child ways of holding you hostage to his eating. Is that what you want?

The plan

Begin at breakfast time. Put out a small quantity of a breakfast food you know he likes — or at least does not hate. Invite him to the table. Since he hasn't eaten since bedtime he should have some hunger pangs. (The best way to find out when your child's hunger pangs kick in is to observe him in the weekend. If he were left to his own devices, when would he become naturally peckish?)

When he has had enough, no matter how much or how little — even if it is nothing! — allow him to leave the table if he wishes. If he wants to stay and enjoy the sociability without eating, let him.

Cover the food and keep it. For young children, I find a plastic compart-mentalised plate (so the yucky food cannot touch the nice food) with a plastic resealable lid easiest. He may have access to this food whenever he wants it — provided he is seated at the table. Deal with any inappropriate behaviour as you would deal with any other matter needing either emotional support or emotional distance.

Likely responses

- Your child: 'This is all yucky. There's nothing I like.' (Crying) You (put an arm around her): 'Isn't that hard for you? Never mind, maybe there will be food you can enjoy later in the day.'
- Your child: 'This is all yucky. There's nothing I like.' (Angry) You: 'I don't like being spoken to like that. You may leave the table and go to another room.'
- Your child: 'I've finished the mandarin but I don't want the toast. Please may I have some more mandarin?' You: 'Sorry, sweetheart. That's what is going for breakfast today. I'll remember that you really like mandarin another time.'
- Your child: 'I don't want any more.' You: 'That's fine, darling. You can get down now and I'll put your breakfast aside in case you are hungry later on.'
- Your child: 'This is all yucky. There's nothing I like.' (Throws the food on the floor.) You: Put him in Time Out, saying, as you move him there, 'You know you are not allowed to throw food. Now, you wait here until I have finished cleaning up.' Clean up slowly.

Some parenting books talk about letting the child experience the conse-quences of his actions by making him clean up. But sloshing milk around a floor with a cloth is usually a pleasant occupation for a young child.

Another attitude involves letting the child clean up in order to preserve the child's self-esteem. It is my self-esteem at stake here. Having thrown the food I carefully prepared onto the floor, my child is in danger of having a mother with shattered self-esteem after she screams at her child and then barely restrains herself from throttling him. (Much better that he should wait in Time Out until I am ready to have him around again.)

Morning tea

At morning-tea time, throw away any remaining breakfast, without comment. Put out a small quantity of morning-tea-type food. It is fine to include a couple of biscuits and, of course, your child will eat those first. Should he become hungry, you know there is some healthy food waiting.

Remember that you are not trying to starve your child into eating. You are merely offering a fresh opportunity, about every two hours, to choose healthy foods. This does not equate to torturing a child — even though he may scream as if it is.

When your child has lost interest in the food he may leave the table, knowing that you will keep that food available till lunchtime.

Should only the biscuit and chippies portion of his stomach have room, and the carrot and apple part be full, he is going to have to make a limited choice. He is going to have to decide whether to eat the less-desired food or wait till lunchtime. By now that is only two hours away and, anyway, the healthy food is available right away if he needs it.

Repeat this pattern with each meal. An hour or two after dinner time the kitchen is closed.

What to expect

Expect a lot of complaining for the first two days. Expect a pathetic little voice saying, 'I'm hungry' while staring at an apple and wishing for chocolate biscuits.

Expect the odd tantrum. Remember that your child may well have had you in the grip of his power trip surrounding food. Suddenly, all his power is gone. Remember, 'No dictator gives up power lightly.'

Expect to feel greatly relieved at not having to spend 24 hours a day thinking about what your child eats or does not eat.

Expect to find it quite hard. You have shifted a pattern of *your* behaviour around your child's eating. Changing our behaviour is always exhausting. It takes 21 days to master a behaviour change.

If I had my time over again, I would love to try bringing a child up with, 'Unless you eat your ice-cream, there is no spinach for you.'

24. Toilet Training

There are many, many words used to describe the bodily functions of elimination. Some are medical, some are technical, some are humorous and some are profane. For the purposes of this chapter I am going to go for the user-friendly terms 'poos' and 'wees'.

Our children are fully toilet trained when they can notice when their body is signalling it needs to eliminate, when they can stop what they are doing (even if it is sleeping), when they can take themselves to the toilet and do what they need to do, all without parental intervention or reminder.

A natural progression

Learning to pay attention to, and act on, our body signals tends to be a progression of awarenesses, although there are some children who appear to train themselves overnight.

Let's look at the steps.

Not a clue

Babies appear to have little awareness that their body is eliminating. They look cute when they go bright red and appear to be straining. They are even cuter when they look amazed at their own body sounds.

However, they do not yet have the ability to know what is going on. At this stage, in a non-tropical environment, we keep them in nappies. In societies where babies are unclothed and carried, mothers appear to be aware when their babies are ready to go and hold them away from their bodies.

Some babies are very fussy about being in wet or soiled nappies and cry until they are changed. Others don't appear to care.

'I've just been'

Sooner or later our toddlers start to tell us when they have 'been'. They are aware that their body has eliminated and they want their nappy changed. (This happens to other people's children. All our three never cared that they were in wet or soiled nappies. However, they did start to announce their activities.)

This is a sign of progress and we should welcome it. Knowing that you have 'been' is an important stage in development, yet we often fail to recognise it. We tend to say, 'Why didn't you tell me and we could have used the potty?'

This is not particularly helpful. We need to recognise that our children, at this stage, only know afterwards. They do not yet have the experience of recognising the signals ahead. It is premature during this stage to keep telling your child, 'You just tell Mummy and we can go to the toilet.'

A better response, to reinforce this wonderful recognition on our child's part, is, 'Good girl for telling Mummy. Let's go and change your nappy.'

'I am going right now'

It is not particularly socially convenient to have our child yelling, in the middle of the supermarket, 'Mum! I'm just doing wees right now!' However, it is a step that we should be pleased about. Our child has now progressed to being aware of what her body is doing as she is doing it.

Again, it is not wise to berate her with, 'Why didn't you tell Mummy?' She *is* telling you — just as soon as she can. She is doing well to tell you and an appropriate way of responding is, 'That's great. You tell Mummy when you are finished and we can go and change you.'

It is around this age — particularly in summer — that our children have the chance to be amazed at the distance they can wee. Boys are well equipped but you may be amazed at just how far little girls with full bladders and tilted hips can reach!

They may also be fascinated by what their bodies can poo. We all have at least one story of finding a child in a cot using her body products for modelling. Don't you just love parenting?

'I need to go — in five seconds'

The next step is when our children know that their body is about to eliminate, but their early-warning system doesn't give much notice. This stage doesn't last long, mercifully. While you are in it, you will find that your sightseeing priorities change. Wherever you go, your first thought is to know the exact location of all toilets within a five-second radius.

Tell your child that she is wonderful for telling you and race for the nearest toilet.

You will not set back your child's progress if you take her out in pull-ups at this stage. This option is great for your blood pressure and peace of mind.

'I will need to go soon'

It is a wonderful stage in a parent's life when you can take your child out without nappies and know that she will tell you in plenty of time, so that you can find the toilet.

Around about this stage, they also get into research. They like to begin a visit to any new house by trying out all the toilets. You are nearly there.

'I can go by myself'

Eventually there comes the wonderful stage when your child takes herself off to the toilet, takes care of her own clothing, flushes, washes her hands and returns to playing without reference to you.

'I don't need night nappies'

Your child can hold on for increasingly long intervals and then go in the right place. When she is really good at hanging on, she may be able to stay dry all night.

There are two reasons why a child might wake up regularly with a dry bed. The first reason is that she has become really good at 'hanging on'. She can go to sleep in the evening and hang on all night until the morning. This is absolutely wonderful, but she is not fully trained.

Your child is fully toilet trained when you are confident that she can recognise, in the middle of the night and in the middle of sleeping, that she needs to go to the toilet, then take herself there and back. Initially, of course, she will have to notify you of this, but eventually she will take care of the entire process by herself.

To go forwards, go backwards

If you are having battles over toileting, it may well be that you have rushed your child too quickly through one of the steps. The easiest way is to go back to the step that has been missed. Parents worry that, if they put a child back in nappies, it will be a backward step. The most important thing is to have your child comfortable with her body processes. It is *her* body and *your* carpet, *her* well-being and *your* blood pressure. Put her in nappies. Let her go back to weeing and pooing when her body dictates. Pretty soon she will be ready to move to the next step.

Frequently occurring problems

Two lovely things happened when Robert was about 15 months. My father-in-law, who was a general practitioner, showed me an article from the *British Medical Journal* that said the reason most mothers went to their doctor about toilet training was because of the pressure from either their mother or mother-in-law.

About the same time my mother said to me, 'Please don't ask me about toilet training. I was never very good at it.'

Since I have been in practice as a family therapist I get a lot of calls about toilet training. I will cover some of the more frequently occurring problems and debunk some myths and legends.

'She likes to go in her nappies'

There are many children who are fully wee-trained (I do know the expression 'have full control over their bladder function', but it just doesn't sound like something a three-year-old would do!) but like to have their nappies put on to poo. When they need to poo, they ask their mum to put on their nappy. They go off to behind the couch and resist any attempt to interpret their crouching position and their red face. When they have finished, they may wish to be changed or they may go off to play.

The first thing I encourage mothers to do is to congratulate themselves. Your child now has full bowel control. As far as pooing goes, she knows when she needs to go, she can hang on till she has her nappy on, she can go in the place of her choice and she knows when she has been. She is trained.

The only thing at issue is location, location, location. I recommend a three-step process.

Firstly, change the location. Everyone else in the house poos in the room with the toilet in it. So can she. When she asks to have her nappy on, put it on and take her to the toilet room. Ask her whether she wants you to stay or go. When she is ready, tell her she is welcome to come out. Tell her she is wonderful for having pooed in the same room as the grown-ups.

If you get a lot of fuss at this stage, you are probably dealing with a compliance issue. Think about the rest of her behaviour. Do you need to insist on a bit more compliance for other than toileting behaviours?

Once she has mastered this step, tell her that she is ready to poo on the toilet with her nappy on. Sorry to be so graphic about this, but many children are wary of the draught on their behind and the big splash that follows. Keeping her nappy on while sitting on the toilet solves both these problems.

Once your child can ask for a nappy, sit on the toilet and do what she needs to do, the rest will follow within a small number of days. She has all the modelling around her of what is expected. One day she will go there and take her own nappy off. She will yell out, 'Quick, come and look,' and you will join all the parents of the world who know how to do cartwheels of delight down the corridor.

When I ask, the answer is always 'no'

If you ask your child whether she needs to go, the answer is usually no. There is a good reason for this. If she recognised that she needed to go, she would have gone. She is either incapable of this recognition or doesn't need to go. If she is incapable, it is not a useful question.

If she is capable but doesn't want to go, there is no point in getting into a verbal battle. Respect the fact that she knows about her own body but accept that sometimes bodies can trick you.

Say, 'I just wondered if there is a sneaky wee hiding there. Let's just go and check.' When you get there, pop her on the toilet and count slowly to 20. Even the most determined 'hanger-on-er' can rarely go past 17 with a full bladder.

If she has a full bladder, she will wee. Say, 'My, that was a sneaky one hiding there so well.' If she doesn't go, say, 'Well, that one fooled me. Let me know when it is ready to come out.'

(If she is hopping around with her legs crossed, don't ask her whether she wants to go. Just say, 'There is a poo (or wee) just waiting to get out. Let's go now.' And take her right away.)

Using this sort of language, you put you and your child on the same side, dealing with the vagaries of a tricky body.

'She gets too busy'

There is a lot of parenting advice around to the effect that one should never show any displeasure around children who wet or soil their pants or your carpet. Now, I am certainly glad that we have left behind the bad old days when parents, in order to facilitate toilet training, would tell a child who had an accident that they were revolting, filthy little grubs. There is no place for berating or humiliating a child who does not have full control of her bodily functions.

However, there does come a point when you become aware that the reason your child has made a puddle or filled her pants is because, although she is perfectly capable of recognising her body's need to go, and she is perfectly capable of going, she simply wanted to carry on playing rather than getting up and leaving what she was doing. Parents often say, 'She's just lazy' or 'She gets too busy'.

The reality is that your child is being mildly non-compliant. She knows what is expected, she is capable of what is expected, but she is choosing not to pay attention to her body's signals.

When you become aware of wet patches or unpleasant fragrances, don't ask her, 'Do you need to go to the toilet?', 'What have you been doing?' 'Are you wet?', or any other question you know the answer to. That is deceitful on your part.

Just tell her she needs to be changed. Change her. Then, take her to her room and say, 'I have a lot of cleaning up to do now. You stay here till I have finished.' Clean up as slowly as it takes to stop being angry, then tell her she can come out. Don't lecture or explain. You have shown mild displeasure. You have mildly inconvenienced your child. Episode over. Your child can do her own learning.

I must stress that this is appropriate only with a child who is already toilet trained. Punishment has no place in training the child who is learning to recognise body signals.

Night-wetting: keep the nappy on

I don't quite understand why anyone allows their child to wet their bed night after night. Of course the odd accident happens, but night after night is not an accident. If there is a wet bed every morning, your child does not have the ability to attend to her body signals in the middle of the night, wake herself up, go to the toilet and get herself back to bed. She needs to be in nappies or protective underpants until she can manage. It is only a matter of time. I cannot think of a good reason for you both to endure the wet sheets, wet blankets and wet mattress, when protective underwear would keep her, her clothing and her bed dry.

Parents worry that protective clothing will somehow humiliate their child. I agree it is not nice for her, but it is a lot less humiliating than an entire washload of bed linen and a mattress drying on the path day after day. Rest assured, she will get there eventually.

To lift or not to lift?

There is no learning for your child in being carried absolutely inert from her bed to the toilet, being parked on it, doing a wee, then being carried equally inert back to her bed. It does save a wet bed, and often that is all you want to do, but if you are interested in training your child, you need her to participate in the process.

Go in and try to rouse your child. If she is in the deepest sleep, go back 15 minutes later and try again. The odds are that she will be coming up into a lighter sleep. Walk or carry her to the toilet and park her on it.

At this point you need her to be aware of the process. This may sound rather unkind, but what I did was put my hands just a little way in front of my child's shoulders. Tipping forward ever so slightly but safely brought my child into a reasonable state of alertness.

When she is finished, walk her back to bed. Leading a child by the hand keeps her reasonably alert and aware of the process. Walking behind holding her shoulders works equally well. Tell her she's just been to the toilet and she's wonderful. Kiss her goodnight and walk out.

What you have done is rehearsed her through the appropriate steps to keeping herself dry at night.

If your child can get through most nights dry with only one lifting, you may decide to put her to bed without a nappy and then, when you have lifted her, pop a nappy on just in case.

When to lift

I work on the basis that after we have eaten, our various digestive processes get to work and one of the by-products is a full bladder. If our children have eaten and drunk fairly early in the evening, they may well have dealt with the full post-dinner bladder before bedtime. If they eat a large meal just before going to bed, they are guaranteed to have a full bladder after an hour to an hour and a half.

The first trick is to establish *when* your child has a full bladder. Most of us think that if we lift her as late as possible, like just before we go to bed, we increase the chances of her getting through. It is a great theory but doesn't work if the child is already wet!

Establish at what time your child wets for the first time. Before this happens is the right time to lift her. Even if it is an hour after she goes to sleep, it is still the right time.

Keep extending the time later and later till you can lift her just before you go to bed.

What if once isn't enough?

With some children, and it certainly happened with our two girls, we could lift them dry at increasingly later times, but they still couldn't get through the rest of the night dry. Clearly, they needed training to take themselves one more time through the night.

One suggestion is to lift your child a second time. It's tough on you but it does work. When you go to bed, set your alarm for two to three hours later. Stagger out and lift your child. Mutter a great deal and go back to bed — and to sleep if you can.

Provided you found your child dry, you can extend the time interval by a quarter of an hour each night. The odds are high that, by the time you have extended the second lifting to 3.30 am she will be able to get through the rest of the night dry.

But she still wets her bed

If your child has reached seven and is still not showing any signs of being able to wake herself in the middle of the night when she needs to empty her bladder, if you are still struggling with wet beds or sodden nappies, speak to your family doctor. If there is no medical reason why she is still wetting, there are things that you can do that may empower your child to train herself.

But she is such a deep sleeper

Children who are deep sleepers do not necessarily wet their beds. Children who wet their beds are almost always deep sleepers.

I think that what happens is that children who find themselves unable

302

to stop wetting their beds absolutely loathe that situation. No matter how nice and discreet we are about it, they always know that this is not appropriate behaviour. Because they seem unable to help wetting they sleep deeper and because they sleep deeper, they wet. It is a vicious cycle.

Provided that our children are relatively co-operative in their daytime behaviours and willing to be enthused by you to try some skills that will help them stay dry at night, there is a way that we can help them develop the skills they need to be dry all night.

Two skills your child will need

In order for our children to be dry all night, they need two skills.

The first skill is to be an excellent 'Hanger-on-er'. They need to be able to hang on with quite a full bladder for quite some time.

The second skill they will need is to be alert for their body signals during the night. This is not easy for a deep sleeper.

Tell your child that you have a plan that will help her stay dry all night. She needs to put her body into training.

Becoming a 'Hanging On' champ

Every day after school, your child drinks two large glasses of water and then hangs on as long as she possibly can. Keep written records, together, of how long she can hang on. A fortnight is a reasonable length of time for your child to discover that she can hang on for increasingly longer intervals. The odds are that she will amaze you and herself at just how long she can hang on. Be very proud of her. She now has conscious knowledge that she is very capable of hanging on to a full bladder.

Teaching your child to sleep alert

Your child needs to attend to her body during the night. She needs to sleep lightly enough to listen to her body's signals. This is a skill and can be learned by a co-operative child. If she is unwilling to engage in the process, she doesn't want to be dry. Check out her compliance on other daytime matters.

You will need a noisy alarm clock. (If it doesn't prove to be noisy enough, put it in a saucepan.) Get your child to set it at whatever time she can just about be guaranteed to be dry. Place it so that it is near enough to her to wake her and far enough away so that she has to get out of bed.

At bedtime, encourage her to 'tell her brain' that it will be listening for the alarm and will wake to it. When she hears it go off, she should get up and turn it off. While she is up, she might as well go to the toilet.

Sometimes you will hear it reverberating through the house while your child sleeps on in deep oblivion. Stagger out of bed and shake her until she is awake enough to get up. You shouldn't need to do this more than three or four nights. After that, she should be sleeping in a much more alert state. If you are dealing with a co-operative child, she will want to wake up and take care of herself.

I have occasionally worked with children who need to reset the alarm for a second wake-up call. There are even clocks around that can be set for two different ringing times.

If your child is managing to wake to an alarm and take herself to the toilet at night, she has made tremendous progress. Be suitably impressed.

This way of helping your child puts you and your child on the same side 'against' the problem. It encourages your child to be self-responsible and to believe that she can develop the skills that will enable her to be like her peers and wake when her body needs her to.

Should this method not be powerful enough to overcome your child's bed-wetting, it is time to talk to your doctor again.

25. Teen Strategies

Raising teens is theoretically simply an extension of everything you have done for the first 12 years. Emotional support is needed just as much — if not more — and holding boundaries to keep them feeling safe and secure is more important than ever as they become increasingly competent and independent.

However, given the addition of hormonal upheavals, increasing connection with support and pressure from their peers, and a media and marketing world that targets them unmercifully, we find ourselves having to call on every parenting skill we have developed up till now — and then some!

The Law of the Farm

Stephen Covey in his wonderful book *First Things First* talks about the Law of the Farm. He reminds us that if we wish to harvest a bountiful crop, we have to plan ahead, prepare the ground, till the soil, plant the seeds at the appropriate time, weed and mulch, feed and prune, and eventually, if we have done it all correctly, we get to harvest a bumper crop. There is no way we can ignore what needs to be done for 11 months, then prepare the soil one day, plant the day after and expect to harvest in a week's time.

Furthermore, we live in an 'instant' age where we expect to be able to do everything faster, harder and smarter — and pay later. Covey goes on to say that real life is not like that. I would like to add that child-rearing is definitely not like that.

A few years ago I had the privilege of attending our older children's graduation ceremonies. Every time I looked around the large auditorium, the centre full of the black gowns of the about-to-graduate, and the rest of the hall dotted with the colour of the admirers and supporters, I was moved to tears.

Every family was there as testimony to the hard work of the previous years as our children had worked their way through a seemingly endless round of lectures and studying and tests. What moved me, however, was not the achievements of the children, but the efforts of all the parents and parent figures who had been part of the process since birth, of raising children with the required self-discipline, perseverance and tenacity. This was definitely harvest time.

It takes a village

The saying 'It takes a whole village to raise a child' has been ascribed to so many people — including Tribal and Anon — that I will not attempt to source it. But I believe it needs to ring in our ears as we raise our children through those teenage years.

Most of us live in an impersonal city, in a slightly less impersonal suburb. The houses in our street often appear deserted for most of the day, as people are involved in their work away from home. In the evenings we know there are people there because there are lights on behind the curtains.

As suburban Western families live their lives, scattered throughout the country or the world, our teens no longer feel themselves guarded and protected by the many adults in their lives. We, as parents, do not feel backed in what we say by the extended family, the church or the state. We experience ourselves in isolation. It is up to us to create the best village we can to provide a safety net around our children.

Networking

Do everything you possibly can to get to know the adults who are raising your children's friends. It is easiest while the teens are still dependent on you for transport.

At the beginning of the intermediate and the high school years it is still absolutely expected and accepted that, when you drop your child at someone's house for the first time, you will go in and make yourself known to the other parent/s. Don't just introduce yourself, but also write down your name, your address and your phone number, give it to them and trust they will reciprocate.

This is one of the best safety nets you can have for your teen: the ability to phone another parent to check arrangements and to find out whether it is true that everyone is allowed to do some particularly hare-brained activity.

Take every chance you get to invite other parents for a cup of coffee when they drop their child to you. Accept every invitation to coffee with them.

Be the centre of the daisy

You may want to flip back to Chapter 10 to remind yourself of the concept of the centre of the daisy. This is the idea that our children make bigger and bigger excursions out into the world but return to their parents periodically for nurture and comfort. As our children grow up, they look more and more independent and may not appear to need us. But what I have found is that although they do operate much more independently they still need our comfort and support — just as two-year-olds do — available the instant that they need it.

They do best when they know exactly where the centre of the daisy is. If it were up to teens, parents would be permanently at home and available 'on tap'. This is not something we are always able or prepared to do, but it behoves us to be mindful that our teens need us at the beginning and end of their day, and any time they have a problem to discuss.

They may even need us to be somewhere else in the house while they discuss the problem with a friend — and will refuse to tell us what is bothering them. It is the fact that we are *there* that is the point, even if they are not taking our advice.

I am not suggesting you sit still in your living room on the off-chance that your teen needs you. I do recommend that, whenever you are absent, your teen knows exactly where you are to be found. This is part of the 'village' concept. You always know where to find Mum or Dad.

Part of being the centre of the daisy is to practise not shutting down a teenager when they do decide to speak. There is a fine line between listening with empathy, asking interested questions, being fully present for them, and interrogating or criticising. I don't have a magic answer for finding that fine line. We all learn from the experience of our teen being in full flow, then we somehow look wrong or utter a wrong phrase and they shut up like a clam and vanish, saying, 'You are always so judgemental.'

It is not useful to become upset or angry. In your now empty room, review what happened and you should find a clue to what was the big turn-off for your child. As they get toward the end of their teens, they will be a lot less touchy.

Parents as role-models

In the tribal village the same rules apply to almost everyone. With the intimacy of a village you cannot get away with 'Do as I say, rather than as I do.' Teens have an extremely sensitive nose for discrepancy, which they translate as 'unfair'.

Remember that they are watching and learning as you model behaviour around eating, drinking, smoking, sexual behaviour, being responsible and being reliable, and although you can get away with a certain amount of 'I am the grown-up and grown-ups are allowed to do this,' we must remember that we are being watched.

Remember also that our teens are watching outrageous behaviour on TV programmes, many of which imply that most difficult problems can be solved in half an hour with advertising breaks in between. It is up to us to model something that has slightly more validity than their favourite soap opera.

Picture the scene: the cookie jar

Mum (having heard the sounds of cupboard door and cookie-jar lid): 'What's that on your face?'

Tot (hoping to stay out of trouble): 'Nothing.'

Mum (dragging tot to a mirror): 'Look.'

Tot (trying to stay out of trouble): 'Must be paint.'

Mum (licking finger, rubbing tot's face, sticking finger in tot's mouth): 'Taste it.'

Tot (trying even harder to stay out of trouble): 'Wow! It's chocolate!'

Mum (getting angrier by the second): 'Well! How did it get there?'

Tot (last valiant attempt to stay out of trouble): 'A witch must have flown in the window and painted it on.'

What happens next is likely to be unpleasant for both. Mum is wondering what on earth she has done to deserve a child who steals and lies. She'll likely be shouting, threatening, lecturing and dragging — probably all of the above. Tot is no doubt shouting or crying or exiled or all three simultaneously.

How do we get into these pickles and what relevance does this have to raising teenagers?

Who told the first fib?

Well, actually, it was Mum. Mum, knowing full well what had caused the brown stuff on Tot's face, asked, 'What's that on your face?' and it all went downhill from there. She would have been better off — and far more honest — saying calmly, 'You have been in the cookie jar. You know you are not allowed to do that without permission.'

Similarly, with our teens, we lose enormous credibility when we interrogate them to obtain 'answers' we already know. If you know where your teen has been or what he has been doing, don't ask if he was there, receive the evasive answer, follow up with, 'Are you sure?' and then accuse him of lying because he was seen there. This will just result in a horrible scene with accusations flying everywhere.

If you know where he has been and what he has been doing and it is outside the framework of accepted family practice, tell him as calmly as you can: 'You were seen in the bar when you told me you were going to the movies.'

Don't leap in with punishment

First, give him the benefit of the doubt. 'I assume there is a perfectly reasonable explanation. What is it?' Wait quite some time for the reply. Your job is to keep the problem with your teen, not to solve it with nagging, whining, pleading or punishing.

Often, the reason is that your teen didn't have the skills to change the arrangements and keep you informed. Keep the problem with him. 'What can we do next time so that it doesn't happen this way? It looked like you were doing something very sneaky. I don't want you to be in that situation again.' This way, you put you and your teen on the same side and together you pit yourselves against the problem — how to make better arrangements next time.

More often, it is likely that your teen has not told you because he knew you would say no, so has gone ahead doing what he wanted, hoping like crazy you wouldn't find out. His bad luck: you did.

The temptation is to leap in and ground him. But be aware that grounding has all the problems of any other punishment. First, you have taken over the problem. You have set up a punishment on the basis that your child will stay grounded for the next week, month, term, and dislike the process so much that he will think again before he breaks any rules. For some children it will work this way.

Other children wildly resent punishment. It gives them just the excuse they need to shift the responsibility for everything that goes wrong in their life onto you. They become sullen, angry, rude and unco-operative and you either take it because you feel they are somehow entitled to do it, or you heap on further punishment for the ghastly behaviour. This is a vicious circle.

Furthermore, you get 10 days, say, out from the episode, and you no longer feel that angry. There are lovely opportunities, social or otherwise, that you wish your child could use. You want to be out and about instead of being a jailer — but there are still six weeks to go.

The alternative to grounding

It is not that different from handling the four-year-old and the cookie jar. Mum could have put the tot into Time Out to express her displeasure. He would be released when Mum was sure he was ready to be in the same house as the cookie jar and leave it alone.

What you want is for your teen to have temptation or opportunity put in front of him and be able to resist it. Until he can resist it, you are going to have a hard time letting him out into the world.

So give him the problem. 'I am concerned about the next time you ask me if you can go out. How would I know that you are going to be where you say you will be?' Leave the problem with him. Tell him to come and find you when he has a good, safe plan.

'But,' I hear you say, 'I don't know what he can do to earn my trust. How can I expect him to work out the answer when I don't know what it is?' And there you have the nub of the problem. Once trust is broken, it is a difficult job to get it back. Give your child the time and space to work that out. In working it out he will come up with small steps toward trust-building. The first step is for him to own the problem. Don't remove this step.

We are simply using the teen version of

Rule broken

↓

Time Out

↓

Child Ready

↓

Relationship restored

With luck, hopefully, with a bit of space to sort things out, your teen can start to plan the steps he can take to regaining your trust and come up with a better plan for his next social activity. If he is not ready to do that, he may not be able to go.

'I'm worried that ...'

When our teens are about to do something we are fairly sure will lead to unpleasantness or danger, we need to find an elegant way of alerting them to the possible consequences of their plan (or lack of plan). Dire predictions delivered in a lecture format have little effect on the typical teen, who considers himself '10-foot tall and invincible' or who is more worried about what his peers will think than his parents' concerns.

We need to find a method to deliver this information in such a way that our teen doesn't immediately begin arguing or switching off. As always, it works best if we take full responsibility for our own thoughts.

I have found that the gentle approach that begins with 'I am worried that …' usually enables us to bring up our concerns and alert our teen to things he may not have fully thought through.

If we are really lucky he may say, 'I hadn't thought of that,' and rethink his plan. If we are less lucky he may say, 'Well, that's your worry.' Our wisest response is to say, 'True, but I needed to give you the information.' Come to think of it, some of my most successful approaches have begun with, 'Forgive me for being a mother, but I am worried that …'

A more likely outcome is when your teen forges on with apparent disregard for what you say. One of two things may happen. One is that whatever it was goes smoothly and well and your teen says, 'See, Mum, you needn't have worried.' This is a good time to apologise for your mistaken fears and be delighted that it all worked out.

The other outcome is that things do go a bit wrong and your child receives a fright — but, hopefully, nothing too drastic. Leave out the 'I told you so'. Commiserate with what went wrong. Your credibility has just risen for the next time you need to say, 'I am worried that …'

'You can't stop me'

Many of us have teens who have waves of getting out of control. We may have said, 'No, you cannot go,' or we may have been the model of the keep-the-problem-with-the-teen method. Either, our lovely teen announces: 'I am going and you can't stop me.'

He has a point. Of course you could hold him back with threats of disinheritance or handcuff him to his bed. But these methods involve threatening and punishing, and also involve your taking on the problem. They keep your child irresponsible and incompetent and will not do much for your relationship with your teen.

What is the alternative? The reality is that you cannot decide what your teen will do, but you can decide what you will do. Very quietly say, 'You are right. I cannot stop you. However, you need to be very clear that you are going without my permission.' Surprisingly, this is very uncomfortable for a teenager to hear. We tend to forget how important we are to them. What we are doing here is creating a situation of emotional distance.

He may storm out. Don't chase and yell after him. Prepare to have a ghastly time while you await his return. He will return — maybe that day, maybe the day after. It is really hard, but just leave him to think it out. When he does return, be rather cool and indifferent. Leave lots of space.

Sooner or later your child will be ready to come closer emotionally. And sooner or later you will be ready to connect with him. Allow him to drift back into the family circle. It is over and you don't need to punish him. He doesn't need to apologise for needing space. He does need to know that his home is his. He also needs the experience that his actions may hurt people and that they may take a while to warm up again. This is a valuable life lesson and who better than a loving parent to teach him?

And you did it all without saying a word.

Lead them not into temptation ...

To return to the cookie jar analogy, one of the things Mum could have done was to recognise that being alone with a visible cookie jar was more temptation than this particular tot could bear. She could have the jar in a less visible place or she could recognise that, when the cookie jar was visible, she would need to be more vigilant.

If we are to keep our teens safe from the temptations that are out there, we need to know what they are up to. How is a parent to get this information? Asking them directly is often not the best way.

Information without interrogation

Under our law, people are not obliged to incriminate themselves. And yet we get very annoyed when our children won't 'own up'. Interrogation to force confessions is not the best way to teach our children responsibility.

You will notice that our tot did not crack under pressure, but Mum lost her cool pretty fast.

If our four-year-olds are so skilled at resisting interrogation, how much skill do you think they will have developed by the time they are 15? We need smarter ways of getting information if we are to keep ourselves well informed about our teens' activities. This way we raise the chances of keeping them safe.

One of the best ways of getting information is by driving two or three teens somewhere in the back seat of your car. The trick is to be so apparently preoccupied with your own thoughts that they assume you are part of the mechanical structure of the car. You can glean amazing information this way because you are not snooping; you are a necessary part of their transport system. Beware, though. If you get carried away and join in their conversation, your source will instantly dry up.

Whenever possible, try to be the parent who does the picking up after the party. I know it is a drag and I know how hard it is for old people like us to stay up that late. However, if you are the parent of a teen who asks you to park down the road so that they can walk into the party without a parent in sight, picking them up afterwards gives you a legitimate excuse for going in. Don't get sucked in to calling them on the cellphone and arranging to meet them a few houses away. You need to know what is going on. It is amazing how much you can learn from observing who is sitting on the footpath edge, who is weaving down the driveway and who is puking in the bushes.

There is a trend for teens to taxi from party to party and to taxi home. This has enormous convenience benefits for parents but leaves many children away from parental influence for too long and leaves parents with too little information to keep their children safe. Being there is much more effective than interrogation the following morning: 'How much did you drink? Smoke? Sniff?'

Don't leave the ladder out

If you don't want your tot in the cookie jar, don't leave the ladder next to the cupboard. And if you don't want your children doing dangerous things, don't be the one who inadvertently provides them with the opportunity or the example.

Don't drive them to parties you know are going to be dangerous for them. Don't let them go without checking on the supervision and the safety precautions. Get your teen used to the fact that you check out the safety systems with responsible grown-ups and don't leave them to chance.

It is inevitable that you are going to find irresponsible grown-ups along the way. Sometimes the reason you have to say 'No' to your child about a particular party or weekend away is simply because you know that the adults involved do not take good enough care.

Don't fund your teenagers' drinking and drug habits. Have a clear accounting system for how much money you give them and roughly how it is spent. Children who learn how to limit their spending and save for things they really want are less likely to spend it on things they cannot remember enjoying. Unlimited opportunities and unlimited financing is a dangerous cocktail for your teens. Don't be the one to set it up for them.

Don't expect your teens to be able to withstand their peer group if you cannot withstand yours. If you are mixing with adults who are doing anti-social or illegal things, you're on very shaky ground when you tell your teens not to. Remember they are watching you and ready to follow your example.

And what about the stolen cookie?

And if you do smell alcohol, nicotine, pot or unwholesome-but-uniden-tified? Humiliating your teen in front of his peers is not likely to enhance his good judgement. Yelling and grounding for life will not improve your relationship.

You are better off — and far more honest — to say calmly, sometime the following day, 'You have been drinking too much/smoking/using illegal substances. You know you are not allowed to do that.' Now is the time to join with your teen to help solve the problem of how he or she can enjoy socialising with peers and still be safe. Try saying, 'We need to come up with a way that you can have a good time and I can trust that you will be safe. What are your ideas?'

Just as with the cookie jar, we need to be more vigilant and to recognise that it may be too much for a teen and a temptation to stare each other in the eye and expect the teen to resist the temptation and walk away.

Remember the village concept and make your 'village' a place of learning, joy, fun and excitement. Make it a place where your teens will find a listening ear, a place to test their courage, a place to discover who they are and what they stand for and a place to increase their competence.

Sex education

Making wise decisions about their sexual behaviour is one of the many challenges facing our teenage children. As parents, we are led to believe that there comes a stage in our children's lives that we should speak to them about sex in such a way that they will feel good about their bodies, keep themselves safe and grow up to lead sexually fulfilled lives. We are led to believe that, if we don't 'get sex education right', we are responsible if our children go off the rails.

I believe that teaching our children about responsible sexual behaviour is very little different from all the other complex behaviours and issues that we are preparing our children for in their adolescent and adult lives — whether we are talking about the decisions they will make about sex, alcohol, driving safely, choosing careers, taking drugs, or choosing friends who are reasonably pro-social in their ways. It doesn't depend on the right chat or the right book or the right Life Education class at school. To raise young adults who are capable of making wise decisions and behaving morally and ethically appropriately is the end-point of 20 years of our raising them.

Having said that, it is hard to imagine a book written about the raising of children, without some specific comment on sex education, so I include a few experiences from home and some observations.

We can split sex education into two very short sections: what they know and what they do with the knowledge.

What they know

All three of our children were and are voracious readers. When Robert and Tanya were preschoolers, they had vast libraries of their own and the rule on library books was 'you can only take out as many as you can carry'. I kept a careful eye on book suitability and some of these books were about how our bodies functioned and some of them were of the 'Where did I come from' variety. Deborah always had access to her older siblings' library, so information on reproduction was easily available to all three.

Being urban rather than rural children and thus rather deprived of any natural examples beyond monarch caterpillars and pregnant mothers, they gleaned most of their knowledge from books and the odd comment from their parents. (They also confessed, once they were in their teens, that when they had baby-sitters who innocently asked them which books they wanted read to them, they always picked at least one book about reproduction! I apologise unreservedly to any of our previous baby-sitters who are reading this.)

When Tanya was about six or seven, she bailed me up one day and said, 'Did you and Dad really do that to make me?' 'Yes,' I said in the carefully neutral tones we parents save for such occasions. 'Ugh. Yuck,' she declared and ran away as fast as she could from the deliverer of the bad news.

My interpretation of this response is that, at three and four and five, she had absorbed the information about human reproduction and experienced it as remote from her own body — nothing much to do with it. Now, suddenly, she identified the behaviour in relation to her own body and being seven, very properly thought 'Ugh. Yuck.'

I assume that, by the time she reached early adolescence, things looked rather different.

When they should know about it

Children need the basic information about how babies are made and born at an early age so that, as they begin to identify the actions with their own bodies, they are not surprised by the information, but know that they have always known. Being a biologist at heart, the books I most liked for my children were those that dealt with all the body systems and included reproduction as just one of them.

As our children near puberty, they need more specific information about the changes that will happen to their own bodies and their likely emotional responses. Society urges them ever earlier to be sexually active so they need the sort of information that will enable them to make wise choices. They need our example and our protection, so they can resist the hype and misinformation that they will inevitably be exposed to.

It is good if we can answer any questions our children ask us but my experience is that most children don't ask too many questions. They glean information about sex as they do about all other matters in their lives — from books, from friends, from school, from magazines, from TV, from movies and, sometimes even from parents.

What they do with the knowledge

As our children move into adolescence the issue is not 'Sex education' as far as I am concerned. The issues are around emotions, relationships, safety, alcohol, drugs, peer pressure, rebellion, conformity, cars, role models, values, ethics and morals and boundaries.

How they respect their bodies, minds and emotions and what they do in relation to their sexuality is largely a product of their upbringing. By the time they are making decisions about how they will express their sexuality, it is best that they should have already had a lot of experience of delaying gratification, making safe mistakes, limited choice, planning and making wise decisions.

The quality of their decision-making also depends a lot on their current friendships — and there is always an element of luck here.

I comfort myself with the thought that, if our children turn out okay, it is a result of their wonderful upbringing, but if our children go off the rails it is because of environmental influences that are outside our control!

Afterthoughts

Parents often worry that when fights suddenly erupt, when the three-year-old — in a fit of temper — throws a plate across the room, when their 10-year-old trips up his younger sister, when the 15-year-old walks in with a nose stud, the parents just don't have an answer on the spot.

In a counselling session they will say to me, 'How come you can come up with these ideas and strategies when all I can do is yell and get flustered?'

The first thing I always point out is that it is easy for *me* to be calm about *their* children. The second thing I point out is that I have done my fair share of hand-wringing, blustering and yelling. However, afterwards I have always thought, 'Diane, that was not a particularly useful way to go.'

The third thing I urge all parents to think about is the concept of 'The General's Tent'.

When we watch old war movies, we become aware of the difference in the lives of those under fire and those who are making the decisions. The foot-soldier is trained to follow orders. When someone yells, 'Forward!' he runs forward. When someone yells, 'Fire!' he fires his gun. He is not expected to think. He is not expected to plan. He is not expected to reason.

When he is under fire, it is reasonable to expect that it is very, very scary and noisy and he will not be able to think straight. He will just follow orders. The person who has to think up the strategies needs a quiet spot to think.

The general's tent is a long way from the battle. He is not in any personal danger. He has people who bring him food and good brandy and cigars. Someone lays out his clothes and attends to his every need. When he is tired, he sleeps. All this is so that he will make wise decisions and plan good strategies.

What about when the general is the foot-soldier and answers to the name Mum? This is the situation most parents find themselves in. It is our job to be the general and make all the strategic decisions. What they will decide in the next 10 minutes will impact on the next day and the next week and the next year. They also need to bear in mind that rearing a child is a 20-year project that requires a 20-year plan. (Generals usually get to retire on a pension. Mums don't.)

At the same time, parents are the foot-soldiers who have all of the detail of daily life to get through — tenderly wiping grubby parts of children's anatomies, listening to upsets, restraining children from dipping the dog's ears in poster paint while making afternoon tea while picking up the answerphone messages while hearing about their day while planning the dinner while finding their swimming togs while listening to their music practice while plonking them all in the car to race one off to tennis while remembering who has books overdue at the library and who needs a birthday present for the party on Saturday.

I remember finding it quite cute — bearing in mind that we had a 13-year gap between the oldest and youngest — listening to French vocabulary while breastfeeding. Four years later it was very un-cute trying to wrap my brain around long-forgotten Year 12 (sixth form, as we remember it) geometry while trying to deal with a lively but exhausted four-year-old.

We cannot expect to make good strategic decisions while driving down the motorway at 4.30 doing the carpool. Our brains simply cannot manage the calm overview while we are under great stress. If there is revolting behaviour going on in the car, it is unlikely that we will come up with the calm, reasoned approach. We are under fire; it is not the time for rational strategy and decision-making.

The most we can hope to do is to make a quiet 'note' in our mind.

When all the children are tucked in — or if you have teenage children, when your child has tucked you in — get out a pen and paper and map out your strategy. What are you going to do the next time that behaviour looks like getting out of control? Is there any way you can use emotional support to avert a crisis? Is there a behaviour that you should be stopping every time? How are you going to stay out of the triangle and not be a rescuer or a persecutor? How can you keep the problem with your child so that your child increases in competence?

These are important decisions. They need to be made in the quiet and security of the general's tent so that, when we are the foot-soldier in the heat of battle, we know exactly what we are going to do.

Ducking arrows

It is a dangerous world out there in Parent Land. There are a lot of children — of varying heights — ready to fire arrows at us.

The first skill is to recognise a verbal arrow — a phrase designed to sting or disable a parent. It might sound like this:

- You're not my friend.
- I don't like you.
- I hate you.
- I'm not going, you know.
- That's a dumb idea.
- You're not the boss of me.
- *Everyone* is allowed to go to the motel for the weekend.
- You are so old-fashioned.

But arrows have the potential to do enormous harm. There are three things you can do with an arrow that has been fired at you.

Take it in the chest

One approach I do *not* recommend is to take the arrow in the chest — or take the comment personally. Don't reprimand her and tell her that it was not a very kind thing to say. Don't begin with phrases like, 'After all I've done for you ...' Don't point out how much you have sacrificed and how much you care. Don't look very, very hurt, sulk, cry or demand an apology.

The problem with taking an arrow in the chest is that there is blood all over the carpet — and it is yours.

Fire it right back

Another approach I do *not* recommend is to fire the arrow right back. Don't tell her she is grounded or that you are never doing anything kind for her again. Don't tell her you won't be her friend either. Don't irritate her by telling her you love her, or that you will ring up every parent in the whole class to check about the weekend. Don't wonder whether she would speak to her classroom teacher or ask how her teacher will feel when you tell her.

The problem with 'firing the arrow right back' is that there is blood all over the carpet and it is *your child's*.

Identify it and let it whistle past

Recognise that the comment is just a response — it does not require your intervention.

Unless you have a real love for battlefields, the best thing you can do is to think, 'That was an arrow,' move your head to one side, and let it whistle past your ear.

Your verbal responses in these situations all need to be mumbled. A small sample would include:

- Uh-huh. (a sort of nondescript grunt)
- How amazing.
- Really? (said in a very puzzled manner)
- I'll have to think about that one.

Four words for exhausted parents

There is a story told about Rabbi Hillel, who was born about 70 BC. One day a man came to him and mockingly asked Rabbi Hillel to teach him the whole of the Torah (Jewish Law) while he stood on one leg. Rabbi Hillel said to him, 'What is hateful unto thyself do not unto another. This is the whole Torah; go and study. The rest is commentary.'

I am not for one moment comparing myself with Rabbi Hillel, but I would like to emulate his example of distilling many, many words down to their essential message.

The ideas in this book can be distilled down to four essential words. I offer these for exhausted parents:

- WOW! — for all the wonderful things our children do that deserve our recognition.
- OH-OH-OH — for the times when our children are upset or angry and need our emotional support.
- GO — for the times when our children need space to sort themselves out.
- UH-HUH — a sort of noncommital grunt for when our children fire arrows that we are going to let whistle past our ear.

Exhausted parents can get a long way with these four words.

Finally, enjoy your child: enjoy yourself

We owe it to our children to help them become the sort of people their family and friends can enjoy being with. In order to be a pleasure to be with, we need our children to be reasonably able to handle ordinary frustrations, reasonably disciplined, growing in their skills and developing their virtues.

Hal Urban, in the last chapter of his book, *20 Things I Want My Kids To Know*, says that being good is the essential ingredient of emotional and spiritual health. As human beings, we need to be good.

If we can guide our children to being good, we give them the key to being happy.

In my introduction I said I wondered whether this portion of the Second Commandment meant even God was keen on reward and punishment: 'I the Lord thy God am a jealous God, visiting the iniquities of the fathers upon the children unto the third and the fourth generation of them that hate me and showing loving kindness unto the thousandth generation unto them that love me and keep my commandments.'

In discovering the importance of emotional support and emotional distance, I now understand this scripture differently. When we are behaving in ways we know are appropriate and worthy — in other words 'good' — we experience ourselves, whether we are religious or secular, in a spiritual alignment with what we should be. If we move too far from this alignment we are unhappy and our well-being is compromised.

The most important and meaningful thing I have done and am doing in my life is raising our three children. I truly believe that we should raise children who are enjoyable to be with — and then enjoy being with them.

The years of parenting go very, very fast, even though some of the days seem endless.

I encourage you all to enjoy your children and so enjoy yourselves.